A Practical Introduction to Research Methods in Psychology

THIRD EDITION

Eugene B. Zechmeister

Loyola University of Chicago

Jeanne S. Zechmeister

Loyola University of Chicago

John J. Shaughnessy

Hope College

The McGraw-Hill Companies, Inc.

New York   St. Louis   San Francisco   Auckland   Bogotá   Caracas   Lisbon
London   Madrid   Mexico City   Milan   Montreal   New Delhi
San Juan   Singapore   Sydney   Tokyo   Toronto

McGraw-Hill

*A Division of The **McGraw-Hill** Companies*

A PRACTICAL INTRODUCTION TO RESEARCH METHODS IN PSYCHOLOGY

4 5 6 7 8 9 QPD QPD 9 0 9 8

ISBN 0-07-072705-8

The editor was Brian McKean;
the production supervisor was Louise Karam.
Quebecor Printing/Dubuque was printer and binder.

http://www.mhcollege.com

To

Roadrunner

E.B.Z.

To

Coyote

J.S.Z.

To the memory of my mother and my father.

J.J.S.

AND

To our students--those whom we meet personally in the classroom, as well as those whom we meet only in these pages.

E.B.Z., J.S.Z., and J.J.S.

TABLE OF CONTENTS

PREFACE

This book was prepared primarily to act as a companion to our textbook, <u>Research Methods</u> <u>in</u> <u>Psychology</u> (Shaughnessy & Zechmeister, 1997, 4th ed.). Students in our research methods classes often ask us for "real" examples of the concepts and methods presented in our textbook and lectures, as well as for additional practice applying the research tools given to them. This book provides students with concrete examples of what to them are often abstract ideas, and gives students the kinds of practical experiences that aid understanding of research methods. There is much information contained herein, however, and some instructors may find it reasonable to use the book without an accompanying research methods text. The present text also could be used as part of a laboratory class or in a statistics class that emphasizes relationships between research methods and data analysis. When not using the book as a companion text, however, the instructor may want to develop certain topics more fully.

This third edition of our book was prepared with the same goals as the second edition, but with a more mundane purpose as well, namely, to put it in sync with the fourth edition of the Shaughnessy and Zechmeister textbook. Thus, some rearrangement of original material has occurred and new material has been added. Previous users will note that material in Unit 9 (Analysis of Experiments) of the previous edition has been assimilated into other units.

Throughout, we have continued to focus on the "working" aspects of understanding and doing psychological research. Every unit contains a rather lengthy overview of a research methods topic with a list of key concepts and their definitions. This is followed in nearly every unit by brief descriptions of published research in psychology with related questions, problems, and exercises. The research examples are real, as are the problems and issues we ask students to consider. Students are asked, in other words, to recognize how concepts are applied in actual research situations. Complete references to published articles are provided should students wish to consult the actual articles for more information about a topic or for ideas that might form the basis of their own research projects. Exercises and problems are based both on key methodological concepts (e.g., identifying a confounding) and on principles of data analysis (e.g., performing and reporting a t test). The goal is to help students develop a working vocabulary along with the necessary skills for doing research in psychology.

In order to complete the problems and exercises related to data analysis, students will need to have been introduced previously to the use of statistics in psychology or, minimally, they need to be taking a statistics course concurrently. Many of the statistical problems can be done successfully using information found in Appendix A (Statistical Methods) of the Shaughnessy and Zechmeister (1997) text; however, for other problems students may find it necessary to have available a statistics book for consultation. Moreover, we encourage students to use a computer and an appropriate statistical software package whenever possible, but especially for the more detailed statistical procedures.

At the end of each unit are several sets of review questions (e.g., multiple choice, matching, or true-false) that test knowledge of the material found in the unit. A complete set of answers to all questions, problems, exercises, and review tests is found at the end of the book. For users of the Shaughnessy and Zechmeister (1997) textbook, we have identified relevant page numbers with the key concepts and test answers to aid students' further review.

New to this edition are questions and problems that provide additional review of material in each unit but do not have answers at the end of the book. These items can be used for class discussion and/or homework assignments.

Students tell us that they find the exercises in this workbook challenging. Most importantly, they also report that they are much more confident about their knowledge of research methods in psychology when they have completed the exercises and problems. This increased competence and confidence has been our main objective for this book.

ACKNOWLEDGMENTS

In order to make this a "practical" introduction to research methods in psychology we have gone directly to the psychology literature for our examples. Readers will see that we have made extensive use of brief summaries of published articles. These summaries are generally paraphrased versions of the original text, and thus we owe a debt of gratitude to the authors and publishers of these works. If this book proves interesting to students it is largely due to the interesting research carried out by the investigators whose work we have liberally cited.

We have included with each article summary a complete citation identifying the author(s), source, and specific volume and pagination of the published work. We wish to thank the many authors who consented to have their work summarized in these pages. We also requested permission to paraphrase the original works from the various journal or book publishers. All consented to our request. Several asked that we formally acknowledge them as publishers. Thus, we want to acknowledge specifically the permission given by the following publishers.

The following summaries were used with permission of the author and Sage Publications, Inc.: (Unit 3) Latané, B., & Bidwell, L. D. (1977). Sex and affiliation in college cafeterias. Personality and Social Psychology Bulletin, 3, 571-574. Copyright 1977; (Unit 3) Crusco, A. H., & Wetzel, C. G. (1984). The Midas touch: The effects of interpersonal touch on restaurant tipping. Personality and Social Psychology Bulletin, 10, 512-517. Copyright 1984; (Unit 4) Simpson, J. A., Campbell, B., & Berscheid, E. (1986). The association between romantic love and marriage: Kephart (1967) twice revisited. Personality and Social Psychology Bulletin, 12, 363-372. Copyright 1986; (Unit 9) Horton, S.V. (1987). Reduction of disruptive mealtime behavior by facial screening. Behavior Modification, 11, 53-64. Copyright 1987; and, (Unit 10) Levitt, L., & Leventhal, G. (1986). Litter reduction: How effective is the New York State Bottle Bill? Environment and Behavior, 18, 467-479. Copyright 1986. Permission was granted by the author and John Wiley & Sons, Inc., to summarize: (Unit 1) Skowronski, J. J., & Thompson, C. P. (1990). Reconstructing the dates of personal events: Gender differences in accuracy. Applied Cognitive Psychology, 4, 371-381. Copyright 1990. The following article was used with permission of the author and the Psychonomic Society, Inc.: (Unit 1) Cunningham, J., Dollinger, S. J., Satz, M., & Rotter, N. (1991). Personality correlates of prejudice against AIDS victims. Bulletin of the Psychonomic Society, 29, 165-167. Copyright 1991. Permission was given by the author and Cambridge University Press to summarize: (Unit 1) Krumhansl, C. L., & Jusczyk, P. W. (1990). Infants' perception of phrase structure in music. Psychological Science, 1, 70-73. Copyright 1990. Permission was given by V. H. Winston & Son, Inc., and the author to summarize: (Unit 5) Kremer, J. R., Barry, R., & McNally, A. (1986). The misdirected letter and the quasi-questionnaire: Unobtrusive measures of prejudice in Northern Ireland. Journal of Applied Social Psychology, 16, 303-309. Copyright 1986.

Finally, we wish to thank the American Psychological Association for permission to reprint an extensive excerpt from the recently published, "Ethical Principles of Psychologists and Code of Conduct." Complete citation and formal acknowledgment appear in Unit 2.

This third edition was built on the excellent foundation provided by several individuals who helped to create and review the earlier editions, and we gratefully acknowledge their contributions. We want to thank specifically Elizabeth J. Zechmeister for obtaining permissions from authors and publishers for use of material presented in this edition.

NOTE TO STUDENT

This book comes with a promise and a warning. (No, the warning is not that learning about psychological research can be hazardous to your health.) The promise is that you will find the topics and problems presented in these pages interesting, challenging, frustrating, tedious, illuminating, and rewarding. We say that with a high degree of confidence because these are the adjectives that most researchers would use to describe psychological research. Our goal has been to reproduce in a textbook as much as we could the taste and feel for the research enterprise. Thus, we must also issue a warning. To the extent that we have been successful, you should experience all of the above. We believe that you will find learning about psychological research interesting; we hope you will find it as interesting as we find doing it (and writing about it). There is no more fascinating topic than that of human behavior and mental processes. But, as you will see, research is a challenging and sometimes even frustrating endeavor. And, yes, there are some tedious aspects also. Ask any detective how cases are solved and he or she will tell you that it is by legwork, by methodically following up leads, by spending time in blind alleys, by checking and rechecking evidence and alibis. These are some of the characteristics of the research process, too. But we believe the outcome is worth it. To illuminate some aspect of behavior or to fit one more piece in the complex puzzle of our existence is a rewarding affair. Good luck.

UNIT 1. INTRODUCTION

I. OVERVIEW

The establishment in 1879 of a formal psychology laboratory in Leipzig, Germany under the direction of Wilhelm Wundt brought the application of the scientific method to problems of psychology. Wundt and his colleagues were interested in a variety of problems, including those of sensation, perception, and cognition (see Boring, 1950). Psychology has changed significantly since these modest beginnings in Wundt's laboratory. Although many psychologists continue to study problems of sensation-perception and cognition, other psychologists study a myriad of topics, including those in such general areas as clinical, social, industrial, counseling, physiological, educational, and developmental psychology. The discipline of psychology is also no longer strictly a laboratory science. Today, psychologists conduct research in schools, clinics, businesses, and hospitals, as well as in other nonlaboratory settings. Psychologists continue, however, to emphasize the scientific method as a basis for investigation.

As an approach to knowledge, people who use the scientific method rely on empirical procedures rather than on intuition, and attempt to control (through manipulation, holding conditions constant, and balancing) those factors believed responsible for a phenomenon (Boring, 1954; Marx, 1963). Those factors that are systematically controlled in an attempt to determine their effect on behavior are called independent variables. The measures of behavior used to assess the effect (if any) of the independent variable are called dependent variables. It is important to recognize when levels of an independent variable have been manipulated and when the levels have been selected, as is the case for individual difference variables, such as age or gender. Suppose an investigator seeks to determine whether listening to music interferes with learning textbook material. She might ask one group of students to study while music is played and ask another group to study without music. Presence or absence of music would be the levels of the independent variable and these levels are manipulated by the researcher. A suitable measure of learning would be needed to serve as the dependent variable. The number of correct answers on a 20-item fill-in-the-blank test covering the information in the textbook would be an example. If an investigator simply compared learning of textbook material between a group of males and a group of females, gender would be the independent variable. In this case, the levels of the independent variable (males and females) are selected rather than manipulated.

Scientists seek to report results in an unbiased and objective manner. Giving operational meaning to concepts helps to achieve this goal (see Marx, 1963). A psychologist might, for example, operationally define expertise based on the time an individual takes to complete a complex task--the shorter the completion time, the greater the expertise. Accuracy and precision of instruments are important to the scientific process, as are both the validity and the reliability of measures. Time to complete a task would be a valid measure of expertise if, in fact, expertise is being measured and not something else, such as previous familiarity with the task. Time would be a reliable measure if individuals' times when measured again on the same or a related task are consistent with their times on the first task.

Psychologists rely on both physical and psychological measurement. Weight and distance, for instance, involve physical measurement because there is an agreed-upon standard and an instrument for doing the measuring. On the other hand, scales or rulers do not exist for measuring such dimensions as aggressiveness, intelligence, or depression. In these cases, psychologists rely on psychological measurement. The basis for psychological measurement is agreement among independent observers. If two observers agree that one individual's severity of depression is high (for example, an 8 or 9 on a 10-point scale of depression) whereas another individual's level of depression is lower (for example, a 3 or 4 on a 10-point scale), then we can say that we have a psychological measure of depression.

Hypotheses are tentative explanations of events. To be useful to the scientist, however, hypotheses must be testable (Marx, 1963). Hypotheses may not be testable for several reasons. The concepts to which they refer, for instance, may lack adequate definition. Hypotheses also are not testable if they are circular, that is, the event itself is used as an explanation of the event. An example of a circular hypothesis would be: People get depressed because they feel "down" most of the time. If depression is essentially feeling down then we have used depression to explain depression. Hypotheses are not testable if they appeal to ideas or forces outside the province of science ("The devil made me do it."). Although some of these hypotheses may be of value to theologians and philosophers, they cannot be evaluated scientifically. Hypotheses often are derived from theories.

More than anything else, scientists are skeptical. A skeptical attitude is not always found among nonscientists, who may rush to accept "new discoveries" and extraordinary claims. It is important to be skeptical about new evidence that is brought forth, even evidence provided by the scientific community. Consider, for example, the task confronting the psychologist interested in explaining human behavior. Behavior is very complex and many factors likely contribute to a particular psychological phenomenon. Some important factors may not even be known and others may be overlooked. Moreover, psychology (like science in general) is a human endeavor. Humans are fallible; they make mistakes. Human judgment is not always perfect. Is it any wonder, then, that a good scientist often wants to examine evidence carefully and to reproduce it again and again under a variety of circumstances before making a conclusion based on the evidence?

The goals of the scientific method are description, prediction, and understanding. Description involves defining, classifying, and categorizing events and their relationships. Both quantitative and qualitative research methods are used to describe behavior. Observation is the principal basis of scientific description. Prediction is based on an analysis of the relationships between events. When two measures correlate we can predict the value of one measure by knowing the value of the other. Understanding is achieved when the causes of a phenomenon are discovered. A causal inference typically is permitted only when we have obtained evidence that two events covary, that a time-order relationship exists (i.e., the causal event comes before the event it causes), and that alternative explanations have been eliminated.

Eliminating alternative explanations (causes) for an event is particularly difficult. Although the experimental method is especially useful when seeking to understand psychological phenomena, it is easy to make mistakes. When two potentially effective independent variables covary such that the independent effect of each on behavior cannot be determined, we say that our research is confounded. Consider, for instance, an educational psychologist who seeks to find out why students make mistakes on mathematical word problems. She manipulates the kind of problem given to two different groups of students. If one group of students were older, more practiced, and in general more proficient at solving word problems than the other group, a confounding would exist. If a difference in problem solving performance between the two groups were obtained, we would not know whether it was caused by the differential abilities of the two groups or by the kind of word problem. Similarly, if the time given to the participants to solve the word problems, or some other aspect of the procedure other than problem type, also differed between conditions, a confounding would be present. A study that provides an unambiguous interpretation for the outcome, one that is free of confoundings, is said to have internal validity. If the results of a research study can be generalized to different populations, settings, and conditions, the findings are said to have external validity.

Psychological research often is done to test a psychological theory, which can be defined as a logically organized set of propositions which serves to define events, describe relationships among these events, and explain the occurrence of these events. Theories have the important functions of guiding research and organizing knowledge (Marx, 1963). Theories differ on several important dimensions, including the scope or the range of phenomena a theory seeks to explain. Generally speaking, the greater the scope of a theory the more complex it is likely to be and, consequently, the more difficult it is to test adequately. Theories frequently make use of intervening processes or variables (Underwood, 1975). An intervening variable is something we infer on the basis of our observations that serves to "mediate" between certain antecedent conditions and behavior. A person who is observed to yell at a spouse, kick the family dog, and otherwise behave uncontrollably during periods when work deadlines are pressing and when many demands must be met, may be judged to be under "stress." Stress is an intervening variable that we infer (we have never "seen" stress) to help explain the individual's behavior. For a theory to be strong scientifically, it is important that these intervening variables be tied to clear antecedent conditions and

4

consequent behaviors (Kimble, 1989). We also can evaluate theories in terms of how closely they follow the scientific rule of parsimony (seeking the simplest of alternative explanations), the precision of their predictions, and the degree to which they successfully pass rigorous tests. A rigorous test is often one that seeks to falsify a theory's propositions rather than simply seeking to confirm them (Cook & Campbell, 1979). While confirming a particular theory's propositions provides support for the theory, confirmation logically does not rule out other, alternative theories of the same phenomenon.

References

Boring, E. G. (1950). A history of experimental psychology. New York: Appleton-Century-Crofts.

Boring, E. G. (1954). The nature and history of experimental control. American Journal of Psychology, 67, 573-589.

Cook, T. D., & Campbell, D. T. (1979) Quasi-experimentation: Design and analysis issues for field settings. Chicago: Rand McNally.

Kimble, G. A. (1989). Psychology from the standpoint of a generalist. American Psychologist, 44, 491-499.

Marx, M. H. (1963). The general nature of theory construction. In M. H. Marx (Ed.), Theories in contemporary psychology (pp. 4-46). New York: Macmillan.

Underwood, B. J. (1975). Individual differences as a crucible in theory construction. American Psychologist, 30, 128-134.

II. KEY CONCEPTS

The following concepts are importantly related to the problems and exercises found in this unit. Use the information found in the **OVERVIEW**, as well as the definitions of the key concepts provided here, to complete the exercises in the following sections. [NOTE: Numbers in parentheses refer to pages in the fourth edition of Research Methods in Psychology by Shaughnessy and Zechmeister (1997), where these concepts are more fully defined.]

causal inference The identification of the cause or causes of a phenomenon, by establishing covariation of cause and effect, a time-order relationship with the cause preceding the effect, and the elimination of plausible alternative causes. (24)

confounding When the independent variable of interest systematically covaries with a second, unintended independent variable. (25)

control A key component of the scientific method whereby the effect of various factors possibly responsible for a phenomenon are isolated; three basic types of control are manipulation, holding conditions constant, and balancing. (10)

correlation A correlation exists when two different measures of the same people, events, or things vary together; the presence of a correlation makes it possible to predict values on one variable by knowing the values on the second variable. (23)

dependent variable Measure of behavior used by the researcher to assess the effect (if any) of the independent variables. (11)

empirical approach An approach to acquiring knowledge that emphasizes direct observation and experimentation as a way of answering questions. (8)

external validity The extent to which the results of a research study can be generalized to different populations, settings, and conditions. (26)

hypothesis A tentative explanation for a phenomenon. (17)

independent variable A factor for which the researcher either selects or manipulates at least two levels in order to determine its effect on behavior. (10)

individual differences variable A characteristic or trait that varies consistently across individuals (e.g., age, depression, gender, intelligence); individual difference variables (subject variables) are often studied as independent variables in the natural groups design. Thus, these variables are sometimes called <u>natural groups variables</u>. (10)

internal validity The degree to which differences in performance can be attributed unambiguously to an effect of an independent variable, as opposed to an effect of some other (uncontrolled) variable; an internally valid study is free of confounds. (26)

operational definition A procedure whereby a concept is defined solely in terms of the operations used to produce and measure it. (14)

reliability A measure is reliable when it is consistent. (16)

scientific method An approach to knowledge that emphasizes empirical rather than intuitive processes, testable hypotheses, systematic and controlled observation of operationally defined phenomena, data collection using accurate and precise instrumentation, valid and reliable measures, and objective reporting of results; scientists tend to be critical and, most importantly, skeptical. (6)

theory A logically organized set of propositions which serves to define events, describe relationships among events, and explain the occurrence of these events; scientific theories guide research and organize empirical knowledge. (28)

validity The "truthfulness" of a measure; a valid measure is one that measures what it claims to measure. (16)

III. EXAMPLE STUDIES

Read the following summaries of published research and attempt to answer the questions found at the end of each summary.

A. INFANTS LISTENING TO MOZART

Reference: Krumhansl, C. L., & Jusczyk, P. W. (1990). Infants' perception of phrase structure in music. Psychological Science, 1, 70-73.

Article Summary: Recent studies have demonstrated that human infants are more cognitively adept than had been thought previously. These cognitive abilities enable infants to discriminate among objects and events in their environment. For example, at a very early point in their development human infants must sort out important noises in their environment. For instance, they must learn to recognize speech. A study was done to find out whether 4½-month-old infants were sensitive to disruptions in the natural structure of music. The infants listened to short selections of simple Mozart minuets that were either natural (pauses corresponded to the phrases in the music) or unnatural (pauses inserted into middle of phrases). A total of 24 4½-month-old infants was tested. An infant sat on a parent's lap inside a three-sided test booth. In the middle of the booth was a green light and on each side was an audio speaker. An observer looked through a peephole in the center panel and recorded direction and duration of head turns. A test trial consisted of the child's attention first being drawn to the center light; then a red light above one of the speakers flashed. When the child turned toward the loudspeaker, one of the two kinds of music was played. The observer measured the length of time the child remained oriented to the speaker. Results revealed that children oriented significantly longer to the naturally segmented music than to the unnaturally organized music. The authors suggested that this finding provides evidence that young children are sensitive to certain natural segmental acoustic cues; these cues may be similar to those the child uses to organize human speech.

Questions:

1. What information in the article summary indicates that the major scientific goal of this study was <u>understanding</u> how children perceive acoustic information in their environment?
2. (a) What are the independent variable and the dependent variable in this study? (b) Identify the specific levels of the independent variable.
3. Were the levels of the independent variable manipulated or were they selected? Explain.

B. PROFILES OF THE EXTREMELY TALENTED

Reference: Colangelo, N., & Kerr, B. A. (1990). Extreme academic talent: Profiles of perfect scorers. Journal of Educational Psychology, 82, 404-409.

Article Summary: Psychologists have long shown an interest in extremely gifted and creative individuals. One way to identify academically talented individuals is through their performance on standardized tests. In this particular study, the authors examined the "characteristics of students who scored perfectly on at least one subtest of the American College Testing Assessment Program (English, Mathematics, Social Studies, or Natural Sciences)." The sample consisted of perfect scorers from a population of 729,606 high school juniors and seniors who took the test in 1985-1986. "Of this group, 5,615 students received perfect scores on at least one scale; 701 received perfect scores on two scales; 384 scored perfectly on three scales and 3 students scored perfectly on all four scales." Perfect scores were most often obtained in Mathematics (3,265) and least often in Social Studies (577). Girls scored perfectly in English at more than a 2:1 ratio relative to boys. On the other hand, boys scored perfectly on the Mathematics subtest at more than a 3:1 ratio compared with girls. "All ethnic minority groups except Asians were underrepresented among perfect scorers." Because so few students scored perfectly on more than one subtest, talent often can be said to be quite specific. Moreover, many perfect scorers in one area tended to be quite average in another area. These results support a model of giftedness that emphasizes multiple intelligences as opposed to a model that emphasizes a global or general intelligence factor. A troublesome (to the researchers) finding was that when asked about possible future careers, most perfect scorers expressed interest in more vocational or applied areas (e.g., engineering, medicine) than in pure areas (e.g., English, mathematics, history). This suggests that relatively few of these talented individuals will seek careers in strictly academic areas where they might use their talents to teach future students.

Questions:

1. What information in the article summary would suggest that a major scientific goal of this study was <u>description</u> of events and their relationships?
2. What is the operational definition of "giftedness" in this study?
3. What evidence might be gathered to support the <u>validity</u> of a perfect score on the ACT subtest in mathematics as a measure of giftedness in mathematics?
4. What evidence would be required to demonstrate the <u>reliability</u> of the ACT test scores as a measure of giftedness?

C. WHO HAS A BETTER MEMORY OF EVENTS AND WHEN THEY OCCUR-- WOMEN OR MEN?

Reference: Skowronski, J. J., & Thompson, C. P. (1990). Reconstructing the dates of personal events: Gender differences in accuracy. Applied Cognitive Psychology, 4, 371-381.

Article Summary: According to the authors of this study, a commonly held stereotype is that women are more concerned with (and attentive to) dates of past events than are men. This stereotype may imply that in general women are better than men at reconstructing the dates of past events. To test this implication, the results of four studies investigating memory for past events were analyzed for gender differences. In all the studies participants were asked to keep a diary for about 3 months. They were instructed to write down each day a short description of one unique personal event. At the end of the 3-month period, participants' memory of the events and their ability to date the events were assessed. The list of personal events was read aloud to participants in a random order. Each participant indicated on a 7-point scale how well the event was remembered (1 = not at all to 7 = perfectly). For events that were remembered, the participant attempted to identify the exact date and day of the week on which the event occurred. Memory for dates was measured using the median error made in estimating the dates for each participant. The means of these error scores for males and females were compared in each of the four studies. In three studies, female mean errors were less than male mean errors. Two of these differences were statistically significant. For the fourth comparison there was a slight and nonsignificant difference in favor of the males. Overall, the investigators viewed the data as suggesting that women are slightly better at reconstructing dates than are men. It is not clear whether this finding occurred because women are better able than men to organize temporal events or because of some artifact of the record keeping process (e.g., women may have written more detailed, and hence more memorable, descriptions in their diaries).

Questions:

1. Have the major scientific goals of description, prediction, and understanding been met in this study?
2. (a) What are the independent variable and the dependent variable in this study? (b) Identify the specific levels of the independent variable in this study.
3. Were the levels of the independent variable manipulated or selected? Explain.
4. Evidence supporting a causal inference is obtained by establishing covariation of cause and effect, a time-order relationship with cause preceding effect, and the elimination of plausible alternative causes. In this study, (a) what specific evidence is provided regarding a causal relationship? (b) What evidence is not provided?

D. ATTITUDES TOWARD AIDS VICTIMS

Reference: Cunningham, J., Dollinger, S. J., Satz, M., & Rotter, N. (1991). Personality correlates of prejudice against AIDS victims. Bulletin of the Psychonomic Society, 29, 165-167.

Article Summary: Despite the obvious suffering of individuals with AIDS, they have sometimes been the object of prejudice. In order to determine the personality characteristics of people who show prejudice against AIDS victims, investigators surveyed 177 male and female college students at a Midwestern university. Five survey items pertained to the respondents' thinking about AIDS and were designed to measure prejudicial attitudes toward people with AIDS. In addition, sets of items were included to assess a respondent's degree of authoritarianism, self-righteousness, sexual liberalism/conservatism, religiosity, and other personality characteristics. Among the significant positive correlations reported were those between measures of self-righteousness and prejudice toward AIDS victims and between measures of authoritarianism and prejudice. The investigators indicated that people showing high degrees of prejudice toward AIDS victims were generally self-righteous and authoritarian males. It is not known whether these types of people also are poorly informed about the nature of AIDS. [Note: A positive correlation indicates that, as the scores on one measure increase, the scores on the other measure also increase. In a negative correlation, as the scores on one measure increase, the scores on the other measure decrease, and vice versa. Quantitative indices of correlations, called correlation coefficients, will be described in Unit 4.]

Questions:

1. What information in the article summary suggests that the major scientific goal of this study was prediction?
2. Given the positive correlation between authoritarianism and prejudice, what kind of prejudice score would you predict for a person with a low authoritarianism score?
3. Assume that two researchers each investigated independently the relationship between measures of self-righteousness and prejudice toward people with AIDS. Assume further that one researcher reported a positive correlation between these measures while the other obtained a negative correlation. What must we know about the measurement of these variables before we conclude that the results of these researchers should be interpreted differently?

IV. PROBLEMS AND EXERCISES

Each of the following descriptions of psychological research contains a major confounding that threatens the internal validity of the study. Read carefully each of the descriptions and attempt to identify the confounding that is present.

A. An investigator developed the idea that an excess of a particular chemical (RTQX) in the brain during infancy produced permanent mental retardation. To gather evidence for this notion, he used 30 infant rats and their mothers in an experiment. The rats (infant and mother) were assigned to two groups of 15 infant-mother combinations on a random basis. In one group, the C Group, the infants were nursed by the mother rats. In the other group, the E Group, infant rats were kept separated from their mothers and fed by bottle. The chemical RTQX was mixed with the milk in the nursing bottle. Tests of mental development were made on both groups at various points in time, even far beyond the nursing period. At every point of the testing the infant rats in the E Group were found to be inferior to those in the C Group. The experimenter concluded that the chemical RTQX causes mental retardation. Do you agree?

B. A psychologist, who also happened to be a musician, decided to test the hypothesis she had always held about the difference between musicians and non-musicians. Specifically, she believed that musicians are born with a "better ear" for music than non-musicians. For instance, she argued that musicians would be better able to detect differences in musical sounds than would non-musicians. She selected two groups, one made up of musicians and one made up of non-musicians. Musicians were selected from members of the local symphony orchestra; non-musicians were selected from members of a local book club (all of whom had never seriously played a musical instrument). As a test of her hypothesis, she gave both groups a task requiring difficult discriminations between similar musical tones. Her results showed that the performance of the musicians was vastly superior to that of the non-musicians. She concluded that her hypothesis that musicians naturally have a better ear for music was strongly supported. Do you agree?

V. REVIEW TESTS

These practice tests will be most helpful in preparing for your classroom tests if you test yourself under conditions that resemble those of your actual tests as closely as possible. We suggest, therefore, that you put away the book after completing the exercises in this unit and then return at a later study session to take the review tests.

A. Matching

In Column A are five features of the process of acquiring knowledge. Characteristics of these features when they are applied in a scientific approach to knowledge are found in Column B. Match the features in Column A with the appropriate characteristics in Column B. Thus, for each feature (Column A), you will want to ask how it is applied (Column B) in a scientific approach to knowledge.

Column A	Column B
_____ 1. Reporting	a. Operationally defined
_____ 2. Instruments	b. Valid and reliable
_____ 3. Observation	c. Systematic and controlled
_____ 4. Measurement	d. Unbiased and objective
_____ 5. Concepts	e. Accurate and precise

B. Identification

For each of the following brief research scenarios, identify the independent variable and dependent variable. Then, identify whether the independent variable is manipulated or selected.

1. An investigator tests a hypothesis about personal space by measuring (unobtrusively) the distance between a speaker and a listener as they are observed conversing in pairs or in groups of three on a campus mall.

IV = _____   Manipulated? Selected?

DV = _____

2. Children from three different grade levels (1st, 3rd, 5th) are presented a moral dilemma (involving a hungry person who steals food) as a test of their moral reasoning ability.

IV = _____   Manipulated? Selected?

DV = _____

3. A clinical psychologist uses two different "prompting methods" with adult patients to determine whether the methods differ in the degree to which memories of childhood abuse are elicited from the patients.

IV = _____   Manipulated? Selected?

DV = _____

4. Employees at a manufacturing plant are asked to work under three different levels of illumination during a month-long study of worker productivity.

IV = _____   Manipulated? Selected?

DV = _____

C. Multiple Choice

1. As an approach to knowledge, the scientific method relies on
   a. intuitive procedures
   b. deductive procedures
   c. empirical procedures
   d. subjective procedures

2. When a researcher is studying an individual difference variable the levels of the independent variable are
   a. manipulated
   b. held constant
   c. balanced
   d. selected

3. Measures of behavior used by researchers to assess the effect of an experimental manipulation are called
   a. reliable variables
   b. independent variables
   c. dependent variables
   d. empiricals

4. Which of the following characteristics applies to a measurement that consistently discriminates between high and low scorers?
    a. validity
    b. reliability
    c. precision
    d. accuracy

5. The tentative explanations scientists use to explain events must be testable and are called
    a. hypotheses
    b. postulates
    c. heuristics
    d. axioms

6. A correlational study is uniquely useful for meeting which of the following goals of the scientific method?
    a. description
    b. modeling
    c. prediction
    d. understanding

7. Which of the following conclusions is possible when a study contains a confounding?
    a. The effect of the independent variable can be unambiguously interpreted.
    b. The effect of the confounding variable can be unambiguously interpreted.
    c. The effect of neither the independent variable nor of the confounding variable can be unambiguously interpreted.
    d. The effects of both the independent variable and the confounding variable can be unambiguously interpreted.

8. When a study is free of confoundings it is said to have
    a. external validity
    b. internal validity
    c. integrity
    d. reproducibility

9. The results of an externally valid study are ones that
    a. apply to a narrow range of subjects, conditions, and settings
    b. apply to a wide range of subjects, conditions, and settings
    c. are likely to replicate if the study is repeated
    d. are likely to be difficult to interpret unambiguously

10. Constructing a psychological theory based on the simplest of several available explanations for a phenomenon illustrates the use of the scientific principle of
    a. confirmation
    b. precision
    c. rigorous testing
    d. parsimony

ANSWERS TO ABOVE EXERCISES AND REVIEW TESTS ARE FOUND

IN THE APPENDIX AT THE END OF THIS BOOK

****

QUESTIONS/PROBLEMS FOR CLASS DISCUSSION

A. Terminology and Concepts

1. Illustrate the distinction between an independent variable and a dependent variable in a simple experiment of your own design.
2. Explain how covariation that occurs with confounding is different from covariation that occurs with a correlation.
3. Operational definitions are used to identify both independent and dependent variables. Give an example of each from the summaries of articles in this unit.
4. Use the summaries of articles in this unit to illustrate the difference between description and prediction, and between prediction and understanding.
5. Using the Skowronski and Thompson (1990) article about men's and women's memory for events, explain why individual differences variables limit our ability to make causal inferences about behavior.

B. Critical Thinking: Analyzing Research

Read the following description of a research study to answer the questions that follow:

IMPROVING THE ACCURACY OF PREDICTIONS ABOUT WHAT WE KNOW

Reference: Maki, R. H., Foley, J. M., Kajer, W. K., Thompson, R. C., & Willert, M. G. (1990). Increased processing enhances calibration of comprehension. Journal of Experimental Psychology: Learning, Memory, & Cognition, 16, 609-616.

__Article Summary:__ When studying in preparation for a later test it is important to be able to judge accurately when we know the material that is to be tested. A judgment that we do not yet know the material should lead us to restudy the material before taking the test. A judgment that the material is sufficiently known to do well on the test will probably lead us to stop studying. But, how good are we at predicting what we know and will remember on a later test? Research in this area has not been encouraging. College students, for example, do not always predict accurately how well they will do on a later test. In an experiment reported herein, prediction accuracy was shown to depend on the ease of processing text material. Students read a series of short paragraphs under one of two conditions. In both conditions the students were told to study the paragraphs in preparation for a later test. In one condition the words in the paragraph contained missing letters. The subjects were told to fill in the deleted letters as they read the paragraphs. In the other condition, the words were intact and students simply studied the material in preparation for a test. At the end of each paragraph, participants in both conditions predicted how certain they were that they would answer correctly questions about material from the paragraph. A 6-point scale (1 = __not at all sure__ to 6 = __very sure__) was used to make predictions. Fill-in-the-blank tests were given to all participants following self-paced study. Results revealed that students in the two conditions did not differ in the amount remembered; but students in the deleted letter condition predicted more accurately what they knew (or didn't know) than did students in the read-only condition. The investigators suggested that requiring individuals to fill in the deleted letters made them think carefully about what the words meant and this increased processing was responsible for increased knowledge about what was known or not known. Apparently, the ability to predict what we know and don't know can be enhanced by more active processing during reading.

Questions:

1. What information in the article summary suggests that the major scientific goal of this study was __understanding__ how people make judgments about what they know?
2. (a) What is the independent variable in this study? (b) Identify the specific levels of the independent variable. (c) Were the levels manipulated or selected? Explain.
3. What is the dependent variable in this study?
4. How do you think the authors would state the research __hypothesis__ for this study?

C.   Creative Thinking: Designing Research

1.   External validity refers to the extent to which research results may be generalized to different populations, settings, and conditions. In the Maki et al. (1990) study, participants were male and female college students from introductory psychology courses at North Dakota State University. Students participated in classrooms. The

materials used in the experiment conditions were articles from the magazine *Science News*.

Design an experiment that is similar to the Maki et al. (1990) study that would test whether their findings can be generalized to a different population, setting, or conditions. Identify on which dimension (population, setting, or conditions) you are seeking to generalize, and explain why it would be important to generalize the Maki et al. (1990) findings over the dimension you have chosen.

2.   A critical aspect of the Maki et al. (1990) study is their explanation that participants who filled in the deleted letters of words thought more carefully about the information. There are many different methods that people use to process information either superficially or more fully. You may wish to consider the different ways that you read or pay attention to different materials, or the factors that influence your own understanding of different materials. These different methods and factors represent potential variables that could be manipulated to see if different levels of processing information influence people's knowledge about what they know.

Identify a variable that you think would influence the type of processing. Design an experiment in which you manipulate this independent variable with at least two levels. Specify the operational definition and the levels of your independent variable, and the operational definition of your dependent variable. What is your research hypothesis?

D.   Statistical Analysis

1.   Based on the summary of the Maki et al. (1990) study, what statistical analysis would be appropriate to test their hypothesis that more active processing during reading enhances people's ability to predict what they know? Explain.
2.   What statistical analysis would be appropriate for the two studies you designed? Explain.

UNIT 2. ETHICAL ISSUES IN THE CONDUCT OF PSYCHOLOGICAL RESEARCH

I. OVERVIEW

An investigator has the responsibility to conduct psychological research in an ethical manner and in accord with governmental laws and regulations. Failure to meet this responsibility undermines the whole scientific process and may lead to legal and financial penalties for individuals and institutions. To conduct research in an ethical manner means that a scientist must carry out the research competently, manage resources honestly, acknowledge fairly those who contributed guidance or assistance, communicate results accurately, consider the consequences of the research for society, and speak out publicly on societal matters that are related to a scientist's particular knowledge and expertise (see especially Diener & Crandall, 1978). And while many of these concerns are relevant to all the sciences, psychologists have special concerns related to the treatment of subjects in psychological research.

The American Psychological Association (APA) has published principles governing research with human and animal subjects (see Section III below). In addition, the federal government has established requirements for institutions, such as colleges and universities, doing psychological research. A major requirement is to set up independent committees to review proposed research. Most institutions, for instance, will have an Institutional Review Board (IRB) that seeks to safeguard the rights and welfare of human participants. Rules for selecting members and guidelines for reviewing research by the IRB are regulated by the government (see Federal Register, June 18, 1991). Similarly, many institutions sponsoring research with animal subjects are required to set up an Institutional Animal Care and Use Committee (IACUC) to help protect the welfare of animal subjects (see Holden, 1987). Investigators must submit their research plan to the appropriate committee for review prior to beginning the research project. All investigators, whether they be undergraduates performing a research project in order to earn a grade in a laboratory course in psychology, or Ph.D.s doing research with the goal of publishing their findings in a scientific journal, must be aware of the ethical rules and regulations governing research at their institution.

An examination of the APA principles governing research with human participants will reveal that there are few "absolutes." The principles attempt to strike a balance between the right--and indeed the ethical responsibility--of the psychologist to seek an understanding of human behavior and the rights and welfare of the individuals who participate in psychological research. The decision to go ahead with a research project rests on a subjective evaluation of the costs both to the individual and to society. Failure to do research may cost society the benefits of research findings and ultimately the opportunity to improve the human condition. To do research may at times exact a cost from individual participants--for example, by exposing them to potentially harmful circumstances or by inducing emotional stress. This dilemma is expressed as the risk/benefit ratio. The risks to the individual must be weighed against the potential benefits to the individual and to society.

Weighing risks and benefits is no easy task. Major ethical issues involving research with human participants include those associated with determining the nature of risk to participants, obtaining informed consent, using deception, safeguarding individuals' privacy, and, as was noted, in the final analysis determining the risk/benefit ratio. Consider, for example, the problem of determining whether a person is at risk in a psychological study. Everything we do involves some degree of risk. Getting out of bed in the morning is an act that unless performed carefully can cause us to fall down and be injured! Clearly, it is not possible to conduct research without some risk to participants. A research participant is said to experience only minimal risk when the likelihood of injury or discomfort in a research project is not greater than that ordinarily encountered in the participant's daily life. Thus, decisions about what constitutes risk must take into account those risks that are part of everyday life, but what is an ordinary risk for some individuals may not be so ordinary for others. Eating a candy bar may not constitute a significant physical risk to many individuals, although it could be a serious risk for someone who is diabetic. Risk also comes in various forms. Though one reasonably might think first about safeguarding participants from physical injury, the potential for social or psychological injury often is present in psychological research. Social risk exists when information gained about an individual through participation in a research study is revealed to others. Most individuals, for instance, would not want information about their sexual practices to be made public; however, this information might be sought by researchers investigating sexual behavior of males and females in different age groups. The potential for psychological injury arises when research procedures are likely to induce mental or emotional stress. Witnessing a crime, for instance, staged by a psychologist studying the circumstances surrounding bystander intervention, may be quite stressful for many participants.

The investigator has the ethical responsibility to minimize any risk and to protect human participants from injury. For example, when substances are to be taken internally, safeguarding subjects against physical risk likely would require careful screening of participants to avoid participation by those who might be especially sensitive to the substance. To protect individuals from social injury, a method of data collection possibly could be used that preserves the anonymity of participants. Safeguards for psychological injury might include extensive postexperiment debriefing of participants by the experimenter to help them understand the goals of the research and their reactions to the situation.

Ethical research practice requires that participants be informed of all features of the research that reasonably might be expected to influence their willingness to participate. As you might expect, this, too, can produce ethical dilemmas for the researcher (see Kelman, 1967, 1972). In some experimental situations, telling a participant about all aspects of a research procedure could negate the effect of a treatment variable. For example, a bystander's reaction to a crime is not likely to be "natural" if the bystander knows that the crime is being staged by the researcher in order to investigate the nature of bystander intervention. The use of deception is also a questionable ethical practice. Although some kinds of research would appear to be impossible to do without uninforming or misinforming the participants, deception runs counter to the principle of openness and honesty that ethical practice says should characterize the relationship between experimenter and participant. As in other areas of ethical decision making, implementing ethical principles requires that the investigator seek to balance the need to investigate human behavior with the rights of the participants. To safeguard these rights, an IRB may decide that alternative methods of inquiry must be substituted. Naturalistic observation or survey methods rather than experimental methods, for example, may be required if the rights or safety of participants are seriously threatened by an experimental intervention.

Whenever deception is used, a researcher has an obligation to inform participants after the experiment of the reasons for deception, to discuss with the participant any misconceptions that the participant may have about the research, and, in general, to attempt to remove any harmful effects of the deception. This experimental debriefing, which we have noted should be part of any research study in order to help participants understand the goals of the research and their role in the research, can benefit the researcher as well as the participant. During the debriefing process the researcher can find out how the participant viewed the situation and determine whether this view was the same as the researcher's. Did an experimental treatment, for instance, that was intended to motivate the participant actually do so? Debriefing can also provide the researcher with leads for future research (see Blanck, Bellack, Rosnow, Rotheram-Borus, & Schooler, 1992). For example, by discussing with the participant the reasons for a particular response, a researcher might learn more about an individual's strategies in a given situation than was revealed by the dependent variable.

Ethical research practices respect the privacy of individuals. But here again decisions about what is ethical are often difficult. It has been suggested that decisions about what information is private and what safeguards should be employed will depend on: the sensitivity of the information, the settings, and the degree of dissemination of information about an individual (Diener & Crandall, 1978). For example, while we might consider information about our sex lives too sensitive to make public, information about our eating habits may not be deemed so sensitive. Publishing individual results in a way that the identity of specific research participants can be identified often would be considered unethical even when the information is not considered to be that sensitive; however, even sensitive information might reasonably be made public when it is reported in the aggregate, for example, in terms of means and proportions. The setting of a research study also plays a role in decisions about what constitutes private information about an individual. Sitting on the lawn at a rock concert, for example, would probably be seen as public behavior; thus, information obtained about an individual in this setting may not be reasonably judged as threatening an individual's privacy. On the other hand, observing an individual's behavior while attending a party at a friend's house after the concert may constitute an invasion of an individual's privacy. As Diener and Crandall (1978) point out, the most difficult decisions regarding privacy involve situations in which there is an obvious ethical problem on one dimension but not on others and situations in which there is a slight problem on all dimensions. Observing individuals at a private party has the potential of revealing sensitive information about them, but by coding the data, for example, by using numbers rather than names, an investigator possibly could prevent others from knowing about any particular individual's behavior. Would this research now be ethical? Such decisions require a subjective evaluation by an independent committee in the context of reviewing the complete research proposal, so that information about the goals of the research, methods of protecting confidentiality, benefits to society of the research outcome, and other important factors can be entered into the risk/benefit ratio.

The use of animal subjects in psychological research also presents vexing ethical dilemmas. Although rodents, especially rats and mice, are the largest group of laboratory animals, researchers use a wide variety of species in their investigations, including monkeys, cats, dogs, and fish. And while the use of animal subjects has often been taken for granted, this is no longer the case (see, for example, Rollin, 1985). Recently, questions have been raised, mainly from outside the scientific community, about the role of animals in laboratory research. These include such a central question as should animals be used at all in research as well as questions about how best to care for animal subjects. Debate over the answers to such questions serves to raise the sensitivity of both the scientist and nonscientist to the problem of balancing the need to improve the human condition through research on animals and the need to safeguard the welfare of animals (see, for example, Goodall, 1987). At present, investigators must meet a host of federal and state regulations aimed at protecting the welfare of the animal subjects. In addition, the APA and other scientific organizations have established guidelines for the treatment and care of animal subjects. Although these guidelines sometimes have been criticized because they deal mainly with the care and treatment of animals and do little to restrict their use, their publication and implementation demonstrate the concern of the scientific community for the welfare of animal subjects. Clearly, until alternatives to animal research can be found, as with most ethical decisions, compromises will be required. The scientist has an ethical responsibility to seek knowledge that will help to eliminate human disease and suffering. This responsibility is joined, however, by one that requires the scientist to protect the welfare of animal subjects used in the pursuit of that knowledge.

Ethical principles related to the treatment of human and animal subjects are a major part of the APA ethical code for psychologists doing research, but there are other important principles as well (see Section III below). These other principles deal with such sensitive issues as sharing and utilizing data obtained in a research project, truthful reporting of results, and assigning authorship on scientific publications describing the research. Plagiarism, which is the presentation of another's work or ideas as one's own, is clearly identified as unethical; however, every year, it seems, the media report instances of plagiarism among professional scientists. Examples of plagiarism among student researchers unfortunately also are not too hard to find. Often the excuse given by those accused of plagiarism is ignorance, for example, a lack of awareness that what was copied actually originated with someone else, or even an ignorance of the rules for properly citing sources. Ignorance does not excuse plagiarism. Both professional and novice researchers must make every attempt to check original sources, to clearly identify, for example, through the use of quotation marks and a correct reference format, all material taken directly from other sources and to become familiar with the rules governing plagiarism as promulgated by various ethics committees. When in doubt about these rules, a researcher has an ethical obligation to seek advice from those who are more knowledgeable.

References

Blanck, P. D., Bellack, A. S., Rosnow, R. L., Rotheram-Borus, M. J., & Schooler, N. R. (1992). Scientific rewards and conflicts of ethical choices in human subjects research. American Psychologist, 47, 959-965.

Diener, E., & Crandall, R. (1978). Ethics in social and behavioral research. Chicago: The University of Chicago Press.

Goodall, J. (1987). A plea for the chimpanzees. American Scientist, 75, 574-577.

Holden, C. (1987). Animal regulations: So far, so good. Science, 238, 880-882.

Kelman, H. C. (1967). Human use of subjects: The problem of deception in social psychological experiments. Psychological Bulletin, 67, 1-11.

Kelman, H. C. (1972). The rights of the subject in social research: An analysis in terms of relative power and legitimacy. American Psychologist, 27, 989-1016.

Rollin, B. E. (1985). The moral status of research animals in psychology. American Psychologist, 40, 920-926.

II. KEY CONCEPTS

The following concepts are importantly related to the problems and exercises found in this unit. Use the information found in the **OVERVIEW**, as well as the definitions of the key concepts provided here, to complete the exercises in the following sections. [NOTE: Numbers in parentheses refer to pages in the fourth edition of Research Methods in Psychology by Shaughnessy and Zechmeister (1997), where these concepts are more fully defined.]

debriefing A process following a research session through which participants are informed about the rationale for the research in which they participated, about the need for deception, and about their specific contribution to the research. Important goals of debriefing are to clear up any misconceptions and to leave participants with a positive feeling toward psychological research. (62)

deception Intentionally withholding information about significant aspects of a research project from a participant or presenting misinformation about the research to participants. (57)

informed consent Explicitly expressed willingness to participate in a research project based on clear understanding of the nature of the research, of the consequences of not participating, and of all the factors that might be expected to influence willingness to participate. (49)

minimal risk A research participant is said to experience minimal risk when probability and magnitude of harm or discomfort anticipated in the research are not greater than that ordinarily encountered in daily life or during the performance of routine tests. (47)

plagiarism The presentation of another's ideas or work without clearly identifying the source. (69)

privacy Refers to the right of individuals to decide how information about them is to be communicated to others. (56)

risk/benefit ratio A subjective evaluation of the risk to a research participant relative to the benefit both to the individual and to society of the results of the proposed research. (45)

III. APA ETHICAL PRINCIPLES GOVERNING RESEARCH

In 1992 the American Psychological Association (APA) published a newly revised code of conduct for psychologists. The Ethics Code is intended to guide the behavior of psychologists across the wide range of activities that constitute the science and practice of psychology. For example, the Code presents Ethical Standards dealing with such diverse issues as sexual harassment, fees for professional services, test construction, and classroom teaching. Students of psychology should become familiar with the Code and the specific Ethical Standards at an early stage in their career and make a commitment to live up to these principles of conduct. Of particular concern to scientists are those principles dealing primarily with the conduct of psychological research. These specific Ethical Standards (6.06 through 6.26 of the APA Code) are reprinted below.

6.06 Planning Research

a) Psychologists design, conduct, and report research in accordance with recognized standards of scientific competence and ethical research.

b) Psychologists plan their research so as to minimize the possibility that results will be misleading.

c) In planning research, psychologists consider its ethical acceptability under the Ethics Code. If an ethical issue is unclear, psychologists seek to resolve the issue through consultation with institutional review boards, animal care and use committees, peer consultations, or other proper mechanisms.

d) Psychologists take reasonable steps to implement appropriate protections for the rights and welfare of human participants, other persons affected by the research, and animal subjects.

6.07 Responsibility

a) Psychologists conduct research competently and with due concern for the dignity and welfare of the participants.

b) Psychologists are responsible for the ethical conduct of research conducted by them or by others under their supervision or control.

c) Researchers and assistants are permitted to perform only those tasks for which they are appropriately trained and prepared.

d) As a part of the process of development and implementation of research projects, psychologists consult those with expertise concerning any special population under investigation or most likely to be affected.

6.08 Compliance With Law and Standards

Psychologists plan and conduct research in a manner consistent with federal and state law and regulations, as well as professional standards governing the conduct of research, and particularly those standards governing research with human participants and animal subjects.

6.09 Institutional Approval

Psychologists obtain from host institutions or organizations appropriate approval prior to conducting research, and they provide accurate information about their research proposals. They conduct the research in accordance with the approved research protocol.

6.10 Research Responsibilities

Prior to conducting research (except research involving only anonymous surveys, naturalistic observations, or similar research), psychologists enter into an agreement with participants that clarifies the nature of the research and the responsibilities of each party.

6.11 Informed Consent to Research

a) Psychologists use language that is reasonably understandable to research participants in obtaining their appropriate informed consent (except as provided in Standard 6.12, Dispensing With Informed Consent). Such informed consent is appropriately documented.

b) Using language that is reasonably understandable to participants, psychologists inform participants of the nature of the research; they inform participants that they are free to participate or to decline to participate or to withdraw from the research; they explain the foreseeable consequences of declining or withdrawing; they inform participants of significant factors that may be expected to influence their willingness to participate (such as risks, discomfort, adverse effects, or limitations on confidentiality, except as provided in Standard 6.15, Deception in Research); and they explain other aspects about which the prospective participants inquire.

c) When psychologists conduct research with individuals such as students or subordinates, psychologists take special care to protect the prospective participants from adverse consequences of declining or withdrawing from participation.

d) When research participation is a course requirement or opportunity for extra credit, the prospective participant is given the choice of equitable alternative activities.

e) For persons who are legally incapable of giving informed consent, psychologists 1) nevertheless provide an appropriate explanation, 2) obtain the participant's assent, and 3) obtain appropriate permission from a legally authorized person, if such substitute consent is permitted by law.

6.12 Dispensing With Informed Consent

Before determining that planned research (such as research involving only anonymous questionnaires, naturalistic observations, or certain kinds of archival research) does not require the informed consent of research participants, psychologists consider applicable regulations and institutional review board requirements and they consult with colleagues as appropriate.

6.13 Informed Consent in Research Filming or Recording

Psychologists obtain informed consent from research participants prior to filming or recording them in any form, unless the research involves simply naturalistic observations in public places and it is not anticipated that the recording will be used in a manner that could cause personal identification or harm.

6.14 Offering Inducements for Research Participants

a) In offering professional services as an inducement to obtain research participants, psychologists make clear the nature of the services, as well as the risks, obligations, and limitations. (See also Standard 1.18, Barter, With Patients or Clients.)

b) Psychologists do not offer excessive or inappropriate financial or other inducements to obtain research participants, particularly when it might tend to coerce participation.

6.15 Deception in Research

a) Psychologists do not conduct a study involving deception unless they have determined that the use of deceptive techniques is justified by the study's prospective scientific, educational, or applied value and that equally effective alternative procedures that do not use deception are not feasible.

b) Psychologists never deceive research participants about significant aspects that would affect their willingness to participate, such as physical risks, discomfort, or unpleasant emotional experiences.

c) Any other deception that is an integral feature of the design and conduct of an experiment must be explained to participants as early as is feasible, preferably at the conclusion of their participation, but no later than at the conclusion of the research. (See also Standard 6.18, Providing Participants With Information About the Study.)

6.16 Sharing and Utilizing Data

Psychologists inform research participants of their anticipated sharing or further use of personally identifiable research data and of the possibility of unanticipated future uses.

6.17 Minimizing Invasiveness

In conducting research, psychologists interfere with the participants or milieu from which data are collected only in a manner that is warranted by an appropriate research design and that is consistent with psychologists' roles as scientific investigators.

6.18 Providing Participants With Information About the Study

a) Psychologists provide a prompt opportunity for participants to obtain appropriate information about the nature, results, and conclusions of the research, and psychologists attempt to correct any misconceptions that participants may have.

b) If scientific or humane values justify delaying or withholding this information, psychologists take reasonable measures to reduce the risk of harm.

6.19 Honoring Commitments

Psychologists take reasonable measures to honor all commitments they have made to research participants.

6.20 Care and Use of Animals in Research

a) Psychologists who conduct research involving animals treat them humanely.

b) Psychologists acquire, care for, use, and dispose of animals in compliance with current federal, state, and local laws and regulations, and with professional standards.

c) Psychologists trained in research methods and experienced in the care of laboratory animals supervise all procedures involving animals and are responsible for ensuring appropriate consideration of their comfort, health, and humane treatment.

d) Psychologists ensure that all individuals using animals under their supervision have received instruction in research methods and in the care, maintenance, and handling of the species being used, to the extent appropriate to their role.

e) Responsibilities and activities of individuals assisting in a research project are consistent with their respective competencies.

f) Psychologists make reasonable efforts to minimize the discomfort, infection, illness, and pain of animal subjects.

g) A procedure subjecting animals to pain, stress, or privation is used only when an alternative procedure is unavailable and the goal is justified by its prospective scientific, educational, and applied value.

h) Surgical procedures are performed under appropriate anesthesia; techniques to avoid infection and minimize pain are followed during and after surgery.

i) When it is appropriate that the animal's life be terminated, it is done rapidly, with an effort to minimize pain, and in accordance with accepted procedures.

6.21 Reporting of Results

a) Psychologists do not fabricate data or falsify results in their publications.

b) If psychologists discover significant errors in their published data, they take reasonable steps to correct such errors in a correction, retraction, erratum, or other appropriate publication means.

6.22 Plagiarism

Psychologists do not present substantial portions or elements of another's work as their own, even if the other work or data source is cited occasionally.

6.23 Publication Credit

a) Psychologists take responsibility and credit, including authorship credit, only for work they have actually performed or to which they have contributed.

b) Principal authorship and other publication credits accurately reflect the relative scientific or professional contributions of the individuals involved, regardless of their relative status. Mere possession of an institutional position, such as Department Chair, does not justify authorship credit. Minor contributions to the research or to the writing for publications are appropriately acknowledged, such as in footnotes or in an introductory statement.

c) A student is listed as an author on any multiple-authored article that is based primarily on the student's dissertation or thesis data.

6.24 Duplicate Publication of Data

Psychologists do not publish, as original data, data that have been previously published. This does not preclude republishing data when they are accompanied by proper acknowledgment.

6.25 Sharing Data

After research results are published, psychologists do not withhold the data on which their conclusions are based from other competent professionals who seek to verify the substantive claims through reanalysis and who intend to use such data only for that purpose, provided that the confidentiality of the participants can be protected and unless legal rights concerning proprietary data preclude their release.

6.26 Professional Positions

Psychologists who review material submitted for publication, grant, or other research proposal review respect the confidentiality of and the proprietary rights in such information of those who submitted it.

IV. APPLYING THE ETHICAL PRINCIPLES

Put yourself in the position of someone serving on an Institutional Review Board (IRB) or Institutional Animal Care and Use Committee (IACUC). Members of these committees are asked to make decisions about the ethical nature of psychological research before it is carried out. In order to do so they must be familiar with the ethical guidelines governing research with human and animal participants. Read carefully each of the following descriptions of psychological research. The research is not unlike that which might be proposed to an ethics committee for review.

NOTE: (1) Both IRBs and IACUCs would require more information regarding the rationale, procedures, and safeguards to participants than can be given here. (2) As you are aware, ethical decision making typically rests with a committee of individuals. We would suggest, therefore, that you consider doing these exercises with a small group of your peers. Thus, the process will resemble more closely what actually occurs when members of an IRB or IACUC meet to evaluate a research proposal. What also should become apparent is that not everyone is going to view the situation in the same way. Issues may be raised that you had not considered or views may be expressed with which you do not necessarily agree. Such is the nature of ethical decision making.

A. Research Proposal 1

A researcher is interested in the important problem of date rape. She proposes to interview male university students about their dating experiences. As part of the interview each student will be asked to read several descriptions of male-female encounters and for each situation judge whether a rape has occurred. Students also will be asked whether they have ever been in a situation similar to any of those described in the written scenarios. The research participants will be recruited by posting signs around campus asking for male volunteers to be interviewed about contemporary college life styles. Five dollars is promised each participant for a 1-hour interview.

What APA principles do you believe are most relevant to this proposal? Focus your review on the following major principles: risk, informed consent, deception, privacy, and the risk/benefit ratio. Make your decision based on the information provided; do not assume that procedures not described are part of the research design.

B. Research Proposal 2

An investigator wishes to explore variables affecting stress. He proposes to ask college students to participate in an anagram task involving competition for points. Anagrams are made by scrambling the letters of words; participants are shown the scrambled letters and the time to identify the word is measured. Participants will be recruited from the introductory psychology classes at the university. Students will be asked to participate in pairs. One member of each pair is randomly designated to be in the experimental condition; the other participant serves as a control. Before meeting each other, the experimental and control participants are given different information about the anagram task. The experimental participant is told that solving anagrams is an important measure of intelligence (IQ). The control participant is told that the anagram task has nothing to do with intelligence. Both students are told that they are in competition with each other for points and that their task is to solve the anagrams as fast as possible. Participants perform the task in the same room; they turn over a card containing the anagram at the signal of the experimenter. Unknown to the students, the version of the anagram given to the experimental participant is always more difficult than that given to the control participant. This ensures that the control participant will win most of the points. The experimenter measures the blood pressure of both control and experimental participants immediately before and after the anagram competition.

What APA principles do you believe are most relevant to this proposal? Focus your review on the following major principles: risk, informed consent, deception, privacy, and the risk/benefit ratio. Make your decision based on the information provided; do not assume that procedures not described are part of the research design.

C. Research Proposal 3

An experimental psychologist wishes to investigate how exposure to certain toxins affects reproductive behavior. As part of the study female rats will be exposed to several different toxins over a lengthy period of time. This will be accomplished by spraying their cages with the experimental agents. Blood will be extracted at weekly intervals to measure blood chemistry. In addition, observations of social interactions will be made when male rats are introduced and physical measures taken of any offspring that result from male-female pairings. Finally, after a 6-month period the female rats will be sacrificed and relevant sections of their brains examined for evidence of changes related to the long-term exposure to toxic agents.

What APA principles do you believe are most relevant to this proposal? Focus your review on the following major principles: subjecting animals to pain, stress, or privation; appropriate use of surgical procedures; termination of an animal's life; procedures ensuring comfort, health, and humane treatment of the animals; prospective scientific, educational, or applied value of the research findings. Make your decision based on the information provided; do not assume that procedures not described are part of the research design.

V. REVIEW TEST

This practice test will be most helpful in preparing for your classroom tests if you test yourself under conditions that resemble those of your actual tests as closely as possible. We suggest, therefore, that you put away the book after completing the exercises in this unit and then return at a later study session to take this review test.

MULTIPLE-CHOICE

1. It is important for researchers in psychology to consider specific ethical issues relevant to their research projects
   a. before beginning the research project
   b. immediately after data collection has begun
   c. only if an ethical issue is raised by a colleague
   d. after the analyses of the data have been completed

2. Researchers must take special safeguards to protect human participants when
   a. behavior is observed in the public domain
   b. informed consent is not required
   c. anonymous questionnaires are used
   d. more than minimal risk is present

3. Which of the following is not one of the types of risk that can be present in psychological research?
   a. economic
   b. psychological
   c. social
   d. physical

4. Whenever deception is used, the researcher has the responsibility to
   a. debrief the participant
   b. inform the participant of the deception before the experiment begins
   c. withhold information from the participant concerning the reasons for having used deception
   d. avoid telling the participant about the deception before, during, and after the experiment

5. Which of the following statements concerning the use of animals in research is true?
   a. Animals may never be subjected to pain or discomfort in research.
   b. Animals may be subjected to pain or discomfort whenever an alternative procedure is not available.
   c. Animals may be subjected to pain or discomfort whenever the goals of the research are judged to justify such procedures.
   d. Animals may be subjected to pain or discomfort only when no alternative procedure is available and when the goals of the research are judged to justify such procedures.

6. According to the APA Ethical Standards, who is ultimately responsible for the ethical conduct of research that is done in psychology?
   a. the Institutional Review Board (IRB)
   b. the individual researcher doing the research
   c. the sponsoring institution (e.g., the university)
   d. the assistants who actually test the participants

7. According to the APA Ethical Standards psychologists must inform participants of the nature of the research and that participants are free to participate or to decline to participate or to withdraw from the research. These requirements (among others) are necessary to ensure the participants'
   a. anonymity
   b. risk level
   c. informed consent
   d. debriefing

8. According to the APA Ethical Standards, which of the following is not a justification for a researcher's making use of deception?
   a. personal value of the research
   b. scientific value of the research
   c. educational value of the research
   d. applied value of the research

9. An overriding principle of the APA Ethical Standards for the care and use of animals in research is that the care of the animals by psychologists be as
   a. inexpensive as possible
   b. humane as possible
   c. efficient as possible
   d. convenient as possible

10. Which of the following statements represents the policy regarding the termination of an animal's life according to the APA Ethical Standards for the care and use of animals?
   a. An animal's life may never be terminated before the time when death by natural causes would occur.
   b. When it is appropriate that an animal's life be terminated, it is done rapidly, with an effort to minimize pain, and in accordance with accepted procedures.
   c. An animal's life may be terminated in whatever way best facilitates the successful completion of the research.
   d. When it is appropriate that an animal's life be terminated, the procedures to be used may be those deemed appropriate by the individual researcher.

DISCUSSION OF THE RESEARCH PROPOSALS AND ANSWERS TO REVIEW

QUESTIONS ARE FOUND IN THE APPENDIX AT THE END OF THIS BOOK

****

QUESTIONS/PROBLEMS FOR CLASS DISCUSSION

A. Terminology and Concepts

1. Describe the nature of the conflict between using deception in research and obtaining informed consent.
2. Explain how the risk/benefit ratio is examined at both the individual and the societal level.
3. Explain how the debriefing procedure in a research study without deception may be similar to the informed consent procedure for the same study. How would the debriefing change if deception is used?
4. What ethical considerations form the basis for the risk/benefit ratio in research involving animals as subjects?
5. Explain why citing original sources only occasionally in a paper may lead to an accusation of plagiarism.

B. Critical Thinking: Ethical Decision-making

Shaughnessy and Zechmeister (1997) suggest several steps to follow when attempting to make an ethical decision. Although these steps are briefly outlined here in the questions below, you may wish to refer to pages 71-72 of the Shaughnessy and Zechmeister text for a more detailed explication.

1. Proposal A

Read the following proposal for a research study from the perspective of someone who is on an Institutional Review Board (IRB). This hypothetical proposal is based on previous research (see, for example, Hetherington, E. M., & Feldman, S. E. (1964). College cheating as a function of subject and situational variables. <u>Journal of Educational Psychology, 55,</u> 212-218).

The proposed study seeks to identify the personality factors associated with cheating behaviors in college students. Participants will be students enrolled in two different sections of introductory psychology at a state university. Students will complete a personality test during the first week of the course. Two situations will be created to give students an opportunity to cheat. Situation 1 will be the first examination in the course, an hour-long multiple-choice test. Students will be allowed to grade their own test in the following class period, unaware that the examination will be graded and scores will be recorded in the interim. Situation 2 will be the second examination in the course, an essay test. A week in advance, students will be given a list of five questions and told that two of the questions will be on the exam. Examination booklets will be made available prior to the exam "for practice." At the time of the test, the examination booklets distributed by the instructor will be unobtrusively marked so that any student substituting a "practice booklet" will be detected.

After the data are collected in the two situations, students will be told about the research study and those students who cheated will be asked to take a make-up examination. Data analysis will consist of trying to determine which personality variables best predict the incidence of cheating.

<u>Outline for ethical decision-making</u>:

1. What ethical issues are relevant in this proposal? [Note: You will need to consult the APA code.]
2. What are the possible consequences (risks <u>and</u> benefits) of this research for:
   a. the participants?
   b. the instructor/researcher?
   c. other students?
   d. other instructors?
   e. society?
3. What alternative methods exist for conducting this research? What are the ethical consequences of these methods (see Step 2)? What are the ethical consequences for <u>not</u> doing this research?
4. As an IRB member, would you consent to this research? Would you ask for any modifications of the research proposal?

2. Proposal B

Read the following proposal from the perspective of someone who is a member of an Institutional Animal Care and Use Committee (IACUC). This research proposal is based on previous research (see, for example, Seligman, M. E. P., Maier, S. F., & Geer, J. H. (1968). Alleviation of learned helplessness in the dog. Journal of Abnormal Psychology, 73, 256-262).

   The proposed study seeks to extend previous research that examined "learned helplessness" in dogs. Results of this and similar studies shed light on possible therapy procedures for humans who have experienced traumatic events and who then show passive responses to future events. These results also provide insight into the nature of depression.

   "Learned helplessness" occurs when dogs who have been given inescapable electric shock while strapped in a harness fail to behave normally when later placed in a situation in which they could avoid electrical shock; that is, the dogs learn to be helpless. Previous research used a shuttlebox apparatus to assess whether the dogs became helpless. In this situation, the floor on one side of the shuttlebox becomes electrified. A dog that has not been previously shocked will learn to jump over a barrier to reach the side of the shuttlebox that is not electrified. Dogs that earlier experienced inescapable electrical shock often fail to learn this, and passively accept the electrical shock.

   The proposed research will examine how helpless dogs can be taught to escape the shock in the shuttlebox. A modeling procedure will be used in which helpless dogs will be paired with dogs that have not been shocked. It is hypothesized that the normal dog will easily learn to avoid the shock in the shuttlebox and correctly model the escape behavior for the helpless dog. The intent of this research is to demonstrate that active escape behaviors can be easily modeled, which has implications for the treatment of humans who are passive following traumatic events, and depressed individuals who respond passively to their own depression.

Outline for ethical decision-making:

1. What ethical issues are relevant in this proposal? [Note: You will need to consult the APA code.]
2. What are the possible consequences (costs and benefits) of this research for:
   a. the subjects?
   b. the researchers?
   c. humans?
   d. society?
3. What alternative methods exist for conducting this research? What are the ethical consequences of these methods (see Step 2)? What are the ethical consequences for not doing this research?

4. As an IACUC member, would you consent to this research? Would you ask for any modifications of the research proposal?

C. Creative Thinking: Designing Ethical Research

Examine the alternative methods you identified for each of the two proposals in Part B. (a) Choose one of the proposals and design a study based on an alternative you suggested. (b) Describe the subjects and procedures of your study, then use the questions in Part B for ethical decision-making to evaluate your own study.

D. Statistical Analysis: Ethics

After data are collected, researchers frequently use statistical analyses to determine whether their hypotheses received support. Additionally, however, researchers will examine their data statistically to determine if any other interesting and important findings emerge that were not predicted. This practice is sometimes called "fishing." In studies with many variables, a large number of inferential statistical tests may be conducted. Because tests of statistical significance rely on probabilities, the more statistical tests that are conducted, the greater the number of statistical conclusions that will incorrectly suggest a statistical difference ("error rate per experiment").

Comment on the ethics involved by identifying the risks and benefits of this use of statistics. What can be done to limit the risks of fishing in one's data?

UNIT 3. OBSERVATION

I. OVERVIEW

Scientific observation generally is made under precisely defined conditions, in a systematic and objective manner, and with careful record keeping. Observational methods differ according to the degree of observer intervention and the manner in which behavior is recorded (Willems, 1969). Observation in a natural setting without observer intervention is called naturalistic observation. In addition to its use by psychologists, naturalistic observation is used in ethology (the study of the behavior of organisms in relation to their natural environment; see Eibl-Eibesfeldt, 1975). A frequent goal of the ethologist is the preparation of an ethogram, which is a complete catalog of the behavior patterns of an organism. An ethogram contains information on the frequency, duration, and context of an organism's behavior.

There are many reasons, however, why a scientist may wish to be more than a passive observer and instead choose to intervene. For example, participant observation may be used to gain access to a situation that is generally not open to scientific observation (e.g., the interaction of cult group members). Both structured observations (frequently used by developmental psychologists) and field experiments (often used by social psychologists) also depend on some degree of observer intervention (see Bickman, 1976). In a structured observation, the scientist may exercise control over events in order to precipitate an event that occurs infrequently in nature, to vary systematically the aspects of the stimulus situation, or to arrange conditions so that important behaviors are controlled and consequent behaviors easily observed. In a field experiment, the observer (experimenter) manipulates one or more independent variables in a natural setting in order to determine their effect on behavior. Field experiments often involve confederates, individuals who are instructed to behave in a certain way in order to help implement an experimental treatment. If naturalistic observation is at one end of the nonintervention-intervention dimension, then the field experiment is at the other end.

The way record keeping is done in an observational study varies according to whether a comprehensive description of behavior is sought or whether a description of only certain predefined units of behavior is desired (see Willems, 1969). Narrative records (including field notes) are used to provide comprehensive descriptions of behavior. The comprehensive description of individuals in everyday contexts is an important goal of ecological psychology; thus, narrative records are very important for this type of investigation. Checklists on the other hand typically are used when the researcher focuses on relatively permanent aspects of the subjects or settings (static checklist) or on whether a specific behavior has occurred or not (action checklist) (see Brandt, 1972). In addition to using checklists, psychologists often record the frequency and duration of behaviors. Observers also are sometimes called on to make subjective judgments (using ratings on a scale) about the quality or degree of a characteristic of the subject or situation. For example, a social psychologist may use a 7-point scale to rate the degree of intensity shown by opponents in a game situation (see Brandt, 1972).

How data are analyzed depends largely on the level of measurement used. Measurement scales are characterized as nominal, ordinal, interval, or ratio scales. The scales differ in the kind of information obtained. A nominal scale is achieved when events are categorized into two or more mutually exclusive categories. Classifying people according to the color of their eyes represents a nominal scale of measurement. An ordinal scale indicates relative importance of events in the form of greater than or less than. Students graduating from high school, for example, often are given a class rank to indicate relative academic position in their graduating class. Class rank is an example of an ordinal scale.

When we specify how far apart two events are on a given dimension we achieve an interval scale of measurement. That is, unlike an ordinal scale, we specify the intervals between events. If you find out that you graduated 10th in your class and a friend graduated 20th (an ordinal measure), you don't know how far apart you and your friend really were on the dimension that was being measured. You simply know your level of performance was greater than hers. However, if you scored 600 on the verbal section of the Scholastic Aptitude Test (SAT) and your friend scored 500, you know that your performance was 100 units above your friend's score. If someone else were found to score 550 you would be correct in saying that 550 is halfway between your score and your friend's score. SAT scores and other kinds of general aptitude measures are examples of an interval level of measurement. Note that though you know the distance your score is from your friend's score, and you even know about the ratio of scale intervals (e.g., a difference between two scores is half that observed between two other scores), there is something missing. That something is an absolute zero point. If you were to score zero on the verbal section of the SAT it would not mean you had zero verbal aptitude. An interval scale lacks a true zero and, therefore, it is not meaningful to express ratios of specific scale values. It is not meaningful, for example, to say that a person who scores 600 on the SAT verbal test has twice as much verbal aptitude as someone who scores 300. When all of the information found in an interval scale is present, as well as an absolute zero, a ratio scale of measurement is achieved. Physical scales measuring time and weight, for instance, typically are ratio scales. In these cases it is permissible to say that one score is twice as great as another score.

Researchers rarely can observe all behavior that occurs. Consequently, some form of sampling of behavior--time sampling, event sampling, situation sampling--must be used. An important goal of each type of sampling is to achieve a representative sample of behavior. When narrative records are used, some type of coding system generally is needed as one step in the process of data reduction. Coding is a stage of data reduction in which behavioral records are classified and categorized according to specific criteria. For example, a narrative description of children's aggressive activities may be coded according to whether the aggression was person-oriented or object-oriented. Coded data, and other measures, such as frequency, duration, and ratings, typically are summarized using descriptive statistics such as percentages or proportions, means, and standard deviations. It is essential to provide measures of interobserver reliability (consistency) when reporting the results of an observational study. Depending on the level of measurement that has been used, either a percentage agreement measure (for nominal data) or a correlation coefficient (for ordinal, interval, ratio data) can be used to assess reliability.

Finally, it is important to control for the possible influence of both reactivity and observer bias in any observational study. Reactivity refers to the influence that an observer has on the behavior under observation. For example, students' classroom behavior may differ when students know their behavior is being videotaped compared with when they do not know their behavior is being recorded. When people know that they are participants in psychological research they also may respond to the demand characteristics of a situation (Orne, 1962). These are the cues or other information that serve to guide the behavior of participants in a way that they feel is expected by the observer. This also may produce results that are not representative of an individual's "usual" behavior. One way that reactivity and demand characteristics can be controlled is by obtaining unobtrusive (nonreactive) measures of behavior (see Webb, Campbell, Schwartz, Sechrest, & Grove, 1981). These are measures that are recorded in such a way that the presence of the observer is not detected by the subjects. Observer bias, the errors in observation that can result from an observer's expectancies about what will occur in a particular situation, also must be controlled (see Rosenthal, 1976). Automating the recording process can help to control observer bias, but the best control may be an investigator's awareness of the fact that results can be influenced by the expectations held by an observer.

References

Bickman, L. (1976). Observational methods. In C. Selltiz, L. S. Wrightsman, & S. W. Cook (Eds.), Research methods in social relations (pp. 251-290). New York: Holt, Rinehart and Winston.

Brandt, R. M. (1972). Studying behavior in natural settings. New York: Holt, Rinehart and Winston; University Press of America, 1981.

Eibl-Eibesfeldt, I. (1975). Ethology: The biology of behavior. New York: Holt, Rinehart and Winston.

Orne, M. T. (1962). On the social psychology of the psychological experiment: With particular reference to demand characteristics and their implications. American Psychologist, 17, 776-783.

Rosenthal, R. (1976). Experimenter effects in behavioral research (Enlarged ed.). New York: Irvington.

Webb, E. J., Campbell, D. T., Schwartz, R. D., Sechrest, L., & Grove, J. B. (1981). Nonreactive measures in the social sciences (2nd ed.). Boston: Houghton Mifflin.

Willems, E. P. (1969). Planning a rationale for naturalistic research. In E. P. Willems & H. L. Raush (Eds.), <u>Naturalistic viewpoints in psychological research</u> (pp. 44-71). New York: Holt, Rinehart and Winston.

II. KEY CONCEPTS

The following concepts are importantly related to the observational methods that are discussed in this unit. Use the information found in the **OVERVIEW**, as well as the definitions of the key concepts provided here, to complete the exercises in the following sections. [NOTE: Numbers in parentheses refer to pages in the fourth edition of <u>Research Methods in Psychology</u> by Shaughnessy and Zechmeister (1997), where these concepts are more fully defined.]

checklist An instrument used to record the presence or absence of something in the situation under observation. (95)

coding The initial step in data reduction, especially with narrative records, in which units of behavior or particular events are identified and classified according to specific criteria. (104)

confederate Someone in the service of a researcher who is instructed to behave in a certain way in order to help produce an experimental treatment. (90)

data reduction The process in the analysis of behavioral data whereby results are meaningfully organized and statements summarizing important findings are prepared. (104)

demand characteristics The cues and other information used by participants to guide their behavior in a psychological study, often leading participants to do what they believe the observer (experimenter) expects them to do. (109)

ecological psychology Has as its goal the comprehensive description of individuals in everyday contexts. (93)

ethogram A complete catalog of all the behavior patterns of an organism, including information as to frequency, duration, and context of occurrence. (83)

ethology The study of the behavior of organisms in relation to their natural environment; generally considered a branch of biology. (83)

event sampling A procedure whereby the observer records each event that meets a predetermined definition; more efficient method than time sampling when event of interest occurs infrequently. (102)

field experiment A procedure in which one or more independent variables is manipulated by an observer in a natural setting to determine the effect on behavior. (90)

field notes Verbal records of a trained observer that provide running descriptions of participants, events, settings, and behaviors. (93)

interobserver reliability The degree to which two independent observers are in agreement. (105)

measurement scale One of four levels of physical and psychological measurement: nominal (categorizing); ordinal (ranking); interval (specifying distance between stimuli); ratio (having an absolute zero point). (95)

narrative records Intended to provide a more or less faithful reproduction of behavior as it originally occurred. (91)

naturalistic observation An observation of behavior in a more or less natural setting without any attempt by the observer to intervene. (82)

observer bias Systematic errors in observation resulting from the observer's expectancies regarding the outcome of a study (i.e., expectancy effects). (113)

participant observation An observation of behavior by someone who also has an active and significant role in the situation or context in which behavior is recorded. (84)

reactivity The influence that an observer has on the behavior under observation; behavior influenced by an observer may not be representative of behavior when an observer is not present. (107)

situation sampling The random or systematic selection of situations in which observations are to be made with the goal of representativeness across circumstances, locations, and conditions. (103)

structured observation A variety of observational methods using intervention in which the degree of control is often less than in field experiments; frequently used by clinical and developmental psychologists when making behavioral assessments. (87)

time sampling The selection of observation intervals either systematically or randomly with the goal of obtaining a representative sample of behavior. (101-102)

unobtrusive (nonreactive) measures Measures of behavior that eliminate the problem of reactivity, because observations are made in such a way that the presence of the observer is not detected by those being observed. (110)

III. EXAMPLES OF OBSERVATIONAL STUDIES

Read the following two summaries of published research carefully. Answer the questions found at the end of each summary. Answering these questions will require use of concepts introduced in this unit and in Unit 1.

A. Need for Affiliation

Reference: Latané, B., & Bidwell, L. D. (1977). Sex and affiliation in college cafeterias. Personality and Social Psychology Bulletin, 3, 571-574.

Article Summary: Latané and Bidwell (1977) sought evidence for a popular assumption, namely, that women are more socially oriented than men. A review of the psychology literature revealed only one study that had relied on an actual field study of affiliative behavior. To investigate further "need for affiliation" in natural settings, Latané and Bidwell observed more than 6,300 people on two college campuses. A major observation site on both campuses was the college cafeteria. Students were observed when entering the cafeterias as well as when eating. Records were made of a student's gender and whether the student was alone or in the presence of other people. A chi-square test was used to assess the reliability of the differences that were observed. On both campuses, females were significantly more likely than males to be in the presence of another person when entering a cafeteria or when sitting in the cafeteria. Gender differences were greater for entering than for sitting behaviors.

The findings that more women than men were observed in the presence of another person in a public setting is consistent with the idea that females have a greater need for affiliation than do males. However, the authors emphasize that alternative explanations are available. For example, observations were made in public settings and it is possible that women are more likely to be alone when in private than are men. Also, gender differences in affiliative behavior may arise because women are more concerned than men are about being seen alone. Females may be especially concerned about unwarranted attributions of unpopularity when they are seen alone. Nevertheless, the data are in agreement with the popular idea that women are more likely than men to interact socially in public settings.

Questions:

1. Would you classify this study as (a) naturalistic observation, (b) structured observation, or (c) a field experiment? Explain why you classified the study as you did.

2. What is the operational definition of "affiliation" used in this study?
3. What scale of measurement was used to measure affiliation: Nominal, Ordinal, Interval, Ratio? Explain why you chose the scale that you did.
4. What information in the summary provides evidence for the external validity of the findings?
5. Although the authors of the study suggest that their findings are consistent with the idea that females have a greater need for affiliation than do males, there are several alternative explanations available. Can you identify one alternative explanation <u>not</u> mentioned in the summary?

B. Interpersonal Touch

Reference: Crusco, A. H., & Wetzel, C. G. (1984). The Midas touch: The effects of interpersonal touch on restaurant tipping. <u>Personality and Social Psychology Bulletin, 10</u>, 512-517.

Article Summary: Through the act of touching someone we communicate a variety of intentions, ranging from love or sexual desire to dominance or aggression. The authors of the study review results of previous research on interpersonal touch, showing, for example, that an innocuous touch of another person can have positive effects, such as increasing ratings of liking a person. There also appear to be differences both in the way that males and females touch one another and in how they respond to being touched. In the present study, the effects of interpersonal touch were examined in a natural setting: a restaurant. Male and female diners were administered either no touch, or one of two kinds of touches, by a waitress immediately before the customers left their tip. The diners were touched briefly either on the hand or on the shoulder during the change-returning transaction. The authors speculated that a touch on the shoulder, which often signals dominance, may be viewed less favorably, especially by male diners, than a touch on the hand. The effects of interpersonal touch were assessed both by measuring the size of the gratuity (tip percentage) and by the results of a brief written survey asking about the customers' dining experience.

Most of the data were obtained at one restaurant and by one waitress who was blind to (unaware of) the research hypothesis. The waitress randomly assigned diners to the experimental conditions after she had collected the money but before she returned the change. The touch was administered at the time the change was returned to the diner. After returning the change, the waitress also asked the customers to complete a restaurant survey and leave it in a sealed envelope on the table.

The statistical analysis revealed that the average percentage tip differed significantly as a function of touch. Specifically, although the mean tip in the Shoulder Touch (M = 14.4) did not differ from the mean tip obtained in the Hand Touch condition (M = 16.7), these two touch conditions did result in larger average tips than did the No

Touch condition (M = 12.2). In addition, the authors reported that male diners tipped significantly more on the average than did female diners (means of 15.3 and 12.6, respectively). When the results of the survey were analyzed, the only significant finding was that males rated their restaurant experience more positively than did females; there were no effects of the touch manipulation on the survey results.

The authors suggested that the failure to find a difference between the two kinds of touches, especially for male diners, was possibly due to the fact that the diners in this setting felt secure in their role and viewed the shoulder touch "benevolently." Several reasons were given to explain why an effect of touch was not observed on the restaurant survey. These included the possibility that the effect of touch is short-lived (and had diminished by the time customers filled out the survey). Nevertheless, the results did show that interpersonal touch had a positive, even if fleeting, effect on behavior. The possibility was raised that the effect may be "subliminal," that is, that the diners were not really aware that they had been touched.

Questions:

1. Would you describe this study as (a) naturalistic observation, (b) structured observation, or (c) a field experiment? Explain why you classified the study as you did.
2. (a) What were the two main independent variables considered in this study? Classify each of these two variables as manipulated or nonmanipulated variables (and show that you understand the difference). (b) What were the two major dependent variables?
3. What measurement scales were used in this study for (a) the tip measure and (b) for the measure of the customers' dining experience (rating)? Be sure to explain why you chose the scale that you did for each measure.
4. What concerns might you have about the external validity of this research? (Base your response only on the information in the summary.)

IV. PROBLEMS AND EXERCISES

Read the following descriptions of observational studies carefully and then answer the questions that follow.

A. Problem 1

<u>Description</u>: An investigator is interested in the relationship between coaching style and success at team sports. She decides to do an observational study wherein certain behaviors of coaches on the sidelines of soccer games are observed. By being very persistent and conscientious she manages to observe 22 soccer games during one fall season. All the games are played in suburbs of a large city and are sponsored by the American Youth Soccer Organization; thus, games are played under similar regulations and referees are present. The ages of the children vary between 6 and 14. (Teams of 6-year-olds always play against other teams of 6-year-olds, etc.) The investigator obtains several measures of behavior, including time spent directing players while they are on the field, whether comments made to players on the field are negative or positive, and number of penalties called against a team. She also records the scores of the game. Her data analysis at the end of her study revealed that the more the coach directed the players on the field the less likely they were to win, and that coaches who made more negative than positive comments to players were more likely to have their team lose the game. She suggests that coaches' comments serve to distract players and thus cause them not to play well.

<u>Questions</u>:

1. Did the investigator use time sampling or event sampling in this study? What aspect of her sampling best indicates the type of sampling she used?
2. The description of the study does not indicate how the observer prevented reactivity from influencing her results. How might she have done so?
3. (a) The results show a relationship between the time coaches spent directing the players on the field and probability of winning. Explain in your own words what the investigator found. (b) The investigator attempted to explain this relationship by saying that the players were distracted by the coaches' comments, and this distraction caused them to not play well. What is the problem with making such a causal inference based on this kind of evidence?

B. Problem 2

Description: An investigator wished to test the hypothesis that students attending School A are more courteous than students attending School B. As a test of her hypothesis, she observed whether or not students at these schools held the door open for another student when entering a building. She observed students entering the door of the student cafeteria on the campus of School A, and students using the door of a main classroom building at School B. In order to make her observations, she positioned herself so that she had a clear view of the door and the people entering the buildings. Observations were made first at School A. For a two-week period she observed students for three hours each weekday, Monday through Friday. The hours chosen for the daily observations were 7:30-8:30 a.m., 11:30 a.m.-12:30 p.m., and 5:30-6:30 p.m. Following the two-week observation period at School A, she conducted observations at School B at the same times (and days) for the next two weeks. Thus, at the end of the study she had observed students at each school for 30 hours. Her results revealed that during the time she observed students at School A, a total of 642 people held the door open. At School B she observed only 352 people to hold open the door. She concluded that students at School A are more courteous than are the students at School B.

Questions:

1. Is reactivity a problem in this study? Explain.
2. What problems can you identify in the way that she made her observations, especially in terms of time and place?
3. Can you identify why the researcher's results are really meaningless as she has reported them? Explain how it may even be possible that just the opposite is true, that is, that students at School B are more likely to hold open the door than are students at School A?

V. DATA ANALYSIS

The following exercises give you practice with some of the statistical procedures common to the analysis of observational data. You will need to refer to Appendix A (Statistical Methods) of the Shaughnessy and Zechmeister (1997) textbook or an introductory-level psychology statistics book in order to do these problems.

A. Descriptive Statistics

1. <u>Measures of relative frequency</u>. Latané and Bidwell (1977) reported different numbers of males and females observed with others or alone in several locations. The data in Table 3-1 below are similar to the data that they reported.

Determine the following from the data in Table 3-1: (a) the proportion of males and the proportion of females observed overall; (b) the proportion of all males who were with others when outside (collapse across sitting and walking) and the proportion when inside (collapse across entering and sitting); (c) the proportion of all females who were with others when outside and the proportion when inside (combine specific outside and inside behaviors as in <u>b</u>). (d) Do inside or outside settings show a larger difference between male-female affiliation behavior?

Table 3-1

<u>Frequency of Males and Females Observed Alone and with Others</u>

Setting	Males		Females	
	Alone	Others	Alone	Others
Sitting Outside	90	140	35	145
Walking Outside	210	60	100	70
Cafeteria Entrance	220	100	120	175
Cafeteria Sitting	110	450	50	400

2. <u>Measures of central tendency and dispersion (variability)</u>. Assume that you have conducted a study similar to that of Crusco and Wetzel (1984). Assume further that in your study you investigated only the effect of a hand touch as compared to no touch of male patrons by a female waitress. The following data represent hypothetical results in the form of tip percentages for 12 male diners in each condition.

Hand Touch: 14, 16, 10, 23, 15, 13, 18, 11, 14, 17, 18, 19

No Touch: 14, 11, 10, 17, 15, 13, 10, 11, 12, 13, 12, 11

Calculate both the mean and standard deviation for each condition; describe verbally the difference between the means.

3. Interobserver reliability. Measures of interobserver reliability differ depending on the way that behavior is measured. When events are classified according to mutually exclusive categories (nominal level of measurement), observer reliability is generally assessed using a percentage agreement measure. The standard formula is: (Number of Times Two Observers Agree)/(Number of Opportunities to Agree) X 100. When observational data are at least of an interval level of measurement, observer reliability is assessed using the Pearson product-moment correlation coefficient (r).

Consider the study described earlier, which reported the results of an investigation of the relationship between coaching style and success at team sports (soccer). (a) How might the investigator provide a measure of interobserver reliability for time spent directing players? (b) For classifying comments as positive or negative? (c) For which of the above two behaviors do you think interobserver reliability will be lower? Why?

4. Measures of interobserver reliability. (a) Calculate a percentage agreement measure for the following sets of observations made by two independent observers. On a cold winter day, observers classified 15 students as male or female when exiting a college library.

Observer #1: M M M F F M M F F M M F M M F

Observer #2: M M M M F M M F M M M F M M F

(b) Calculate the appropriate measure of interobserver reliability for data reported by two individuals who made observations of the time (seconds) that it took 10 college students to walk between two points on a campus sidewalk.

Observer #1: 12, 14, 12, 7, 18, 22, 14, 15, 13, 24

Observer #2: 10, 14, 10, 9, 20, 22, 14, 17, 10, 23

5. Graphing. Using data from Table 3-1, draw a bar graph showing proportions of males and females who were with someone as a function of the four different settings. (Hint: Your graph should show eight different bars.)

B. Inferential Statistics

1. <u>Chi-square test of association (contingency test)</u>. An investigator observed college students on a college campus when eating alone or with others as a function of meal (breakfast, lunch, dinner). [This example was suggested by reading Smith, G. F., & Adams, L. (1982). Sex and time of day as determinants of whether people enter the cafeteria together or alone. <u>Psychological Reports, 51</u>, 837-838. Data in Table 3-2 are similar to data reported in Table 2, p. 838, of the Smith and Adams study.] The data in Table 3-2 show overall frequencies of students (males and females are combined) entering a cafeteria together or alone. Perform a chi-square test of association on these data. Indicate level of significance (and critical value) and state your conclusion based on the outcome of the statistical analysis.

Table 3-2

<u>Number of Students Observed Entering Cafeteria Alone or Together for</u>

<u>Each of Three Meals</u>

	Meal		
Observation	Breakfast	Lunch	Dinner
Together	225	630	1150
Alone	220	460	300
Total	445	1090	1450

2. <u>Test for difference between means</u>. Carry out a <u>t</u>-test for independent groups comparing the difference between means in the hypothetical data set shown earlier (V. DATA ANALYSIS A.2), which presented results from the two conditions of interpersonal touch: Hand Touch and No Touch. Identify the critical value that you chose for your test and report the results of your inferential test both statistically and verbally.

VI. REVIEW TESTS

These practice tests will be most helpful in preparing for your classroom tests if you test yourself under conditions that resemble those of your actual tests as closely as possible. We suggest, therefore, that you put away the book after completing the exercises in this unit and then return at a later study session to take the review tests.

A. Matching

On the following pages you will find five brief descriptions of observational research. Read each description carefully. Then, identify the type of observational study used by choosing the appropriate letter from Column A. Next, look over the concepts in Column B. Identify the concepts that are illustrated in the research description. Place the appropriate letters from Column B beneath the research description. Letters from both Columns A and B may be used one time, more than one time, or not at all.

Column A	Column B
a. naturalistic observation	a. ethology
b. participant observation	b. ethogram
c. structured observation	c. confederate
d. field experiment	d. narrative records
	e. ecological psychology
	f. field notes
	g. checklist
	h. time sampling
	i. event sampling
	j. situation sampling
	k. data reduction
	l. coding
	m. interobserver reliability
	n. reactivity
	o. demand characteristics
	p. unobtrusive measure
	q. observer bias (expectancy)

1. Sally is interested in the behavior of field mice. She decides to observe their behavior from a distance using a powerful telescope. There are four fields near the university she attends that contain colonies of mice. She observes the mice in the four different fields according to a schedule that she makes up. On each observation day, six 15-minute periods during the day are randomly selected from the times when the daylight is sufficient to permit her to see the mice. She makes written descriptions of many activities of the mice. Later, she organizes the behavioral descriptions according to well-defined categories of behavior.

   Type of observational study from Column A: _____

   Concepts from Column B that are illustrated:_____, _____,_____, _____, _____, _____, _____

2. Luther wants to find out whether college students are influenced by how someone dresses. To do so, he asks one of his male friends to approach students on campus and ask for directions to a well-known restaurant located on the other side of the city. His friend is asked to be well dressed and neat in appearance when approaching some students and to dress in old, dirty clothes, and to look like he has not washed in a week when approaching other students. Otherwise, his friend is told to make the request in exactly the same way to all students. Every 20th student exiting the library on Monday and Wednesday is approached by the neat dresser, and on Tuesday and Thursday by the shabby dresser. The friend reports to Luther how many people were willing to give directions when he approached them in the two different types of dress.

   Type of observational study from Column A: _____

   Concepts from Column B that are illustrated: _____, _____

3. Students in an introductory psychology class are assigned to observe at a busy intersection and to record whether or not cars enter the intersection when the light has changed to red, and if so, to record whether the car was high-priced, moderate-priced, or low-priced. Students are asked to observe in pairs from the window of a second-story office in a building near the intersection. The data from the pairs of observers are later compared.

   Type of observational study from Column A: _____

   Concepts from Column B that are illustrated: _____, _____, _____

4. A psychologist investigates the response of 20 different 4-year-old boys to being separated from their mothers. A mother and child are brought into a large playroom. The child is allowed to play by himself for 10 minutes. At that time, the mother is signaled by the psychologist to get up and leave the room. The psychologist observes the child through a one-way mirror, recording everything the child does for the next 5 minutes.

Type of observational study from Column A: _____

Concepts from Column B that are illustrated: _____, _____

5. Mary is an educational psychologist studying classroom behavior. She sets up a study to observe boys and girls during their regular class periods at school. She is interested in whether boys and girls differ in their "out of seat" behavior in the classroom. Because she expects boys to be out of their seats more often than girls she observes from a position in the front of the classroom where she can see the most boys clearly.

Type of observational study from Column A: _____

Concepts from Column B that are illustrated: _____, _____, _____

B. Classification

Classify each of the following variables according to the level (scale) of measurement (Nominal, Ordinal, Interval, Ratio) that was used.

_____ 1. Number of wrong turns made by rat in a maze.
_____ 2. Time it takes a car to leave an intersection when the light changes.
_____ 3. Self-reported level of frustration using a 7-point scale (1 = not at all frustrated; 7 = extremely frustrated).
_____ 4. Whether or not a person uses a self-referent ("I," "me," "we," or "us") in 10-minute conversation.
_____ 5. Scores on a paper and pencil test measuring depression (maximum score is 100).
_____ 6. Student's ranking of 5 topics in terms of his/her relative knowledge of the topics (ranked from "most" to "least" knowledge).
_____ 7. Child's choice of "ugly toy" or "pretty toy."

C. Multiple Choice

1. When observers classify events according to mutually exclusive categories, interobserver reliability is usually assessed using a
   a. Spearman correlation coefficient
   b. percentage agreement measure
   c. Pearson correlation coefficient
   d. percent reliability measure

2. Which of the following is <u>not</u> a characteristic of the naturalistic observation method?
   a. observation in a natural setting
   b. systematic observation of behavior
   c. major goal is description of behavior
   d. manipulation of events by an experimenter

3. The influence that an observer has on the behavior under observation is called
   a. reactivity
   b. observer bias
   c. demand characteristics
   d. expectancy effect

4. In observational studies situation sampling is a technique most often used to ensure the study's
   a. internal validity
   b. external validity
   c. construct validity
   d. inferential validity

5. Which of the following characteristics of observers would most likely be associated with high interobserver reliability?
   a. observers are unclear about what is to be observed
   b. observers are well trained
   c. observers are tired or bored
   d. observers differ in outcome expectancy

6. The person who assists the experimenter by carrying out a role essential to implementing an experimental treatment is called a(n)
   a. accomplice
   b. helper
   c. confederate
   d. experimenter

7. An investigator who provides a written description of the situation surrounding a child's temper tantrum, as well as characteristics of the event itself, is implementing the technique of a
    a. narrative record
    b. field experiment
    c. participant observation
    d. checklist

8. Which of the following procedures would be an example of using <u>coding</u> in the process of data reduction?
    a. obtaining an arithmetic mean for a time measure
    b. finding proportions of respondents in various groups
    c. classifying observational records using specific criteria
    d. measuring interobserver reliability

9. When people know that they are participants in a research study they often try to figure out what it is that the researcher expects them to do. The cues participants use to help guide their behavior in a research situation are called
    a. unobtrusive effects
    b. reactive cues
    c. experimenter effects
    d. demand characteristics

10. An observer who sets out to study car drivers' reactions to being "pulled over" by a highway patrol officer would most likely use what type of behavior sampling procedure?
    a. time sampling
    b. event sampling
    c. situation sampling
    d. random sampling

ANSWERS TO EXERCISES AND REVIEW TESTS ARE FOUND

IN THE APPENDIX AT THE END OF THIS BOOK

****

QUESTIONS/PROBLEMS FOR CLASS DISCUSSION

A. Terminology and Concepts

1. How might a calculation of interobserver reliability be used to help detect whether observer bias exists in a study?
2. When does a "structured observation" become a "field experiment"?
3. What is the relationship between demand characteristics and reactivity?
4. Does the use of a confederate make "naturalistic" observation impossible?
5. Suppose you are interested in observing "tipping" behavior. Use the basic setting and conditions of the Crusco and Wetzel (1984) study to make up an example of how you could observe tipping using (a) situation sampling, (b) time sampling, and (c) event sampling.

B. Critical Thinking: Analyzing Research

Refer to Section III, Examples of Observational Studies (pp. 40-42), to answer the following questions:

1. Latané and Bidwell (1977) observed that women were more likely than men to be in the presence of another person in a public setting. One interpretation of this finding is that women have a greater need for affiliation than do males; that is, women's need for affiliation causes them to be with others relative to men's need for affiliation. Comment critically on accepting this conclusion on the basis of these data.

2. Latané and Bidwell (1977) also suggested the idea that the public nature of their observations influenced their results, and that it is possible that women may be more likely than men to be alone in private situations. Identify the types of observations one would need to test this hypothesis, and discuss why these data may be difficult to obtain.

3. The summary of the Latané and Bidwell (1977) study indicates that they coded their observations into two categories: "alone" or "others present." Can you think of other information that could have been coded? What type of scale would you use to measure this information?

4. One problem with the external validity of the Latané and Bidwell (1977) study is that their observations were limited to college students, and it is possible that their findings are unique to this population. Can you think of reasons why traditional-age male and female college students may differ in their need for affiliation compared to individuals in other age groups?

5. Despite the observation that diners were apparently unaware of being touched in the Crusco and Wetzel (1984) study, why is it possible to conclude that the touch <u>caused</u> the diners to leave a larger tip?

6. Crusco and Wetzel (1984) were interested in examining the factors that influence the amount of money left for a tip. Explain why it was important to use the percentage of the bill left for a tip as the dependent variable rather than the amount of money left for the tip. What potential variable is controlled for by using the percentage tip as the dependent variable?

7. The researchers held conditions constant in their experiment by employing one female wait-staff person as their confederate. Explain how this might have influenced the results they observed.

C. Creative Thinking: Designing Research

1. Design a naturalistic observation study to examine the idea that traditional-age male and female college students may differ in their need for affiliation compared to individuals in other age groups. What age groups will you consider? How will you operationally define these groups? What will you use as your dependent variable? Describe the setting and procedures you will use to make your observations. What are your hypotheses?

2. Male and female diners may differ in the percentage tip they leave in response to being touched by male versus female wait-staff. That is, opposite-sex pairs (wait-staff person and diner) may respond differently to touch compared to same-sex pairs. Using the shoulder-touch condition and the no-touch condition, design a field experiment to examine this hypothesis. What are your independent variables? Are they selected or manipulated? Describe the setting and procedures you would use to conduct your field experiment. What is your hypothesis?

D. Statistical Analysis

1. Create a table with hypothetical data that would lend support to your prediction in the study you designed in C.1. (see Table 3-1 on page 45 for help with this; you may wish to substitute "Age Group" for "Setting"). Describe the statistical analysis you would choose to analyze these data.

2. Assume that for the study you designed for C.2. that you collected data for 10 participants in each of your conditions. Develop hypothetical data (i.e., percentage tip) for each participant that would support your prediction. Calculate the mean and standard deviation (estimate the population standard deviation) for each condition. Why would it be impossible to use a single t test to determine whether your hypothesis received support?

UNIT 4. CORRELATIONAL RESEARCH: SURVEYS

I. OVERVIEW

Survey research represents a general approach to psychological research called correlational research. Unlike experimental research (see Unit 6), in which independent variables are manipulated, correlational research assesses the covariation among naturally occurring variables that are measured by the investigator. The primary goal in correlational research is to identify predictive relationships between variables by using a quantitative index known as the correlation coefficient. One frequently used correlation coefficient used with interval or ratio data is the Pearson product-moment correlation (r).

The direction of a correlation coefficient can be either positive or negative. A positive correlation between two measures indicates that, as scores for one measure increase, scores for the other measure also increase. A negative correlation indicates that as scores for one measure increase, scores for the other measure decrease. Knowing scores on either measure allows us to predict scores on the other measure. The magnitude (degree) of correlation coefficients can range in absolute value from 0.0 to 1.00. A correlation of zero indicates that there is no relationship between measures of two variables, a correlation coefficient of +1.00 indicates a perfect positive correlation, and a correlation of -1.00 indicates a perfect negative correlation between two measures. Usually, however, variables are not perfectly correlated, and correlation coefficients can vary in magnitude. The higher the value of a correlation coefficient, the stronger the predictive relationship. Remember that the sign of a correlation only indicates its direction: A correlation of -.50 indicates a stronger relationship between two variables than a correlation of +.20. The magnitude and direction of a correlation between two variables measured using interval or ratio scales can be represented graphically using a scatterplot.

Although results of correlational studies are useful for prediction, a serious limitation of correlational studies is that they do not allow causal inferences about the relationship between variables. For example, Myers and Diener (1995) demonstrated there is a positive correlation between being outgoing and being satisfied with one's life. This correlation allows us to predict a person's satisfaction level if we know she is outgoing, or we can predict the extent to which someone is outgoing if we know his level of life satisfaction. We do not know, however, what causes this relationship. Three possibilities exist. It could be that being outgoing causes people to be more satisfied with their lives. Or people may be more outgoing because they are more satisfied with their lives, or a third variable may be responsible for the correlation. For example, people who have more friends may be more outgoing and more satisfied with their lives. A correlation between two variables that can be explained by a third variable is called a spurious relationship (Kenny, 1979). Although correlational evidence alone is not sufficient for making causal inferences, sophisticated statistical techniques can help to make causal interpretations from correlational studies (Baron & Kenny, 1986). One such technique is to identify moderator variables. A moderator variable affects the direction or strength of the correlation between two variables.

Questionnaires are often used in survey research. Demographic variables are frequently measured to describe the characteristics of people who respond to the survey. Examples of demographic variables include age, race, ethnicity, and occupation. The sample of people who respond to the survey are used to represent the population from which the sample was drawn. Well-selected samples will provide data that estimate the characteristics of the population, but there will always be some error. Frequently, survey results are reported with this error in mind. For example, a poll may report that 55% of a sample of respondents state they will vote for candidate X, but the margin of error may be 5%. This means that the actual percentage of people in the population (from which the sample was drawn) who will vote for candidate X falls between 50% and 60%. The margin of error is primarily determined by the size of the sample--the larger the sample, the smaller the error-- and the confidence we want to have in our estimate. The higher the desired level of confidence, the larger the margin of error.

Reliability and validity are vital characteristics of all psychological measurement, including surveys and tests. The goal of psychological measurement is to assess the degree to which some attribute (e.g., intelligence, depression) is present in a population, sample, or individual. Reliable measures are consistent, and will yield similar results each time a person completes the measure. "Test-retest reliability" can be determined by computing a correlation coefficient between the scores at two administrations of a measure. Reliability is increased when we use many items to assess an attribute, by including different types of items to measure an attribute, when there is greater variability on the factor or attribute in the sample being tested, and when the administration of the test or questionnaire is free of distractions and the instructions are clear. Reliability of a measure is easier to determine and achieve than validity. Validity refers to the extent to which a questionnaire or test measures the theoretical construct it is intended to measure. Using correlations between measures, "construct validity" can be assessed by examining the degree to which two measures of a construct (e.g., depression) lead to the same conclusion ("convergent validity") and the extent to which two measures of different constructs lead to different conclusions ("discriminant validity").

Because correlations allow us to make predictions, the results of correlational research have implications for decision making. Psychologists involved with psychotherapy, for example, frequently rely on clinical prediction to diagnose a client's problem. Clinical prediction is a judgment made about an individual based on careful review of evidence such as case study material as well as the clinician's prior experience with this type of client. Meehl (1954, 1992) has contrasted this type of decision making with that based on actuarial prediction, which involves the use of correlational research to develop statistical predictive relationships. Information about the client is entered into this predictive system and a statistical decision is made regarding the diagnosis. Actuarial prediction is based on empirical evidence rather than on the individual judgment of a clinician. In many situations it turns out that decision making based on actuarial prediction is more accurate than that based on clinical prediction (see also, for example, Dawes, 1988).

Surveys are an efficient way to obtain information needed to describe people's thoughts, opinions, and feelings. Surveys differ in purpose and scope, but they generally involve some form of sampling. The general goal of sampling is to identify a group of individuals whose responses can be generalized to the population of interest (see, for example, Campbell, 1981). How well responses can be generalized depends on the representativeness of the sample, that is, on how well the characteristics of the sample (e.g., gender, age, race, ethnicity, etc.) correspond to those of the population. Surveys also involve the use of a predetermined set of questions, generally in the form of a questionnaire. The construction of a good questionnaire often is time consuming, but it is a vital part of survey research.

A sample typically is formed by drawing a specified number of elements from an actual list of the possible elements in the population. The list of population elements is called a sampling frame. For example, if students attending a particular university are the elements of interest, then the registrar's list of currently enrolled, full-time students might serve as a sampling frame. A representative sample is best achieved by using probability sampling rather than nonprobability sampling. Probability sampling allows one to identify the probability that any one element in the population will be selected. In simple random sampling (the most common type of probability sampling) every element is equally likely to be included in the sample. Stratified random sampling is an alternative when simple random sampling is not sufficient. Accidental samples and purposive samples are two examples of nonprobability samples. Whereas the former is based on convenience and availability, the latter is based on expert judgment of some kind. An investigator, for example, wanting to assess the opinions of a university's best students, might obtain a purposive sample by asking professors and deans to identify the best students on campus. An accidental sample of the school's best students might be obtained by noting those students who are attending a meeting of a campus honorary society. Nonprobability samples do not allow the researcher to estimate the probability of an element's being included in the sample.

There are three general survey methods: mail surveys, personal interviews, and telephone interviews. Mail surveys avoid problems of interviewer bias, or the effect the interviewer has on the responses obtained, and are especially well suited for examining personal or embarrassing topics. A serious limitation of mail surveys, however, is the potential for response bias (see, for example, Babbie, 1989). This type of bias occurs because of the generally low response rate associated with mail surveys. Not everyone answers a mail survey, and we must assume that those who do respond are different in important characteristics from those who do not respond. Thus, the actual sample obtained from a mail survey may not be representative of the population. Personal interviews and phone surveys usually have much higher response rates and provide greater flexibility. Two major disadvantages of personal interview surveys are their high cost and the opportunity for interviewer bias. The telephone survey is the method of choice for most brief surveys, although there is still a problem with interviewer bias. Moreover, selection bias exists due to the fact that not everyone has a phone. Selection bias is a problem whenever some segment of the population is over- or underrepresented at the time the sample is selected.

Three survey research designs are the cross-sectional study, the successive independent samples study, and the longitudinal study. Cross-sectional surveys focus on describing the characteristics of a population or the differences between two or more populations. A survey of voters in California and in Florida regarding their attitudes toward national gun control legislation would represent a cross-sectional survey design. Describing changes in attitudes or opinions over time requires the use of successive independent samples. A successive independent samples design involves just what the name implies, approaching different (independent) samples of individuals in succession (over time). On the other hand, a longitudinal study requires that the same individuals be contacted at two or more points in time. The longitudinal study generally is preferred because it allows the assessment of changes for specific individuals and often avoids the problem of noncomparable successive samples.

Assume, for example, that a researcher uses a successive independent samples design to measure changes over time in the attitudes of people entering the military. In 1980 the researcher samples from new recruits at a large Marine base in California. In 1990 the same researcher obtains a sample of new recruits from an Army base located on the east coast. People entering the military in California may differ in important ways from those entering on the east coast; moreover, individuals enlisting in the Marines also may differ from those choosing the Army. Results from this study would be difficult to interpret due to the problem of noncomparable successive samples. Noncomparable samples can also arise in a longitudinal survey. Sometimes all respondents in a longitudinal survey do not complete all phases of the research; they drop out for one reason or another. Respondent mortality is one term used to describe a situation in which research participants begin a study but do not finish. When respondent mortality is present it is not always known whether the final sample in a longitudinal survey is comparable to the original sample. Those respondents who do complete all phases of the survey may differ systematically from those who drop out. The final sample, in other words, may differ in important ways from the original sample because some individuals who were part of the original sample are no longer included in the final sample.

One threat to the validity of survey results is the pressure on respondents to give socially desirable responses; thus, people's behavior does not always conform to what they say they would do (see Kidder & Judd, 1986). It may be important to supplement survey results with data based on direct observation or other, nonreactive measures.

References

Babbie, E. R. (1989). The practice of social research. Belmont, CA: Wadsworth.

Baron, R. M., & Kenny, D. A. (1986). The moderator-mediator variable distinction in social psychological research: Conceptual, strategic, and statistical considerations. Journal of Personality and Social Psychology, 51, 1173-1182.

Campbell, A. (1981). The sense of well-being in America. New York: McGraw-Hill.

Dawes, R. M. (1988). Rational choice in an uncertain world. San Diego, CA: Harcourt, Brace Jovanovich.

Kenny, D. A. (1979). Correlation and causality. New York: Wiley.

Kidder, L. H., & Judd, C. M. (1986). Research methods in social relations (5th ed.). New York: Holt, Rinehart, and Winston.

Meehl, P. E. (1954). Clinical versus statistical prediction: A theoretical analysis and review of the literature. Minneapolis: University of Minnesota Press.

Meehl, P. E. (1992, June). Philosophy of Science: Help or Hindrance? Paper presented at the Fourth Annual Convention of the American Psychological Society, San Diego, CA.

Myers, D. G., & Diener, E. (1995). Who is happy? Psychological Science, 6, 10-19.

II. KEY CONCEPTS

The following concepts are importantly related to the correlational research studies that are discussed in this unit. Use the information found in the OVERVIEW, as well as the definitions of key concepts provided here, to complete the exercises in the following sections. [NOTE: Numbers in parentheses refer to pages in the fourth edition of Research Methods in Psychology by Shaughnessy and Zechmeister (1997), where these concepts are more fully defined.]

accidental sample A type of nonprobability sample that results when availability and willingness to respond are the overriding factors used in selecting respondents; generally low in representativeness. (139)

actuarial prediction A prediction of people's typical or average behavior based on reliable correlations between variables (e.g., predicting students' college GPA based on SAT scores). (130)

biased sample A sample in which the distribution of characteristics is systematically different from that of the parent population. (136)

correlation A correlation exists when two different measures of the same people, events, or things vary together; the presence of a correlation makes it possible to predict values on one variable by knowing the values on the second variable. (120)

correlation coefficient A statistic that indicates how well two measures vary together; absolute size ranges from 0.0 (no correlation) to 1.00 (perfect correlation); direction of covariation is indicated by the sign of the coefficient, a plus (+) indicating that both measures covary in the same direction and a minus (-) indicating that the variables vary in opposite directions. (120)

correlational research Research which has the goal of identifying predictive relationships among naturally occurring variables. (119)

cross-sectional design A survey research design in which one or more samples of the population is selected and information is collected from the samples at one time. (146)

element Each member of the population of interest. (136)

interviewer bias Occurs when the interviewer tries to adjust the wording of a question to "fit" the respondent or records only selected portions of the respondent's answers. (144)

longitudinal design A survey research design in which the same sample of respondents is interviewed more than once. (150)

margin of error In survey research, an estimate of the difference between a result obtained from a sample (e.g., the sample mean) and the corresponding true population value (e.g., population mean). (125)

nonprobability sampling A sampling procedure in which there is no way to estimate the probability of each element's being included in the sample; two common types are accidental sampling and purposive sampling. (138)

population The set of all the cases of interest. (135)

probability sampling A sampling procedure in which the probability that each element of the population will be included in the sample can be specified. (138)

purposive sample A type of nonprobability sample in which the elements to be included in the sample are selected by the investigator on the basis of special characteristics of the respondents. (139)

representativeness A sample is representative to the extent that it has the same distribution of characteristics as the population from which it was selected; our ability to generalize from sample to population is critically dependent on representativeness. (136)

response bias A threat to the representativeness of a sample which occurs when some participants selected to respond to a survey systematically fail to complete the survey (e.g., due to failure to complete a lengthy questionnaire or to return a phone call). (141)

sample Something less than all the cases of interest; in survey research, a subset of the population actually drawn from the sampling frame. (136)

sampling frame A specific listing of all the members of the population of interest; an operational definition of the population. (135)

selection bias A threat to the representativeness of a sample which occurs when the procedures used to select a sample result in the over- or underrepresentation of a significant segment of the population. (136-137)

simple random sample A type of probability sample in which each possible sample of a specified size in the population has an equal chance of being selected. (140)

social desirability The pressures on survey respondents to answer as they think they should respond in accordance with what is most socially acceptable, and not in accordance with what they actually believe. (153)

stratified random sample A type of probability sample in which the population is divided into subpopulations called <u>strata</u>, and random samples are drawn from each of these strata. (140)

successive independent samples design A survey research design in which a series of cross-sectional surveys is done and the same questions are asked of each succeeding sample of respondents. (147)

III. EXAMPLES OF SURVEY STUDIES

Read the following summaries of published research carefully. Answer the questions found at the end of each summary. Answering these questions may require use of concepts introduced in previous units as well as those concepts found in this unit.

A. The Intelligence Test Controversy

Reference: Snyderman, M., & Rothman, S. (1987). Survey of expert opinion on intelligence and aptitude testing. American Psychologist, 42, 137-144.

Article Summary: The measurement of intelligence (IQ) and the use of intelligence or aptitude tests in school and employment settings are controversial. Critics suggest, for example, that these tests "measure nothing but test taking skills" and that they are culturally biased against certain groups in society. Observers outside the fields of psychology and education also sometimes perceive experts as showing wide disagreement over these issues. But what do the experts think? To find out, researchers asked 1,020 social scientists and educators to respond to a 16-page questionnaire containing 48 questions about the IQ controversy. The sample was carefully chosen from among scholarly organizations whose members would likely have an intimate knowledge of IQ measurement and testing. Primary groups included, for instance, relevant divisions of the American Psychological Association and the American Educational Research Association. Examples of other groups sampled were the Behavior Genetics Association and the Cognitive Science Society. The sample was drawn randomly from the membership directories of these groups. Envelopes containing the questionnaire, a stamped return envelope, and cover letter introducing the nature of the study and assuring confidentiality of responses were mailed in September, 1984. About two weeks after the initial mailing a reminder postcard was sent to individuals who had not yet returned the questionnaire. Four weeks later a complete second set of materials was sent to those who still had not responded. A total of 661 individuals responded (65%).

Fifty-three percent agreed somewhat or strongly that a consensus existed among psychologists and educators "as to the kinds of behaviors that are labeled 'intelligent'." When asked to identify specific traits associated with intelligence, more than 90% of those responding selected "abstract thinking or reasoning," "problem solving ability," and "capacity to acquire knowledge." "General knowledge" and "mathematical competence" were identified by about two-thirds of those answering. When asked whether intelligence should be described in terms of some general factor with possible special abilities or entirely in terms of separate faculties, 58% said that intelligence is best described as some form of general factor. Only 13% said separate faculties, and 16% said the data were not clear on this issue. Because respondents were given the opportunity to respond "not qualified" to any question, not everyone answered every question. Of those responding to a question about sources of evidence for the heritability of IQ, 94% indicated that such evidence existed. However, experts also tended to agree that IQ tests are somewhat biased against American Blacks as well as members of lower socio-economic groups.

The researchers indicated that when responses to all items were considered, experts held "generally positive attitudes about the validity and usefulness of intelligence and aptitude tests," but experts also acknowledged that there were problems due to the influence of nonintellectual factors on test performance (for example, anxiety, motivation, physical health), and to the frequent misinterpretation of and overemphasis on test scores in the schools.

Questions:

1. Which of the following three research designs was used by Snyderman and Rothman: cross-sectional design, successive independent samples design, or longitudinal design?
2. The Snyderman and Rothman survey is based on probability sampling. (a) What specific procedures indicate that this survey was based on probability sampling? (b) Show with a hypothetical example how the sample obtained by Snyderman and Rothman could have been obtained through nonprobability sampling, for example, by purposive sampling.
3. Ninety percent of those responding identified a relatively small set of specific traits associated with intelligence. Fifty-three percent agreed that a consensus existed about "intelligent" behaviors. Explain how it could be possible that fewer people contributed to the 90% value than to the 53% value.
4. Results of surveys sometimes are reported in the popular media with subtle but important qualifying statements. Consider, for example, the following statement: "More than two-thirds of *those surveyed*..." Another example is: "More than three-fourths of *those responding*..."   Each of these statements alludes to a different and important number that must be reported if survey data are to be interpreted meaningfully. (a) What value (i.e., the size of what group) serves as the denominator for computing a proportion such as "two-thirds of those surveyed? What value serves as the denominator for computing "three-fourths of those responding? Why is it so important that both numbers always be reported with survey data? (b) What specific aspect of Snyderman and Rothman's instructions to respondents indicates the need for careful reporting of numbers of those responding?
5. Although it was not included in the article summary, Snyderman and Rothman did something very interesting as part of their survey procedure. They randomly sampled 40 names of persons who did not return the questionnaire after three mailings. These individuals were contacted by phone and asked some demographic questions as well as some of the important substantive questions from the questionnaire. The researchers also asked the nonrespondents why they had not returned the questionnaire they had received in the mail. The results of questionnaire items for this sample of nonrespondents were then compared with results for those who returned the questionnaire. The reasons people did not respond were also summarized. What do you think Snyderman and Rothman were trying to accomplish by using this procedure?

B. Love and Marriage

Reference: Simpson, J. A., Campbell, B., & Berscheid, E. (1986). The association between romantic love and marriage: Kephart (1967) twice revisited. Personality and Social Psychology Bulletin, 12, 363-372.

Article Summary: The authors remind us that American society has changed a great deal in the last several decades, and they suggest that some of these changes can be expected to have influenced Americans' attitudes toward love and marriage. For example, although romantic love is widely assumed to be an important condition for initiating and maintaining marital relationships, data obtained by social scientists have not always been consistent with this assumption. According to the authors, in the 1960s, Kephart (1967) reported that males and females differed substantially in their attitudes toward love and marriage. College men and women were asked the following question: If a boy (girl) had all the other qualities you desired, would you marry this person if you were not in love with him (her)? Although about two-thirds of the men surveyed said no, less than one-fourth of the women answered no. (Undecided was another possible response.) At that time, Kephart (1967) reportedly stated that considerations such as economic security, family background, and professional status may have influenced women's marital choices more than men's.

The authors sought to determine whether the ideas expressed by college students had changed since the mid-1960s. They conducted two surveys, one in 1976 and another in 1984, of college men and women at the University of Minnesota. Both their samples (n = 246 in 1976, and n = 339 in 1984) were more than 90% "white," and at least 93% were between the ages of 18 and 24. Kephart's (1967) original question was reworded slightly ("boy, girl" was changed to "man, woman") for the more recent surveys. In 1976, 86.2% of the males (n = 116) and 80.0% of the females (n = 130) responded no to this question; in 1984, 85.6% of the males (n = 173) and 84.9% of the females (n = 166) surveyed said no. A second survey item was designed to assess students' attitudes toward romantic love as a prerequisite for maintaining a marital relationship. Students were asked to respond (agree, disagree, neutral) to the following statement: If love has completely disappeared from a marriage, I think it is probably best for the couple to make a clean break and start new lives. In 1976, 57.0% of males (n = 114) and 61.9% of females (n = 130) agreed; in 1984, 46.2% of males (n = 169) and 44.3% of females (n = 165) agreed with this statement.

In 1976 and 1984, a large majority of both college men and women viewed "romantic love as a necessary prerequisite to establishing a marital relationship"; in both surveys, men and women were likely to say that romantic love was also necessary for maintaining a marital relationship. The authors discuss several reasons for these changes in attitudes since the Kephart (1967) survey, including possible decreasing societal pressures on men and women to marry early (thereby allowing people more time to find someone they truly love), growing importance of family values, and systematic changes in the ratio of available men to women. Because the changes in attitudes have been most dramatic for women, the authors emphasize that one important reason likely is the increasingly greater "independence" (legal, economic, social) experienced by women over the past decades. However, another possibility is an increase in the general "importance of positive emotional experiences in people's lives." [NOTE: Kephart, W. M. (1967). Some correlates of romantic love. Journal of Marriage and the Family, 29, 470-474.]

Questions:

1. Based only on the information provided in the summary, would you characterize the samples in the Simpson et al. (1986) study as probability samples or nonprobability samples? Explain your choice.

2. What concerns might you have regarding the representativeness of the college students surveyed by Simpson et al., assuming the population of interest was U.S. college students?

3. The 1967 survey by Kephart, combined with the 1976 and 1984 surveys by Simpson et al., could be viewed as constituting a successive independent samples design. Explain why the successive independent samples design may be a good description of the present study and indicate the important characteristics of this type of survey design. (For example, how does this design differ from a longitudinal design?)

4. A potential problem with the successive independent samples design is that of noncomparable successive samples. Describe the nature of this problem and indicate whether you believe it is a problem in the Simpson et al. study.

5. Another subtle but important limitation of the successive independent samples design appears when we attempt to determine how people have changed over time. For example, Simpson et al. reported that 61.9% of the women surveyed in 1976 agreed that it was important to make a clean break when love had disappeared from a marriage, but that in 1984 only 44.3% of the women (a decrease of about one-fourth the total in 1976) agreed with this idea. One might be tempted to make the following conclusion regarding these findings: The results show that about one-fourth of the women who agreed with this statement in 1976 no longer agree. Explain why such a conclusion can not be made on the basis of these data.

IV. PROBLEMS AND EXERCISES

Read the following descriptions of survey research studies carefully and then answer the questions that follow.

A. Problem 1

<u>Description</u>: The registrar's office of a small college was asked to prepare a report for a national association of colleges regarding the job placement of their graduates. The college registrar decided to conduct a mail survey of recent graduates. A brief questionnaire asking about the employment status of the graduates was constructed and mailed to the 682 graduates who appeared on the graduation rolls in the last two years. A total of 504 completed questionnaires was returned. A tabulation of the survey results revealed that 88 percent of the graduates indicated that they were employed in a field of their choice. The average time reported to obtain a first job after graduation was 1.2 months. The registrar was quite enthusiastic about these results and quickly forwarded them to the national association. He underscored in his summary letter to the association the fact that at his college nearly 9 out of 10 graduates are successfully employed within fewer than 6 weeks!

<u>Questions</u>:

1. (a) What was the sampling frame used in this study? (b) Was the survey study based on a probability sampling procedure or a nonprobability sampling procedure?
2. (a) What survey research problem is possible because of the return rate in this study? (b) How is this problem likely to affect the conclusion that nearly "9 out of 10" graduates had jobs?
3. Although it is possible that the actual percentage of recent graduates from this school who have jobs in fields of their choice is 88 percent, the percentage is likely somewhat less than 88 percent. If we assume that those graduates who responded to the survey answered truthfully, what <u>could be</u> the actual percentage of graduates holding jobs?

B. Problem 2

<u>Description</u>: A physician read a newspaper article stating that the incidence of child abuse in this country is on the rise. The article provided estimates of the percentage of children who were abused during the past year in the U.S. The physician was quite skeptical that the number of abused children was as high as that reported in the article. She decided to conduct a survey of all the physicians specializing in children's medicine who worked at the five hospitals in her community. She obtained a list of all such physicians, a total of 103. She then made up a short list of questions

regarding the physicians' personal experiences with cases of child abuse. A paid research assistant attempted to contact by telephone each of the physicians. By being persistent, the assistant reached 91 physicians by phone and asked each about his or her experiences with child abuse. Every physician who was contacted agreed to answer all the questions. The researcher found that the number of child abuse cases seen by her respondents was considerably fewer than would be expected given the population of her community and the percentage estimates provided in the newspaper article. She concluded that the author of the newspaper article was seriously overestimating the incidence of child abuse.

Questions:

1. What was the sampling frame used in this study?
2. It seems likely that the results of this survey are biased. What type of bias is apt to be present: response bias or selection bias? Define each of these types of bias and explain your choice.

V. DATA ANALYSIS

A. Survey Results

Survey data, such as those obtained by Simpson et al. (1986), are often described in the form of cross tabulations. Specifically, results are presented in a table with columns and rows defined by crossing two or more variables. One variable typically represents the columns of the table, while a second variable represents the rows. In the Simpson et al. study, for example, one variable was sex of respondent (male and female), and the other variable was type of response (agree, disagree, neutral). In 1984, Simpson et al. obtained the following distribution of responses to the statement about maintaining a marital relationship: Men, 46.2%, 26.7%, 27.2%; Women, 44.3%, 33.3%, 22.4% (agree, disagree, neutral, respectively).

1. Construct a data matrix by showing proportions of men's and women's responses in the six cells created by crossing the sex of respondent (rows) and type of response (columns). NOTE: Remember to change percentages to proportions before entering the numbers in the matrix.
2. Consult the article summary in order to obtain the sample sizes of men and women associated with this question in 1984. The sample sizes for different questions are slightly different, so be sure to use the sample sizes for the question on maintaining relationships. Use the sample size information to calculate the frequency of responses in each of the six cells. Enter the frequencies in the matrix by putting them in parentheses next to the relevant proportions.
3. Formalize the data summary by constructing a table in the format recommended by the American Psychological Association (APA). Make sure,

for instance, that both rows and columns have appropriate labels and that you indicate to the reader, perhaps with a footnote to the table, that proportions are reported outside parentheses and frequencies are found inside parentheses.

B. Correlations

It is important when developing a test or questionnaire to provide information about the measure's reliability. A common way of measuring reliability is to compute a measure of test-retest reliability. This usually consists of a correlation obtained when the same test (or highly similar forms of the test) is administered to the same group of individuals on two different occasions. Generally, test-makers like to see test-retest reliability coefficients of .80 or greater. The data shown below represent hypothetical scores on a test measuring students' belief in extra-sensory perception (ESP). Assume that the test was developed by a psychology student who is planning an independent study investigating high school students' beliefs in ESP. After designing the test, the psychology student administered the test to 15 high school seniors at the beginning of the semester and then again near the end of the semester, about 14 weeks later. [If this were a real study the student would want to test more than 15 subjects in order to obtain valid results. An example of an actual test developed to measure ESP beliefs is reported by Tobacyk, J., & Milford, G. (1983). Belief in paranormal phenomena: Assessment instrument development and implications for personality functioning. Journal of Personality and Social Psychology, 44, 1029-1037.] The seniors' results (based on a maximum score of 40; higher numbers indicate greater belief) on the same test given at two different times are reported below in the 2nd and 3rd columns. Does the test show an acceptable level of test-retest reliability?

Participant	ESP (1)	ESP (2)
1	26	30
2	18	17
3	33	29
4	36	34
5	12	11
6	23	29
7	27	27
8	31	29
9	14	15
10	33	28
11	19	17
12	20	22
13	36	32
14	22	19
15	39	35

VI. REVIEW TESTS

These practice tests will be most helpful in preparing for your classroom tests if you test yourself under conditions that resemble those of your actual tests as closely as possible. We suggest, therefore, that you put away the book after completing the exercises in this unit and then return at a later study session to take the review tests.

A. Matching

1.   The following brief descriptions of survey studies represent examples of the three major survey designs that have been introduced in this unit: cross-sectional design; successive independent samples design; longitudinal design. Identify the type of design used in each survey. Write the first letter of the first word in each design name (C, S, L) next to the appropriate description. (Some designs appear more than once.)

_____ a.   Children from the 4th grade, 6th grade, and 8th grade of a public elementary school are asked about the number of hours that they watch TV each week. Twenty children, 10 males and 10 females, are surveyed in each grade.

_____ b.   First-year students attending a small Midwest college were asked whether or not they smoke cigarettes. Responses were obtained from a total of 215 students in 1970 and from 313 students in 1990.

_____ c.   All the faculty members of a large public university are surveyed regarding their attitudes toward changes in the university's core curriculum.

_____ d.   Students enrolled in a large introductory psychology class are asked at the beginning of the semester and at the end of the semester about their intentions to major in psychology.

_____ e.   Responses to a questionnaire containing items asking about the use of animals in scientific research are compared between members of two different scientific organizations.

2.   At the heart of any survey study is its sample. However, as you have seen, samples come in different shapes and sizes. Four types of samples discussed in this unit were the: (1) simple random sample, (2) stratified random sample, (3) purposive sample, and (4) accidental sample. Each of the following sample descriptions illustrates a different type of sample. Match the four sample types with the four sample descriptions by placing the appropriate number (1-4) from the above list next to each sample description.

_____ a.   A total of 60 patients in a psychiatric hospital is selected for a survey about hospital treatment. Equal numbers (20) of patients are selected from three different categories defined by length of stay in the hospital. Selection from these three categories is done in such a way that each individual in each category had an equal chance of being selected.

_____ b.   Psychologists attending a convention are asked as they enter the convention hall whether or not they belong to more than one national psychology association.

_____ c.   A researcher contacts 10 clinical psychologists who have treated a serial killer in their private practice. The psychologists are asked questions about the psychopathology of serial killers, and the results are used to create a profile of this type of individual.

_____ d.   A questionnaire is sent to 1,000 members of the American Psychological Society (APS). Individuals were identified by selecting names randomly from the membership list of this organization.

B. True-False

_____ 1. A Pearson product-moment correlation coefficient is used with nominal scale data.

_____ 2. Valid tests are characterized by consistency.

_____ 3. In general, the reliability of a test increases with the number of items on the test.

_____ 4. Obtaining a correlation coefficient (r) of 1.42 would indicate an error in calculation.

_____ 5. A reliable test is one that measures what it is supposed to measure.

_____ 6. A correlation coefficient of +.46 indicates a stronger relationship than a coefficient of -.56.

_____ 7. Causal inferences are problematic when based only on correlational evidence.

_____ 8. Clinical prediction relies heavily on correlational evidence obtained from large data sets describing individuals with characteristics relevant to the problem under study.

C. Multiple Choice

1. Responses from a sample can be generalized to the population of interest when which of the following characteristics of the sample is present?
    a. efficiency
    b. representativeness
    c. responsivity
    d. uniqueness

2. The actual list of the possible elements that provides an operational definition of the population of interest is called the
    a. sampling frame
    b. sampling index
    c. population listing
    d. population catalog

3. For which of the following types of sampling do we know the probability of any one element's being selected?
    a. equiprobable sample
    b. accidental sample
    c. purposive sample
    d. simple random sample

4. Which of the following survey methods is best suited for the study of personal or embarrassing topics?
    a. personal interview
    b. telephone interview
    c. mail survey
    d. accidental sample

5. When not everyone answers a mail survey it is reasonable to assume that those who do respond are different in important ways from those who do not respond. The term used to describe this problem in survey research is
    a. inadequate response rate
    b. response bias
    c. selection bias
    d. differential response rate

6. In which of the following survey research designs is the focus on describing the characteristics of a population or the differences between two or more populations at a certain point in time?
    a. cross-sectional design
    b. successive independent samples design
    c. longitudinal design
    d. accidental samples design

7. A major threat to the validity of results obtained from a successive independent samples design is
    a. respondent mortality
    b. nonrandom sampling
    c. noncomparable successive samples
    d. interviewer bias

8. Which of the following is a major threat to the validity of results obtained from a longitudinal survey design?
    a. respondent mortality
    b. interviewer bias
    c. selection bias
    d. nonprobability sampling

9. A survey using the Internet to contact people about attitudes toward mental health services would most likely be criticized for
    a. response bias
    b. interviewer bias
    c. social desirability bias
    d. selection bias

10. Surveys play an important role in a type of research that is intended to assess the covariation of naturally occurring variables. This general type of research is called
    a. experimental research
    b. correlational research
    c. analytical research
    d. qualitative research

ANSWERS TO EXERCISES AND REVIEW TESTS ARE FOUND

IN THE APPENDIX AT THE END OF THIS BOOK

****

QUESTIONS/PROBLEMS FOR CLASS DISCUSSION

A. Terminology and Concepts

1. Suppose you were to survey students regarding attitudes toward the value of a college education. Identify a variable that you believe would correlate positively with the belief that a college education is valuable, and a variable that would correlate negatively with this belief.
2. Suppose you are seeing a therapist for anxiety. Explain how the therapist could use clinical prediction to decide on a treatment. How could actuarial prediction be used?
3. Explain why a purposive sample may be more representative of the population of interest than an accidental sample. How are these two samples different from a simple random sample?
4. Illustrate how selection bias and response bias could have played a role in the Snyderman and Rothman (1987) study described in this unit.
5. How are cross-sectional and successive independent samples designs different from longitudinal designs? How are successive independent samples and longitudinal designs different from cross-sectional designs? Give specific examples of each type of research design using ideas obtained from reading the summaries of articles in this unit.

B. Critical Thinking: Analyzing Research

Refer to Section III, Examples of Survey Studies (pp. 63-67), to answer the following questions:

1. In the article by Snyderman and Rothman (1987) summarized in this unit, experts were surveyed regarding their opinions of intelligence and aptitude testing. The authors of this study also measured the political perspective of the experts. Higher numbers on their political perspective measure indicate political conservatism, and lower numbers on the scale represent political liberalism. Three measures were shown to be correlated significantly with political perspective: test usefulness (higher scores represent the belief that tests are useful), test bias (higher scores indicate that tests are rated as biased), and test misuse (higher scores represent the belief that tests are misused). The correlations between political perspective and these three measures were .31, -.38, and -.17, respectively. Based on these correlations, describe the relationships between political perspective and beliefs about intelligence and aptitude tests.

2. Snyderman and Rothman (1987) concluded that "those with expertise in areas related to intelligence testing hold generally positive attitudes about the validity and usefulness of intelligence and aptitude tests." Consider the correlations that were summarized in the preceding paragraph (B.1.). Based on those additional correlations, do you agree with their conclusion? Why or why not?

3. The samples in the Simpson, Campbell, and Berscheid (1986) study were probably not representative of all people of marrying age. Instead, the samples were probably somewhat representative of white college students, ages 18-24, who attend college in the Midwest. Describe the characteristics of the population of interest which, ideally, you would like the study sample to represent. Consider in your description the following questions:
    a. Should the sample consist only of college students?
    b. What age range should be considered?
    c. Should the sample consist only of never-married individuals?
    d. Are variables such as race, ethnicity, and religiosity important?
    e. Should the attitudes of homosexual and bisexual individuals be included?

4. Given that there are various characteristics of individuals that may be related to attitudes regarding love and marriage, how might stratified random sampling be used to investigate relationships between these characteristics and attitudes?

5. One interpretation of the findings in the Simpson et al. (1986) study is that the societal pressure to marry at an early age has decreased over time, which gives people more time to find someone to marry whom they truly love. If this is correct, one might expect that older individuals (who perhaps see themselves as having less time to find that special someone) may differ from traditional-age college students in their endorsement of the question, "If a man (woman) had all the other qualities you desired, would you marry this person if you were not in love with him (her)?" What survey design would you use to examine this hypothesis?

C. Creative Thinking: Designing Research

Based on your analysis of the Simpson et al. (1986) study on love and marriage, develop a survey design that examines differences in attitudes that may exist for males and females with different characteristics (e.g., religiosity, sexual preference). What is your research hypothesis? Describe how you will conduct your survey (e.g., identify your sampling frame, how you will identify elements for your sample, your survey method, the questions you will ask, etc.). How do you think your findings will compare to those observed by Simpson et al. (1986)?

D. Statistical Analysis

Simpson et al. (1986) used two items to examine respondents' attitudes regarding what should happen when love disappears in a marriage:

1. "If love has completely disappeared from a marriage, I think it is probably best for the couple to make a clean break and start new lives."
2. "In my opinion, the disappearance of love is not a sufficient reason for ending a marriage, and should not be viewed as such."

Responses to these two items could be used to assess a "belief in divorce" construct. Suppose that respondents indicated the extent to which they agreed with these statements on a 5-point scale, with "1" indicating "totally disagree" and "5" indicating "totally agree." How should respondents' ratings for these two statements correlate in order to obtain evidence for convergent validity of this construct?

Presented below are hypothetical data for 10 individuals who responded to these two statements. Do the data indicate convergent validity for the "belief in divorce" construct?

Respondent	Statement 1	Statement 2
1	4	1
2	5	1
3	2	5
4	3	4
5	4	2
6	1	5
7	3	1
8	5	2
9	1	3
10	2	4

UNIT 5. UNOBTRUSIVE MEASURES OF BEHAVIOR

I. OVERVIEW

The use of physical traces and archival data in psychological research represents an important alternative to direct observation and surveys (see Webb, Campbell, Schwartz, Sechrest, & Grove, 1981). Physical traces are the remnants, fragments, and products of past behavior. A psychologist, for instance, who examines the arts-and-craft projects made by patients residing in a mental hospital would be making use of physical traces in the form of products of past behavior. In addition to examining the creations or products of past behavior, researchers may choose to measure the nature of physical use. Physical use traces are based on the accumulation of evidence (accretion measures) or are the result of selective wear (erosion measures) (Webb et al., 1981). Use traces can either result naturally, without any intervention by the investigator, or be planned by the investigator. Recording the amount of litter on a college campus, for instance, might be an indirect measure of students' concern for the appearance of their campus (or, perhaps, the efficiency of the college's groundskeepers). Amount of litter would represent a natural physical use trace resulting from accretion. On the other hand, a researcher who intentionally drops litter on the walkways of a college campus and then measures whether or not the litter is picked up by students in a specified interval of time would be using a planned physical use trace.

When obtaining physical traces, an investigator must be aware of possible biases in the way in which traces accumulate or survive over time (see Webb et al., 1981). A measure of the amount of litter on a college campus, for example, made at the same time that a large off-campus group is using campus facilities may not be a valid measure of the student population's concern for the appearance of their campus. An investigator who controls the amount of litter appearing on a campus walkway by depositing it at various intervals may not obtain a valid measure of student concern if weather conditions are such that much of the litter is displaced by high winds.

Archival data are found in records and documents that recount the activities of individuals, institutions, governments, and other groups. Although archival data are often in the form of written communications, radio, television, and other forms of electronic media can be sources of archival data. Archival records, like physical traces, constitute nonreactive approaches to hypothesis testing (Webb et al., 1981). These sources of information are valuable because they provide a way of investigating the external validity of laboratory findings, assessing the effect of a natural "treatment" (such as a political assassination), analyzing the content of communications (for example, letters to the editor of a school newspaper), and describing trends (such as might be documented by noting sales of exercise equipment in a particular company). A researcher, for instance, might analyze the contents of a personal help column, such as "Dear Abby," in order to test a laboratory-derived theory of human behavior. Do rationalizations for actions described in a personal help column match those obtained from participants in laboratory studies of this topic? (See, for example, Fischer, Schoeneman, & Rubanowitz, 1987.) If the pattern of results from the archival analysis is similar to that obtained from laboratory studies, the external validity of the laboratory results is increased.

The analysis of archival data typically requires some form of content analysis, a process that can involve problems of sampling and coding that are not unlike those that arise in the analysis of narrative records (see Holsti, 1969). Content analysis typically is a three-stage process involving identification of a relevant source, sampling from that source, and coding the contents of the source. Coding requires that relevant descriptive categories and appropriate units be defined and measured. Consider a researcher who is interested in investigating bias in the way news is reported on television news shows. The investigator will need to provide definitions for what is "news," what constitutes "bias," and other relevant categories. Amount of time, for instance, given to a particular news event might represent a measure of the event's importance.

Problems of selective deposit and selective survival must be investigated when archival data are used, just as they are when physical traces are used (Webb et al., 1981). Suicide notes illustrate the problem of selective deposit -- fewer than one-fourth of all suicides leave notes, so it is possible that those who leave notes are not representative of those who do not. The analysis of the contents of advice columns illustrates the problem of selective survival. Advice columnists print only a fraction of the letters they receive, and the "survivors" may not be typical of the entire set of letters received. Whenever possible, evidence should also be presented showing that spurious relationships have not been obtained. A spurious relationship exists when data falsely indicate that two variables are associated when, in fact, they are not directly associated. This can occur when improper or inadequate statistical procedures are used or when variables are accidentally related (see Judd, Smith, & Kidder, 1991). For example, a researcher may find that frequency of daily traffic accidents in a given month and average daily temperatures are positively associated. However, before concluding that temperature and traffic accidents are directly related ("when the temperature gets hot drivers get 'hot'"), the investigator would need to demonstrate that more traffic accidents do not occur on warm than cold days simply because there are more cars on the road when the temperature is warmer.

Physical traces and archival data can provide important nonreactive (unobtrusive) measures of behavior and may be used as the sole dependent variable or in combination with other measures of behavior. You may remember that a measure is nonreactive when the participant under investigation is unaware of the presence of an observer or that he or she is the object of a scientific study. When use measures or measures based on the analysis of archival data are combined with other measures of behavior, the investigator often can increase the internal validity of a scientific study. Multimethod approaches to the study of behavior reduce the chance that results are due to some artifact of the measurement process (Webb et al., 1981).

References

Fischer, K., Schoeneman, T. J., & Rubanowitz, D. E. (1987). Attributions in the advice columns: II. The dimensionality of actors' and observers' explanations for interpersonal problems. <u>Personality and Social Psychology Bulletin, 13</u>, 458-466.

Holsti, O. R. (1969). <u>Content analysis for the social sciences</u>. Reading, MA: Addison-Wesley.

Judd, C. M., Smith, E. R., & Kidder, L. H. (1991). <u>Research methods in social relations</u> (6th ed.). Fort Worth, TX: Holt, Rinehart, and Winston.

Webb, E. J., Campbell, D. T., Schwartz, R. D., Sechrest, L., & Grove, J. B. (1981). <u>Nonreactive measures in the social sciences</u> (2nd ed.). Boston: Houghton Mifflin.

II. KEY CONCEPTS

The following concepts are importantly related to the methods that are discussed in this unit. Use the information found in the **OVERVIEW**, as well as the definitions of the key concepts provided here, to complete the exercises in the following sections. [NOTE: Numbers in parentheses refer to pages in the fourth edition of <u>Research Methods in Psychology</u> by Shaughnessy and Zechmeister (1997), where these concepts are more fully defined.]

archival data A source of evidence that is based upon records or documents relating the activities of individuals, institutions, governments, and other groups; used as an alternative to or in conjunction with other research methods. (160)

content analysis Any of a variety of techniques for making inferences by objectively identifying specific characteristics of messages, usually written communications but may be any form of message; used extensively in the analysis of archival data. (173)

multimethod approach An approach to hypothesis testing that seeks evidence by collecting data using several different measures of behavior; a recognition of the fact that any single measure of behavior can result from some artifact of the measuring process. (161)

physical traces A source of evidence that is based on the remnants, fragments, and products of past behavior; used as an alternative to or in conjunction with other research methods. (159)

selective deposit The bias that results from the way physical traces are laid down and the way archival sources are produced, edited, or altered, as they are established; when present, the bias severely limits generality of research findings. (178)

selective survival The bias that results from the way physical traces and archives survive over time; when present, the bias severely limits the external validity of research findings. (179)

spurious relationship Exists when evidence falsely indicates that two or more variables are associated. (179)

unobtrusive (nonreactive) measures Measures of behavior that eliminate the problem of reactivity, because observations are made in such a way that the presence of the observer is not detected by those being observed. (159)

III. EXAMPLES OF STUDIES USING UNOBTRUSIVE MEASURES

Read the following two summaries of published research carefully. Answer the questions found at the end of each summary. Answering these questions will require use of concepts in this unit as well as those in previous units.

A. Self and Social Perception

Reference: Frank, M. G., & Gilovich, T. (1988). The dark side of self- and social perception: Black uniforms and aggression in professional sports. Journal of Personality and Social Psychology, 54, 74-85.

Article Summary: As Frank and Gilovich (1988) point out, there is a strong association between the color black and bad or evil things. It is evident in our language when we speak of people being "blackballed," "blacklisted," or "blackmailed," or a reputation being "blackened." When terrible things happen we call it a "black day." Moreover, research has shown that an association between the color black and evil or death is found in numerous cultures, including those of Western Europe, Asia, and central Africa.

Frank and Gilovich (1988) wanted to determine whether this strong cultural association between black and evil would affect the way people behave. One way to find out, they reasoned, was to see whether professional sports teams that wear black uniforms are more aggressive than those wearing nonblack uniforms. Using the running records kept by the central offices of the National Football League (NFL) and the National Hockey League (NHL), the researchers analyzed penalty records of each of the major professional teams in these sports between 1970 and 1986. Yards penalized were analyzed for the NFL teams, and minutes that a player was assigned to the penalty box were calculated for the NHL teams. A uniform was considered as black if the colored part of the team's uniform (the one used typically for away games in the NHL and for home games in the NFL) was at least 50% black. (An exception was made for the Chicago Bears of the NFL, who wear dark blue uniforms which many people mistakenly remember as black.)

If there is an association between black and aggression then teams wearing black should be penalized more than would be expected simply by chance. And they were. Teams with black uniforms, such as Oakland, Chicago, and Cincinnati in the NFL, and Philadelphia, Pittsburgh, and Vancouver in the NHL, were reliably more aggressive than many other teams. The investigators also examined the archives for penalty records of any teams that switched their uniform color from nonblack to black sometime during the period under observation. An interesting question is whether a team that switches from nonblack to black becomes more aggressive after it starts wearing black. The analysis of the archival data suggested that this indeed was the case. Data provided by two NHL teams revealed that when these teams donned black uniforms they were penalized more. In addition, one team in the NHL that switched from a nonblack color to a different nonblack color did not show any increase in aggressiveness. This latter finding helps to rule out an effect of simply switching uniforms, as, for example, might occur if players compete more energetically after any change.

The investigators suggested that these results are due to both "social-perception" and "self-perception" processes. Specifically, they argued that referees "see" players in black as more aggressive than those players not wearing black and consequently award more penalties to players in black. And it is suggested that the players themselves tend to act more aggressively when they put on a black uniform. These conclusions were supported by both the analysis of archival data as well as the results of two laboratory experiments also carried out as part of this study. The experiments examined actual referees' judgments of aggressiveness of football teams wearing black- or white-colored uniforms, and college students' choices of games varying in aggressiveness (e.g., "dart gun duel," "block stacking") after putting on black or white uniforms. In addition to illustrating an ingenious use of nonreactive measures based on archival data, the Frank and Gilovich article is a nice illustration of the multimethod approach to hypothesis testing.

Questions:

1. How do the authors operationally define: (a) "black" and (b) "aggression"?
2. Identify the research hypothesis of this archival study. You will find it stated explicitly in the summary of the Frank and Gilovich article. (Remember that a research hypothesis should state clearly the expected relationship between the major variables of interest.)
3. (a) How does this study illustrate a multimethod approach to hypothesis testing? (b) Why is a multimethod approach especially recommended?
4. Archival records, like physical traces, can be biased, for example, by selective deposit or selective survival. There is no evidence to indicate that either of these types of bias was present in the Frank and Gilovich study. However,

consider the following hypothetical situations and decide which best illustrates selective deposit and which illustrates selective survival:

a. Coaches of 8th grade football teams in a community football league keep records of their teams' performances. These records are collected by a community official at the end of each year. A psychologist investigating level of youth activity in sports in this community finds that over the years the records were "edited" by a local community official after they were received.

b. When analyzing a report to the school superintendent on frequency of injuries in high school athletics, a social psychologist finds that the frequencies of serious injuries apparently were not recorded in the same way by coaches of different athletic teams. Thus, for example, the records revealed that the relative frequency of serious injuries among tennis players was similar to that of football players!

5. A spurious relationship between two variables exists if two variables are accidentally related or are related due to a "third variable." In the context of the Frank and Gilovich study, a spurious relationship between color of the uniform and number (or time) of penalties would be present, for example, if a third factor was identified that varied with black and nonblack uniforms and was actually responsible for the difference in penalty records between teams wearing black and nonblack uniforms. The authors discussed such a variable. What do you think that variable might be? That is, can you think of a reason that an association between color (black/nonblack) and aggressiveness might be found that is not related to self- or social-perception of players wearing black? HINT: Keep in mind that professional teams are controlled by the owners or management. [NOTE: This is a difficult question and do not be frustrated if you are not able to identify a possible third variable. Our goal in asking it is to demonstrate how difficult it sometimes is to identify spurious relationships. Give the question some thought and then look up the answer in the appendix and decide if you think the variable Frank and Gilovich identified in their article is a plausible alternative for their results.]

B. Prejudice

Reference: Kremer, J.R., Barry, R., & McNally, A. (1986). The misdirected letter and the quasi-questionnaire: Unobtrusive measures of prejudice in Northern Ireland. Journal of Applied Social Psychology, 16, 303-309.

The authors of this study point out that the "lost letter technique" has been used successfully over the past few decades as an unobtrusive measure of people's attitudes and behavior. The technique has been used, for example, to study voting preferences, racial prejudice, and political attitudes. Investigators using this method randomly distribute stamped, addressed letters or postcards that vary in some significant way. For example, letters addressed to a well-known conservative political group along with letters addressed to a more liberal organization might be dropped in various neighborhoods. The dependent variable is the return rate of these "lost" letters and is considered a measure of the community's attitudes towards such organizations. Presumably, someone would be less likely to place a letter in a mail box when the letter is addressed to an organization that the person dislikes than when a letter is addressed to an organization that is favored by the person finding the letter.

Kremer and his colleagues also point out, however, that one of the problems with the lost letter technique is that "the researcher is never sure precisely who returns the letter." Also, in some situations it may be difficult to drop letters without attracting unwanted attention from residents of the area or others who happen to be near the chosen drop sites. Researchers have developed another technique that circumvents these problems. It is called the misdirected letter technique. This technique involves sending letters addressed to particular households but with a fictitious name as the addressee. A return address is printed on the letter and the dependent variable is once again the rate of return of these, not lost, but "misdirected" letters. The method has been used, for example, to assess attitudes toward people with surnames (i.e., the addressees) that are associated with particular ethnic groups.

In the first experiment reported in this study, the authors used the misdirected letter technique to investigate religious prejudice among citizens of Northern Ireland. Specifically, two areas of West Belfast were chosen, one exclusively Catholic and one exclusively Protestant. "Misdirected letters were posted to households at random in each area, half of each batch addressed to William Scott and half to Patrick Connolly." [Prior to the actual study the authors had presented a list of common Catholic and Protestant names to judges and obtained ratings of degree of Protestant and Catholic association. Patrick Connolly was rated as having a strong association with Catholic; William Scott was a name rated as strongly associated with Protestant.] While only 26 percent of the letters overall were returned, significant differential rates of return were found from Catholic households. Thirty-five percent of the letters addressed to the fictitious Patrick Connolly were returned whereas only 15 percent of the letters addressed to the fictitious William Scott were returned. No difference in return rates was evident from Protestant households.

In a second experiment, the authors used a different unobtrusive measure, which they called the "quasi-questionnaire technique." This method involves sending a cover letter addressed simply to "resident" at a particular address and a brief questionnaire on some general topic. In this case, the questionnaire asked for respondents' views about transportation in urban areas. In addition to the questionnaire and the cover letter, a stamped, return envelope is included. The authors used either the name Patrick Connolly or William Scott on the cover letter and return envelope. These individuals were further identified as researchers at a nearby university who were carrying out a survey on transportation problems in the area. A total of 72 households (half Protestant and half Catholic) in a town with a history of sectarian conflict received letters that contained questionnaires from either Patrick Connolly or William Scott; questionnaires from the two different fictitious persons were also sent to 106 households (half Catholic and half Protestant) in a town that had been relatively free of conflict.

The results of the second experiment revealed that about 50 percent of the questionnaires were returned from each town. The return rate was similar for both Protestant and Catholic households in the town with no significant history of conflict, and rates did not differ in this town as a function of the name on the questionnaire and return envelope. However, in the town with a history of religious strife, Catholics were twice as likely to return the questionnaire from the fictitious Patrick Connolly as they were those from the equally fictitious William Scott. As was found in the first experiment, return rates from the Protestant households did not differ as a function of the sender's name. The authors suggest that unobtrusive measures such as those derived from the misdirected letter and quasi-questionnaire techniques can be particularly useful in helping to understand the complex forms that prejudice takes.

Questions:

1. Identify the independent variables in the two experiments reported in this study.
2. The dependent variable in these experiments was whether or not a letter was returned. What scale of measurement does this dependent variable represent: nominal, ordinal, interval, or ratio?
3. In the first experiment, which was based on the misdirected letter technique, the investigators ran into an interesting problem. Specifically, one-third of the letters were returned by the Post Office before reaching the intended household. Alert postal workers presumably spotted the unfamiliar name of the addressee and returned the letters rather than delivering them. [The quasi-questionnaire technique was created partly in response to this problem.] Can you identify at least one way that other forms of intervention by postal workers might bias the results obtained with the misdirected-letter technique?
4. The authors mention that return rates using the quasi-questionnaire technique might also be affected by people's attitudes toward the institution or agency sponsoring the survey. They did not believe this was a factor, however, in the present experiment because both Protestant and Catholic students attended in equal numbers the university that was identified with the questionnaire study. Describe how institutional sponsorship could be an independent variable in a study using the quasi-questionnaire technique. Can you identify one or more other factors that might be meaningfully manipulated as independent variables when using this nonreactive method to study prejudice?

IV. PROBLEMS AND EXERCISES

Read the following descriptions of physical trace and archival studies carefully and then answer the questions that follow.

A. Problem 1

Description: A researcher believes that college students are not as romantic as they used to be. Specifically, he believes that students in the "fifties" were much more romantic than they are in the "nineties." To test his hypothesis he decides to examine the frequency of personal ads placed in several college newspapers on Valentine's Day. From the college archives he samples the appropriate issues of the college papers over the period from 1950 to the present. He finds that the number of personal ads placed in the newspapers has declined dramatically.

Questions:

1. What major concept in this study must be given clear operational meaning prior to collecting data?
2. Which seems more likely as a possible source of bias in this study: selective survival or selective deposit? Explain your answer.
3. Identify an important variable not controlled in this study that could produce a spurious relationship between year of newspaper publication and frequency of personal ads.

B. Problem 2

Description: A student researcher has come up with what she believes is an ingenious unobtrusive measure of student anxiety before exams. Specifically, she finds out that large introductory sections of courses in the social sciences (e.g., psychology, political science) and natural sciences (e.g., biology, chemistry) at her university make use of standardized tests scored by a computer. Students in these classes are given small, No. 2 pencils prior to each exam. Students return the pencils by dropping them in a box on the way out of the classroom. The researcher suggests that biting or chewing on a pencil is a sign of anxiety. Her hypothesis is that students enrolled in natural science courses (mainly pre-med students) are more anxious about exams than are those taking courses in the social sciences. She decides to collect data after the first exam in each of these large classes because at the time of the first exam the pencils are new and have not been previously used by students. She obtains permission from the instructors to examine the pencils following the initial exams in these courses. She then counts the number of pencils with teeth marks. Her results appear to support her hypothesis. A greater proportion of pencils in the natural science classes have teeth marks than do pencils in the social science classes.

Questions:

1. What is the student's operational definition of "anxiety"?
2. Which of the following physical use measures was employed in this research situation?
   (a) planned accretion measure
   (b) natural accretion measure
   (c) planned erosion measure
   (d) natural erosion measure
   (It is possible that more than one description of physical use measures can be reasonably defended. Be sure to explain why you selected the measure that you did.)
3. Illustrate how selective deposit might operate in this situation to produce a spurious relationship between type of class (natural science or social science) and the unobtrusive measure of anxiety.

V. DATA ANALYSIS

NOTE: You may find it necessary to consult an introductory statistics textbook in order to answer the following questions completely. We wish to emphasize that it is a good idea to keep a statistics textbook, as well as a research methods textbook, close at hand when reading descriptions of original research. So many different statistical measures, types of inferential tests, and research methodologies exist that it is necessary for even the most advanced researcher to consult a relevant reference book occasionally in order to understand a research article fully.

1. In order to analyze statistically the penalty records of the black and nonblack teams, Frank and Gilovich had to come up with a measure of aggressiveness based on the archival data. They chose to use z scores based on each year's penalty records for each team. Specifically, for each of the 17 years, 1970-1986, they converted each team's penalties (treating NHL and NFL teams separately) to a z score. Then, they found the average z score of each team that wore black and each team that wore nonblack for this 17-year period. Provide both a statistical definition and a verbal definition of a z score.
2. Why do you believe that the authors chose to use z scores to measure each team's performance in a year rather than the mean number of yards (or minutes) penalized for each team in each year during this period?
3. Table 5-1 contains fictitious data; however, the data are similar to those reported by Frank and Gilovich (see their Table 3). Table 5-1 shows average z scores for 15 NHL teams. (Frank and Gilovich compared a total of 23 NHL teams.) Five teams that wear black uniforms (all capitalized entries) are among these 15 teams. Calculate the mean z-score for the black and nonblack teams.

Table 5-1

<u>Mean Number of Penalty Minutes (in z Scores) for NHL Teams</u>

Team	z Score
PHILADELPHIA	2.24
PITTSBURGH	0.90
VANCOUVER	0.88
Detroit	0.66
BOSTON	0.55
Quebec	0.22
CHICAGO	0.12
Washington	-0.06
St. Louis	-0.11
Los Angeles	-0.24
Winnipeg	-0.30
Hartford	-0.33
Calgary	-0.45
Buffalo	-0.68
Montreal	-0.76

VI. REVIEW TESTS

These practice tests will be most helpful in preparing for your classroom tests if you test yourself under conditions that resemble those of your actual tests as closely as possible. We suggest, therefore, that you put away the book after completing the exercises in this unit and then return at a later study session to take the review tests.

A. Completion

Underline the correct ending to the following sentences:

1. Physical traces are the remnants, fragments, and products of (past behavior / present behavior).
2. Use traces can result naturally or they can be (spontaneous / planned).
3. Measuring the number of words underlined in a textbook as a measure of a student's study activity would be an example of an (erosion measure / accretion measure).
4. Experimenters testing students participants from introductory psychology courses do not always record instances when the student is a "no show." This is an example of (selective deposit / selective survival).
5. Content analysis of archival data involves three major steps: (1) identification of a relevant source; (2) sampling; and (3) (tallying / coding).
6. A spurious relationship exists when data are (intentionally falsified / accidentally related).
7. A research article that reports the results of a laboratory experiment with manipulated variables as well as those of an investigation based on the analysis of physical use traces would be an example of an approach to research best characterized as (multihypothesis / multimethod).

B. Multiple Choice

1. Data that are found in records and documents that recount the activities of individuals, institutions, governments, and other groups are called
   a. archival data
   b. index data
   c. social data
   d. codified data

2. One of the major advantages of using data found in records and documents is that these data are most likely to be
   a. nonreactive
   b. unbiased
   c. valid
   d. reliable

3. Which of the following characteristics of the results of a laboratory experiment increases when the pattern of results of a study based on data found in records and documents is similar to the pattern of results of the laboratory experiment on the same topic?
   a. interpretability
   b. external validity
   c. sensitivity
   d. reliability

4. Respondent mortality in survey research corresponds most closely to which of the following problems in the use of physical traces?
   a. selective deposit
   b. selective survival
   c. accretion
   d. erosion

5. An investigator who was trying to show that the frequency of traffic accidents increases when it is warmer would need to consider whether there are more cars on the road when it is warmer. The number of cars variable needs to be checked to be sure that the original relationship is not a(n)
   a. contaminated relationship
   b. redundant relationship
   c. orthogonal relationship
   d. spurious relationship

ANSWERS TO EXERCISES AND REVIEW TESTS ARE FOUND

IN THE APPENDIX AT THE END OF THIS BOOK

****

QUESTIONS/PROBLEMS FOR CLASS DISCUSSION

A. Terminology and Concepts

1. Provide an example of an erosion measure and an example of an accretion measure that would provide evidence that a textbook has been read.
2. Explain how letters that appear in "Dear Abby" regarding marital troubles could represent selective deposit or selective survival.
3. Explain why the Frank and Gilovich (1988) study is considered an archival study and why the Kremer, Barry, and McNally (1986) study is considered a physical trace study.
4. Describe the three stages of content analysis that Frank and Gilovich (1988) conducted in their study of team uniform color and aggressiveness.
5. Explain why the Kremer et al. (1986) study on prejudice would be called a nonreactive study.

B. Critical Thinking: Analyzing Research

1. Explain why it is not possible to show that wearing black uniforms causes teams to play more aggressively based on the archival data analyzed by Frank and Gilovich (1988). Why might the experimental evidence mentioned at the end of the summary provide more convincing causal evidence?

2. Suppose that at some point during the time period analyzed by Frank and Gilovich (1988) there was a change in the football rules that influenced when a penalty is called, making the occurrence of the penalty more frequent. Would this change threaten the analysis of penalties based on team color (i.e., would this serve as an alternative explanation for why teams with black uniforms seem to play more aggressively)? Explain.

3. Use the methods involved with the lost-letter and the misdirected-letter techniques described in the study by Kremer et al. (1986) to illustrate problems of selective deposit and selective survival.

C. Creative Thinking: Designing Research

1. Kremer et al. (1986) used experimental manipulation involving the misdirected-letter technique and the quasi-questionnaire technique to observe religious prejudice. Design an archival study that could be used to investigate the occurrence of religious prejudice. What source(s) would you use? What would be the nature of your content analysis (e.g., how might you categorize incidences of prejudice)? How would you avoid problems of selective deposit and selective survival?

2. Using archival data, Frank and Gilovich (1988) demonstrated that teams with black uniforms played more aggressively, as measured by penalties, than teams with non-black uniforms. A reasonable question to ask is whether this aggressiveness extends to the fans who attend the home games for these teams. Thus, one could hypothesize that fans at home games for black-uniformed teams are more rowdy and aggressive than fans at home games for teams with non-black uniforms.

Design a study that uses <u>physical trace</u> measures to examine this hypothesis. Choose accretion measures and erosion measures to operationalize rowdy or aggressive behavior of fans. Describe your plan for making your observations. Discuss how your measures could be affected by selective deposit and selective survival.

D. Statistical Analysis

Choose either your archival study based on the work of Kremer et al. (1986) or your physical trace study based on the work of Frank and Gilovich (1988) and describe more fully the data you would collect. How would you record your observations? Develop a sample "coding sheet" that you could use to record your observations. Specify what type of scale (i.e., nominal, ordinal, interval, ratio) each dependent variable represents.

Next, prepare a sample table in APA format to report a summary of your data, including hypothetical data that would support your hypothesis. Be sure to specify whether you are presenting frequency counts, proportions, percentages, means, etc. Write a short paragraph that describes the results of your study.

UNIT 6. INDEPENDENT GROUPS DESIGNS

I. OVERVIEW

The experimental method is ideally suited to identifying cause-and-effect relationships. The logic of the experimental method is as follows. Two or more conditions are compared such that the conditions differ only with respect to the factor of interest. This factor is called the independent variable and the conditions represent levels of the independent variable. In the most common experimental design, the random groups design, separate groups of subjects are formed by randomly assigning subjects to conditions. Random assignment seeks to establish equivalent groups at the start of the experiment. Except for the factor under investigation, a researcher attempts to maintain the equivalence of the groups throughout the experiment. Then, if the groups perform differently on the dependent measure, it can be presumed that the independent variable is responsible.

Consider the following hypothetical example. Two equivalent groups of students are formed through random assignment, and one group is taught a specific study technique and the other group is not. Amount of instruction is the independent variable. It has two levels: some and none. Then, both groups are given an identical passage to read in preparation for a test. Number of correct answers on the test might serve as the dependent variable. If both groups are treated alike except for level of instruction, and if a difference in correct answers for the passage material is observed, the logic of the experimental method suggests that a difference in test scores is due to instruction in the particular study technique.

A researcher always seeks to conduct an experiment properly. Properly done experiments are internally valid, reliable, sensitive, and externally valid. An internally valid experiment provides an unambiguous interpretation for the outcome of the experiment and is generally achieved through the control techniques of manipulation, holding conditions constant, and balancing. An experiment lacking internal validity is said to be confounded. A confounding is present when a second independent variable is permitted to covary with the intended independent variable. If, in our example above, students in the instruction condition were given an easier passage to study than were students in the no instruction condition, then the results would be ambiguous with respect to what produced a difference in test performance. A difference in favor of the instruction group on the dependent measure could be explained <u>either</u> by the variable of instruction or by the variable of passage difficulty.

Of course, to be internally valid, an experiment must begin with equivalent groups. If one group of subjects was brighter or more motivated than another group, our experiment also would be confounded. As was noted, balancing through random assignment is the most common means of forming comparable groups. By distributing subjects' characteristics equally across the conditions of the experiment, random assignment ensures that the differences among the subjects are balanced. The most common technique for carrying out random assignment is block randomization.

The experimental method is ideally suited for making causal inferences due to the high degree of control. Remember that causal inferences require three conditions to be met: covariation, time order, and elimination of alternative causes. The covariation condition is met when we observe systematic changes in the dependent variable as a function of the independent variable. In our study technique example, covariation would be present if test performance was greater in the instructed group than in the noninstructed group. Because the independent variable of instruction was manipulated <u>before</u> we measured test performance, the time-order condition is also met. Finally, by holding conditions constant (e.g., giving students in both groups the identical passage to study) and by balancing subject characteristics (e.g., by randomly assigning subjects to conditions) we eliminate alternative causes for any difference that is obtained.

Although random assignment contributes to the internal validity of an experiment, external validity, or the degree to which results can be generalized, must be established in some other way. One approach to enhancing external validity is to select representative samples of all dimensions on which you wish to generalize. Sampling college students randomly from all colleges and universities across the United States might be a way to ensure representativeness of a group of U. S. students. Of course, such an approach is impractical and, as it turns out, unnecessary. External validity in this case would most likely be established on the basis of the continuity assumption or on the basis of replication (or both) (Underwood & Shaughnessy, 1975). The continuity assumption asserts that behavior is relatively continuous across time, subjects, and settings unless there is reason to assume otherwise. Simply speaking, a researcher studying learning processes will most likely make the assumption that the learning of college students in Illinois, for instance, is similar to that of students in California or elsewhere. Confidence in the continuity assumption can be increased through replication of an experiment. If we obtain the same outcome when a replication of an experiment is performed in a setting different from that of the original experiment, our confidence in the external validity of that finding increases. Replication also provides evidence of the reliability of experimental findings. An experiment is reliable if the same results are obtained each time the experiment is repeated. Finally, the limits of the continuity assumption can be tested directly by performing a replication of an experiment while also varying a factor on which we wish to generalize. This provides perhaps the best way to establish the external validity of research findings.

Testing intact groups threatens the internal validity of experiments involving the independent groups design (see Cook & Campbell, 1979). Intact groups are those that were formed prior to the start of the experiment. For example, if participants in the experimental condition were students from one section of general psychology and students in the control condition were students from another section of general psychology then the groups could not be considered equivalent. As we have seen, random assignment of subjects to conditions is used to balance subject characteristics, thereby establishing equivalent groups. Extraneous factors, such as different rooms or different experimenters, also must not be allowed to confound the independent variable of interest. Even when such factors are controlled, however, they can affect the sensitivity and generality (external validity) of an experiment. A sensitive experiment is one that is likely to detect the effect of an independent variable even when that effect is a small one. Holding extraneous factors constant increases sensitivity and decreases generality, whereas balancing extraneous factors decreases sensitivity and increases generality.

A serious threat to the internal validity of the random groups design arises when subjects are lost differentially across the conditions and some characteristic of the subject that is related to the outcome of the experiment is responsible for the loss (Underwood & Shaughnessy, 1975). This problem is called selective subject loss. Suppose we compared the learning of two groups of students under two different rates of presentation: fast and slow. If some students in the fast condition were not able to keep up and thus were not able to view all of the material then they would not be able to complete the task. By not including these participants' data in the analysis of results we have introduced a potential threat to the internal validity of the experiment. By selectively excluding students from one condition because they had difficulty keeping up with the material we have destroyed the initial equivalence of the groups. We can help prevent selective loss by restricting participation to those likely to complete the experiment successfully or we can compensate for it by selectively dropping comparable subjects from the group that did not experience the loss. Selective subject loss typically is a threat to the internal validity of an experiment. Mechanical subject loss, on the other hand, does not usually affect internal validity. Mechanical loss represents loss of subjects due to accidents during testing, such as the breakdown of experimental equipment or the inadvertent mistakes of an experimenter.

An experimenter also must be alert to the possible contribution to experimental results of demand characteristics and experimenter effects. Demand characteristics are the cues and other information used by participants to guide their behavior in an experiment (Orne, 1962). Demand characteristics may lead participants to do what they believe the researcher wants them to do, thus artificially corroborating the experimental hypothesis. Experimenter effects occur when an experimenter's expectations lead to differential treatment of subjects in different groups or cause the experimenter to record the data in a biased manner (Rosenthal, 1976). Both demand characteristics and experimenter effects can be minimized through the use of proper experimental procedures; they can best be controlled by using placebo control and double-blind procedures.

The matched groups design is another type of independent groups design. It is an alternative to the random groups design when only a small number of subjects is available and when we can identify a good matching task. In a true matched groups design the researcher first obtains scores for each subject on a measure known to be correlated with the dependent variable. These scores often are based on the same task or a task from the same class of tasks as that used for the dependent variable. Once these measures are obtained, the researcher constructs pairs (or triplets, etc.) of subjects who have similar scores on the matching variable. Finally, subjects from the matched sets are randomly assigned to the separate experimental conditions. The goal of a matched groups design is to attempt to make the groups comparable on the dependent variable prior to collecting data.

There are a number of practical problems associated with the matched groups design. For instance, it is important that the variable used to match subjects be correlated significantly with the dependent variable. Obtaining such a variable is not always easy (for example, it may require careful pretesting or searching archives for previous test scores), and without empirical evidence a researcher should not assume that a variable is correlated with the dependent variable. Because subjects are assigned randomly to conditions after matching takes place (presumably balancing important subject characteristics), we generally turn to the matched groups design only when we have a relatively small number of subjects from a heterogeneous population. With such small numbers of subjects we may not want to trust that random assignment will produce equivalent groups on all factors other than the matching variable.

Another important independent groups design is the natural groups design. In this design researchers select the levels of the independent variable (usually an individual differences variable) and look for systematic relationships between the independent variable and other aspects of behavior. Investigating the memory abilities of young adults and elderly adults would require a natural groups design. The levels of the independent variable (age) would necessarily have to be selected from preexisting natural groups. Essentially, the natural groups design involves looking for correlations between subjects' characteristics and their performance. Such correlational research designs pose problems in drawing causal inferences. Unlike the random groups design in which the independent variable is manipulated by the researcher, the natural groups design involves selection of levels of the independent variable. In the natural groups design, therefore, we cannot be sure that the groups are equivalent on important characteristics other than the independent variable. It is likely, for instance, that young adults and old adults differ in important ways other than in terms of age, for instance, in terms of experience, physical abilities, general knowledge, and other relevant variables.

The analysis of independent groups design experiments begins with a summary of descriptive statistics in a table or figure. In fact, some researchers (e.g., Loftus, 1993) argue that descriptive statistics, if used properly, are sufficient for the analysis and interpretation of experiments. Such a situation exists when the standard error of the mean can be used to describe how much sampling error there is when estimating the population mean based on a sample mean. The plot-plus-error-bar procedure allows us to compare differences between means by examining the span of the error bars associated with each mean. Nonoverlapping error bars provide evidence that the means are really different from each other.

The traditional approach to the problem of error (chance) variation, however, is the use of inferential statistics (i.e., null hypothesis testing) to determine whether the obtained differences are larger than would be expected on the basis of error variation alone. The inductive and indirect process of null hypothesis testing provides a set of guidelines for deciding on the statistical significance of a finding. The process is indirect because it begins by assuming the null hypothesis, specifically, that the independent variable has had no effect. Probability theory is used to determine the likelihood of obtaining the difference that we did IF the null hypothesis is true. Should this likelihood turn out to be small, then we reject the null hypothesis and conclude that the independent variable did have an effect in our experiment. Researchers generally set this level of significance (alpha) at .05. Thus, experimental outcomes that are judged to occur fewer than 5 times in every 100 tests, if the null hypothesis is true, lead us to reject the null hypothesis and to conclude that the outcome is due to the effect of the independent variable. The results, in other words, are said to be statistically significant.

We will begin our discussion of null hypothesis testing by looking at the logic behind the most popular test of statistical significance, the $\underline{F}$-test or analysis of variance (ANOVA). We will emphasize the ANOVA for a random groups design; however, the general rationale underlying ANOVA is the same no matter what type of experimental design is used.

There are two sources of variation in any random groups design. The first is variation within groups. Because of individual differences among subjects, the scores in each group will not be the same even though in each group subjects are treated alike. These differences within each group should represent only error variation. The second source of variation in the random groups design is variation between groups. When the null hypothesis is true--the independent variable did not have an effect--then differences among group means can also be attributed to error variation. Differences among means are expected due to random error even if the independent variable did not have an effect. This is why we cannot simply examine the differences among sample means and conclude that the independent variable worked. When the null hypothesis is true both sources of error variation in the random groups design (within groups and between groups) should be similar.

When the null hypothesis is false--the independent variable did have an effect--systematic variation across the group means will be added to the differences among group means that arise from chance. This systematic variation does not affect error variation within groups. The $\underline{F}$-test takes advantage of these relationships to create the following statistic:

$$F = \frac{\text{variation between groups}}{\text{variation within groups}} = \frac{\text{error variation + systematic variation}}{\text{error variation}}$$

If the null hypothesis is true, then there is no systematic variation and error variation (i.e., error variation + 0) gets divided by error variation. The expected value of the F ratio in this case is 1.00. If the null hypothesis is false, then systematic variation is present and the numerator of the F-ratio will be larger than the denominator. The expected value of F in this case will be greater than 1.00. How much greater than 1.00 does the F-ratio need to be before we can be relatively sure that systematic variation is present? The F-ratio needs to be large enough that its probability of occurring if the null hypothesis were true is less than the chosen level of significance (alpha), which we have seen is traditionally set at .05. A statistically significant F-ratio is one that is larger than the critical value corresponding to alpha = .05.

The initial overall analysis of an experiment is called an omnibus F-test. The first step in such an analysis is generally to state the research question or hypothesis. This generally takes the form of asking: Did the independent variable have an effect? For example, in the study instruction experiment, the research question was: Did the type of instruction received by the participants (i.e., some or none) have an effect on test performance? The next step is to state the null hypothesis. When only one independent variable is present, the null hypothesis for this omnibus F-test is that all the group means are equal. The null hypothesis is always stated in terms of the means of the populations from which the sample means were obtained. In the instruction experiment, the null hypothesis would be that the population mean represented by the sample mean for the instructed participants is equal to the population mean represented by the sample mean for the noninstructed students. The alternative hypothesis, of course, is that the population means are not equal. This, of course, is what we would expect if the answer to the research question was yes, the independent variable did have an effect.

The calculations necessary to carry out an ANOVA are best done with the aid of a computer and an appropriate statistical software program. The computer output associated with an ANOVA is typically in the form of an Analysis of Variance Summary Table. This table summarizes the results of the computations required to construct the F-ratio. In the set of exercises that follow this Overview, you will have the opportunity to practice learning to "read" ANOVA summary tables. At this point we wish to pursue further the interpretation of a significant omnibus F-ratio.

Suppose that the results of an ANOVA for an experiment with four conditions yielded an F-ratio with a probability less than the chosen significance level of .05. Accordingly, we would reject the null hypothesis. We might see the outcome of the test expressed as follows: $F(3, 156) = 5.23$, $p < .05$. The numbers within the parentheses refer to the degrees of freedom associated with the numerator and denominator of the F-ratio. (The concept of degrees of freedom is generally defined as the number of entries of interest minus one. This concept will be discussed more fully in the exercises that follow this Overview.) The number 5.23 is the obtained F-ratio and the probability of obtaining an F-ratio this large if only error variation were present is less than .05. Thus, the results of this omnibus F-test are statistically significant.

What have we learned from this analysis? We now are in a position to state with some confidence that the independent variable did have an effect. We can conclude that the variation among the sample means represents more than simply error variation, something that we could not conclude merely by visually inspecting the mean differences. We must refer to the means, however, to help us understand exactly what happened. Did Condition A result in a larger mean than Condition B, and so forth? The descriptive statistics accompanying our analysis, in this case the means for each group in our experiment, are used to guide our interpretation of the results. The omnibus F-test, however, does not tell us the source of the significant effect. On the basis of the omnibus test we can only conclude that systematic variation is present; we cannot pinpoint the source of this variation on the basis of the omnibus test alone. In other words, we are NOT permitted to say that the mean for Condition B is significantly different from the mean for Condition C, or to make any statements about significance between any other pairs of means.

Analytical comparisons are one way to track the source of the significant effect obtained in our omnibus test. These particular statistical procedures are used to "follow up" the results of an omnibus analysis in a way that is guided by the initial research hypothesis. The first step in doing an analytical comparison is to state the null hypothesis. For example, in a four-group experiment, it could be that the (population) mean of Condition A is not different from the (population) mean of Condition C. An analytical comparison always contrasts only two means. The computational procedures for analytical comparisons produce an F-ratio which is interpreted in the same way as is the F-ratio associated with the omnibus test. If the probability associated with the F-ratio for the analytical comparison is less than the significance level, then we can reject the null hypothesis and conclude with some degree of confidence that the difference between these particular two sample means is not due to error variation alone. Computational procedures for conducting analytical comparisons can be done on a computer using a statistical software package or by following step-by-step procedures outlined in a statistics or research methods book. You will also find that there are many other statistical procedures, usually referred to as "post hoc" tests, that allow you to follow up the results of an omnibus test. Post hoc tests are often used to test for statistical significance in all possible pairs of experimental means. The choice of a particular post hoc test, such as the Scheffé or Tukey test, depends on certain assumptions regarding your research plan. Many introductory statistics textbooks provide information that will help you make a decision about the appropriateness of these tests for your experiment. [See also Keppel (1991) for an informative discussion of both analytical comparisons and post hoc tests.]

Strictly speaking, the process of null hypothesis testing can never prove beyond a shadow of a doubt that an effect is present (or, for that matter, not present). It is always a matter of probabilities. No matter what decision you reach--the null hypothesis is true or the null hypothesis is false--you could be wrong. When we judge that the outcome is statistically significant because its probability of occurring under the null hypothesis is less than .05 we acknowledge that 5 times out of every 100 tests the outcome could occur even if the null hypothesis were true. Rejecting the null hypothesis when it is true is called a Type 1 error and is equal to the level of significance we have chosen for our test (e.g., alpha = .05). On the other hand, we can also err by accepting the null hypothesis when it is false (Type 2 error). Given this situation you should be able to see why researchers generally avoid the word "prove" when describing the results of an experiment and, instead, use phrases such as "consistent with the hypothesis," or "supporting the hypothesis." The probabilistic nature of inferential statistics is also a reason why researchers will always look to replication of an experimental finding as confirmation of the reliability of a research finding.

We must not confuse a "statistically significant" finding with the significance of the conclusion based on that finding. Our ability to draw appropriate conclusions rests first on the internal validity of the experiment. Another way of stating this is that experiments with poor internal validity can easily produce statistically significant outcomes. We must also be aware that the probability of obtaining statistical significance is directly related to the sample size used in an experiment. In other words, even if the null hypothesis is false to a tiny degree, a large enough sample will produce a significant result. Statistical tests tell us only whether or not an effect of the independent variable is present. Thus, researchers have sought a measure of the strength of the relationship between the independent variable and the dependent variable that is independent of sample size. One popular measure of effect size is d. The measure d is a ratio that assesses the difference between means relative to the degree of "error" due to individual differences as measured by the standard deviation of scores. Because effect sizes are measured in standard deviation units, we can make meaningful comparisons of effect sizes across experiments using different dependent variables (and different sample sizes). Measures of effect size permit us, for example, to rank independent variables in terms of the relative strengths of their effects. Consider two experiments that each test the effect of a particular psychotherapy program on clients' well-being. In each experiment a treatment program (A or B) is compared with an untreated control group. Assume that in both experiments the results are statistically significant (i.e., $p < .05$). A measure of effect size could then be used to determine which program (A or B) produced a greater effect on clients' well-being. Moreover, effect sizes are also important to calculate even if the null hypothesis is not rejected (i.e, $p > .05$). As we have mentioned, it is possible to obtain a statistically significant effect even when the effect size is very small (for example, when an experiment is particularly sensitive or a very large sample of subjects is tested); it is also possible not to find statistical significance even when the effect size is very large (for example, when there is poor experimental sensitivity or a small sample size). By measuring effect size you are in a position to judge whether the statistically significant effect you found is also large enough to be of practical or clinical significance. You will also be able to judge whether the effect that was not statistically significant is large enough to warrant further study, perhaps using a more sensitive experiment or a larger sample size.

Finally, measuring effect size is important when conducting a meta-analysis. A meta-analysis summarizes the results of different experiments investigating the same independent variable. Results of these experiments are summarized using measures of effect size. Meta-analysis is a way to find out if a particular independent variable has been shown to be effective across experiments carried out by different investigators, using different subject populations under different experimental conditions. For example, there is a large body of psychological research investigating cognitive therapy for depression. A meta-analysis might be usefully employed to determine the size of the treatment effect typically obtained for this type of therapy. A meta-analysis is not easy; sophisticated statistical procedures must be mastered and many difficult decisions must be made, ranging from which studies should be included in the analysis to what specific measure of effect size should be used. Nevertheless, the outcome of a meta-analysis can go a long way in telling us what variables are effective in producing behavior change.

References

Cook, T. D., & Campbell, D. T. (1979). Quasi-experimentation: Design and analysis issues for field settings. Chicago: Rand McNally.

Keppel, G. (1991). Design and analysis: A researcher's handbook. Englewood Cliffs, NJ: Prentice Hall.

Loftus, G. (1993). A picture is worth a thousand p values: On the irrelevance of hypothesis testing in the microcomputer age. Behavior Research Methods, Instruments, & Computers, 25, 250-256.

Orne, M. T. (1962). On the social psychology of the psychological experiment: With particular reference to demand characteristics and their implications. American Psychologist, 17, 776-783.

Rosenthal, R. (1976). Experimenter effects in behavioral research. (Enlarged ed.). New York: Irvington.

Underwood, B. J. & Shaughnessy, J. J. (1975). Experimentation in psychology. New York: Wiley. (Robert E. Krieger, 1983.)

II. KEY CONCEPTS

The following concepts are importantly related to the design and analysis of independent groups experiments that are discussed in this unit. Use the information found in the **OVERVIEW,** as well as the definitions of the key concepts provided here, to complete the exercises in the following sections. [NOTE: Numbers in parentheses refer to pages in the fourth edition of Research Methods in Psychology by Shaughnessy and Zechmeister (1997), where these concepts are more fully defined.]

analytical comparison A statistical technique that can be applied (usually after obtaining a significant omnibus F-test) to locate the specific source of systematic variation in an experiment. (228)

block randomization The most common technique for carrying out random assignment in the random groups design; each block includes a random order of the conditions and there are as many blocks as there are subjects in each condition of the experiment. (201)

confounding When the independent variable of interest systematically covaries with a second, unintended independent variable. (197)

demand characteristics The cues and other information used by participants to guide their behavior in a psychological study, often leading participants to do what they believe the observer (experimenter) expects them to do. (209-210)

dependent variables Measures of behavior used by the researcher to assess the effect (if any) of the independent variables. (192)

double-blind experiment Both the subject and the observer are kept unaware (blind) of what treatment is being administered. (210)

effect size An index of the strength of the relationship between the independent variable and dependent variable that is independent of sample size. (229)

experimenter effects The experimenters' expectations that may lead them to treat subjects differently in different groups or to record data in a biased manner. (210)

extraneous variables Potential independent variables that are not directly of interest to the researcher but serve as possible sources of confounding. (206)

F-test (Analysis of Variance) A statistical test based on the ratio of variation between groups and variation within groups; under the null hypothesis both sources of variation represent error variation only and the expected value of F is 1.00. (225)

independent groups design Each separate group in the experiment represents a different condition as defined by the level of the independent variable. (197)

independent variable A factor for which the researcher either selects or manipulates at least two levels in order to determine its effect on behavior. (192)

inferential statistics A means to test whether the differences in a dependent variable that are associated with various conditions of an experiment are reliable, that is, larger than would be expected on the basis of error variation alone. (219)

matched groups design A type of independent groups design in which the researcher forms comparable groups by matching subjects on a pretest task and then randomly assigning the members of these matched sets of subjects to the conditions of the experiment. (211)

mechanical subject loss Occurs when a subject fails to complete the experiment because of equipment failure or because of experimenter error. (208)

meta-analysis The analysis of results of several (often, very many) independent experiments investigating the same research area; the measure used in a meta-analysis is typically effect size. (231)

natural groups design A type of independent groups design in which the conditions represent the selected levels of a naturally occurring independent variable; for example, age is an individual differences (subject) variable. (213)

null hypothesis The assumption used as the first step in statistical inference whereby the independent variable is said to have had no effect. (219)

placebo control Procedure by which a substance that resembles a drug or other active substance but that is actually an inert, or inactive, substance is given to subjects. (210)

random assignment The most common technique for forming groups as part of an independent groups design; the goal is to establish equivalent groups by balancing subject characteristics. (199)

random groups design The most common type of independent groups design in which individuals are randomly selected or randomly assigned to each group such that groups are considered comparable at the start of the experiment. (199)

replication Repeating the exact procedures used in an experiment to determine whether the same results are obtained. (203)

selective subject loss Occurs when subjects are lost differentially across the conditions of the experiment as a result of some characteristic of the subject that is related to the outcome of the study. (208)

statistically significant When the probability of an obtained difference in an experiment is smaller than would be expected if error variation alone were assumed to be responsible for the difference. (219)

III. EXAMPLES OF EXPERIMENTAL STUDIES (Independent Groups Designs)

Read the following two summaries of published research carefully. Answer the questions found at the end of each summary. Answering these questions will require use of concepts introduced in this unit and previous units.

A. Mindfulness

Reference: Langer, E. J., & Piper, A. I. (1987). The prevention of mindlessness. Journal of Personality and Social Psychology, 53, 280-287.

Article Summary: According to the authors, "mindlessness" is characterized by a "rigid use of information," treating information as if it had a single meaning and could be useful in only one way; a consequence is that the individual fails to recognize potential novel uses of information. On the other hand, "mindfulness" is characterized by "active distinction making and differentiation." One who is mindful engages in the process of creating new categories while making finer and finer distinctions. It is possible that mindlessness arises in part because of the way that information is presented to us. For instance, people are often educated about the world by naming objects absolutely ("this is an X"). If people were introduced to information conditionally ("this could be an X"), perhaps they would produce more creative use of objects and ideas.

Several experiments were conducted to test the hypothesis that subtle linguistic cues lead people to act mindfully or mindlessly. In one experiment (Exp. 3), students were told they were participating in a study of stress management and were taken to a room where they were asked to answer questions about several pictures. An experimenter described various objects in the room, including an unfamiliar black rubber object which (unknown to the participant) was the target object. The unfamiliar object was described in one of three ways: Unconditionally ("This is a precision propel."); Conditionally ("This could be a precision propel."); and Conditionally Unknown ("I do not know what this is."). There were 20 Harvard University undergraduates assigned randomly to each of the three experimental conditions. When the participants had answered the questions about the pictures, they were told by the experimenter that the answers had been recorded in the wrong section of the book and that there were neither additional forms nor an eraser. The goal of this experimental procedure was to create a "need" for a solution to the problem of the misrecorded answers. The target solution was to make an eraser available (i.e., identifying the black object as a potential eraser). In keeping with the theory of mindlessness/mindfulness, it was predicted that the different ways in which the unfamiliar black object had been introduced would affect the likelihood of students meeting the need, that is, solving the problem. Specifically, the authors predicted that more students would respond creatively in the two conditional groups than in the unconditional group. And they did. Sixty-five percent of the students in the Conditional group and 55 percent of the students in the Conditional Unknown group solved the problem by suggesting that the unfamiliar black object could be used as an eraser; only 25 percent of the students in the Unconditional group came up with this creative solution to the problem. The authors suggested that the Conditional participants had learned to think flexibly about the object.

Langer and Piper (1987) argue that too often we teach children to treat the world unconditionally, and that cognitive flexibility, and hence, creative solutions to problems, might result were we to educate children more conditionally. According to this view, giving information in absolute terms encourages the mindless use of it.

Questions:

1. (a) Identify clearly the independent variable (including its levels) in this experiment. (b) Is the independent variable a manipulated variable or a natural groups variable? Why? (c) Identify the dependent variable. (d) What level of measurement was used for the dependent variable?
2. Based on your reading of the research summary, provide examples of how the two control methods of balancing and holding conditions constant were used in this study.
3. (a) Can you imagine a way that experimenter effects could affect the results of this study? Explain. (b) What specific control procedure might be used to protect against undesirable experimenter effects?
4. Assume that an experimenter decided to replicate the Langer and Piper study, but rather than randomly assigning individual students to the three conditions of the study the experimenter randomly assigned three different psychology classes to the conditions of the study (that is, each class represented a different condition). What criticism would you have of this procedure involving intact groups?
5. Assume that Langer and Piper used a block randomization procedure to assign individuals to the conditions of their study. [NOTE: In order to answer the following questions you may find it necessary to review in a research methods text the specific procedures associated with the experimental technique of block randomization.]
    (a) What experimental goals are achieved by block randomization?
    (b) Specify exactly how students in the Langer and Piper study would be assigned using block randomization. Be sure to indicate the number and the size of the blocks required for this procedure.
    (c) Assume that Langer and Piper hired two different undergraduate assistants to test the 60 students in their study. How would the use of two different experimenters affect both the sensitivity and generality of the experiment?

(d) Explain how block randomization would be used in the situation where two different experimenters are employed so that the extraneous factor of experimenter is controlled. That is, specify exactly what changes you would need to make in the block randomization procedure used above (5.b) in order to balance the effect of experimenter.

B. Anorexia Nervosa

Reference: Clinton, D. N., & McKinlay, W. W. (1986). Attitudes to food, eating and weight in acutely ill and recovered anorectics. British Journal of Clinical Psychology, 25, 61-67.

Article Summary: Anorexia nervosa is a condition characterized by chronic failure to eat for fear of gaining weight. The chief symptom is extreme loss of weight brought on by refusing food. Other symptoms include periods of overactivity and distorted attitudes toward food and eating. The anorexic (British: anorectic) is typically female and between the ages of 12 and 18 at time of onset. Severe cases of anorexia nervosa, unless treated, may result in death.

The authors of the present study suggested that although clinical intervention may result in improved weight gain among acutely ill anorexics, nevertheless the "recovered" anorexic is likely to continue to show evidence of "distorted attitudes to food, eating and weight." To test this idea the investigators administered the Eating Attitudes Test (EAT) to four groups of females: acutely ill anorexics (n = 15), recovered anorexics (n = 14), psychiatric controls (n = 10), and normals (n = 24). Both the acutely ill and recovered anorexics were shown to be similar at time of onset of their illness, although the recovered group had been slightly younger (15.7 years) at time of onset than the currently ill group (17.3 years). For example, the average weight loss (in terms of percentage of matched population mean weight) was 31.1 percent for the acutely ill and had been 34.4 percent for the recovered group. To identify participants for the recovered sample, 26 former patients meeting the study's selection criteria were contacted; 6 could not be located, 2 refused to participate, and 4 failed to make appointments, resulting in 14 recovered individuals who received the EAT. Mean length of time since discharge for the recovered group was 42.6 months. The psychiatric controls were patients hospitalized for a variety of disorders, including schizophrenia and depression, but who showed no evidence of eating disorder. The normals were nursing students who showed no evidence of eating disorder or other psychiatric disturbance based on responses to a brief questionnaire designed by the authors. The mean ages of the four groups were not significantly different based on a between-subjects ANOVA.

The EAT is intended to measure both behavioral (e.g., vomiting, dieting) and attitudinal aspects of anorexia nervosa. Participants respond to 40 statements using a 6-point scale ranging from "very often" to "never." Mean scores (and standard deviations in parentheses) for the four groups (higher numbers indicate more extreme responses) were: anorexics, 51.5 (30.7); recovered anorexics, 31.8 (28.8); psychiatric controls, 13.6 (10.5); normals, 7.9 (4.7). The results of a one-way ANOVA were statistically significant. A post-hoc test (Scheffé) revealed that the acutely ill females had statistically higher EAT scores than did the psychiatric females or the normal females. The EAT scores of the currently ill and recovered individuals were not significantly different, and the recovered group had significantly higher scores than did the normals. The authors concluded that present treatments for anorexia nervosa, although successful in treating gross physical and behavioral symptoms, leave the distorted attitudes associated with this condition relatively unaltered. Important questions for future research are whether these attitudes serve to slow down treatment, contribute to relapse rates, or are distressing in themselves to the individuals.

Questions:

1. Identify the independent variable (and its levels) in this experiment.
2. (a) What is the dependent variable? (b) What level of measurement was used for the dependent variable?
3. The natural groups design is not a true experiment; rather, the design is basically correlational in nature. Explain why causal inferences based on results of a natural groups experiment such as the Clinton and McKinlay (1986) study are problematic.
4. Comment critically on the external validity of the Clinton and McKinlay study based on the samples taken, the procedure employed, and the results obtained.

IV. PROBLEMS AND EXERCISES

Read the following descriptions of experimental studies carefully and then answer the questions that follow.

A. Problem 1

Description: Executives at a large corporation hired a psychologist to evaluate two physical fitness programs that differed specifically in the degree to which diet and nutritional suggestions were part of the program. Plan N included diet/nutritional requirements for all participants. Plan E emphasized a regular exercise program for all participants but did not require participants to change their eating habits. The nature and amount of exercise required in the two programs were essentially the same. The psychologist obtained a list of all employees who, as part of a previous survey, had indicated their desire to take part in a fitness program while at work. These people were contacted and 85 percent of the original group of employees were still working at the company or had not changed their minds about participating. Two hundred employees from this remaining group were randomly assigned in equal numbers (100) to either

Program N or Program E. Each program lasted 6 months, during which time employee absenteeism in each group was monitored. At the end of the program, participants were given a questionnaire designed to assess attitudes toward the company and the fitness program. Because of transfers within the company, firing and quitting of employees, and other reasons not able to be documented, only 75 out of 100 employees in Group E finished the program, and only 50 of the original 100 participants from Program N completed the 6-month program. The psychologist judged that these sample sizes were still sufficiently large to assess adequately the effect of the program. A statistical comparison of participants from the two groups revealed that employees enrolled in Program N showed significantly less absenteeism than persons completing Program E. Moreover, the attitude assessment at the end of the program revealed that employees who completed Program N had significantly better opinions of the company and the program than did persons in Program E. On the basis of these results, the psychologist concluded that Plan N was better than Plan E.

Questions:

1. What is the independent variable (and its levels) in this study?
2. What is the dependent variable? (Note: There may be more than one dependent variable associated with this experiment.)
3. Can you identify a serious threat to the internal validity of this experiment? Identify the threat and explain why it is a threat.

B. Problem 2

Description: A social psychologist wants to test the implications of a theory of personal space. He thinks that people will differ in their reaction to others who intrude in their personal space depending on the perceived status of the intruder. Specifically, he predicts that people who are viewed as having higher status in some way will be permitted to move closer than those who are not viewed as having higher status. Thus, the investigator arranges to conduct an experiment using undergraduate students as participants wherein he manipulates status by controlling the manner in which individuals are introduced to a participant. Confederates of the researcher (all male graduate student research assistants) are introduced as observers in one of three ways, as: "an undergraduate student working for the psychology department"; "an undergraduate honors student working for me" (i.e., the faculty member); or "a graduate student working for me." Prior to testing any participants, three different confederates were randomly assigned one of the three roles to play and subsequently kept that same role throughout the experiment. Students were scheduled in groups of three and were assigned randomly to one of the three introduction conditions when they appeared for the experiment. Each participant was taken to a different small room with two chairs, supposedly to work on an experimental task. The confederates were introduced by the psychologist to participants while they were working on their project. After being introduced to each participant the confederate-observer took the second chair and placed it within 6 inches of a participant, made what looked like observations for 5 minutes, and then left. The confederate-observer actually measured how many participants moved their chairs away, even slightly, when he moved next to them. After many individuals were tested in this manner, the psychologist found that significantly fewer people adjusted their seating position when the observer was introduced as a graduate student than when the observer was introduced as an undergraduate. There was no difference in the number of moves made by participants in the two conditions in which the observers were introduced as undergraduates. The investigator concluded that his hypothesis was supported.

Questions:

1. What is the independent variable (and its levels) in this study?
2. What is the dependent variable?
3. Can you identify a confounding that threatens the internal validity of this experiment? Identify the confounding and explain why it is a threat to the study's internal validity.
4. What specific control technique should the experimenter have employed in order to protect the internal validity of this experiment?

V. DATA ANALYSIS

A. Descriptive Statistics

Assume that the data presented in Table 6-1 represent EAT scores from four groups similar to those tested in the study by Clinton and McKinlay (1986).

Table 6-1

Performance on the EAT for Four Groups of Females

Acutely Ill	Recovered Anorexic	Psychiatric Control	Normal Control
44	38	22	6
54	44	19	19
61	55	7	22
36	39	11	5
55	45	6	10
51	49	12	9
49	32	11	12
56	48	5	9
35	56	10	8

1. Calculate the mean and standard deviation for each of the four groups in Table 6-1.
2. Draw a bar graph summarizing mean scores of the groups found in Table 6-1. Construct your figure according to the stylistic requirements of the American Psychological Association.

B. Inferential Statistics

The analysis of variance is the proper inferential test for analyzing the results presented in Table 6-1 (p. 111). In most cases, the computation for this analysis would be done on a computer using appropriate statistical software.

Questions:

1. The means calculated from the data in Table 6-1 clearly are not the same. What prevents us from concluding, based on an examination of these differences among the means, that the independent variable has had an effect?
2. In your own words, state both the null hypothesis and the alternative hypothesis for an inferential test of the difference among these sample means.
3. Explain why you could find a statistically significant outcome on the basis of an analysis of variance of these experimental results but be wrong when you concluded that the independent variable had an effect. Be sure to indicate what "type" of error you would be making.

1. Independent Groups Design: ANOVA Summary Tables

As we mentioned in the Overview, an ANOVA is typically carried out with the aid of a computer. The output generated by a statistical software program will usually include an ANOVA Summary Table. Thus, it is important that you become familiar with the construction of such tables and learn to "read" them in order to determine what happened in an experiment. The precise format of these tables will vary depending on the particular design that was used and on the number of variables. The following example illustrates an ANOVA Summary Table for a random groups design. After the summary table is illustrated, a problem emphasizing the interpretation of the summary table is presented.

2. Independent Groups Design: Illustration of ANOVA Summary Table

We will use hypothetical results from a fictitious product commercial experiment. The experiment investigated people's interest ratings of a breakfast food after viewing one of four product commercials (A, B, C, and D). Thus, the independent variable, type of commercial, had four levels. There were 160 participants; 40 people were randomly assigned to view each of the four commercials. The mean interest ratings following the four commercials were: A, 6.2; B, 5.7; C, 7.3; D, 6.1. The results as they might appear on a computer screen following an ANOVA are as follows:

Table 6.2 ANALYSIS OF VARIANCE SUMMARY TABLE

Source of Variation	df	SS	MS	F	p
Between Groups (Commercial)	3	45.67	15.22	5.23	.002
Within Groups	156	453.96	2.91		
Total	159				

The left column of the table lists the sources of variation. The independent variable, type of commercial, is a source of variation between groups and the within groups differences provide an estimate of error variation. The degrees of freedom (df), defined as the number of entries of interest minus one, are shown in the next column. Because there are four commercials, there are three df for the between groups (4 - 1 = 3). There are 40 participants in each group and so there are 39 df within each group. Thus, the df for within groups can be obtained by multiplying the number of groups by the df for each group (4 X 39), which yields 156. The total df for a random groups experiment is always the total number of subjects (N) minus one. The sum of squares (SS) must be calculated in order to obtain the mean square (MS), which becomes part of the F-ratio. The MS is defined as the SS divided by its df. The MS between groups is the numerator of the F-ratio and the MS within groups is the denominator of the F-ratio. The probability of this particular F-ratio assuming the null hypothesis is true is shown in the last column. Because the p value of .002 is less than the conventional level of significance (.05), the null hypothesis is rejected; the results of the F-test reveal a statistically significant outcome. We can conclude that the independent variable had an effect. The researcher will likely follow up the results of the omnibus F-test with analytical comparisons in order to test additional hypotheses about differences between specific pairs of means.

3. Random Groups Design: ANOVA Summary Table Problem

In order to evaluate your understanding of these concepts, first examine the following ANOVA Summary Table; then, answer the questions that follow.

TABLE 6.3 ANALYSIS OF VARIANCE SUMMARY TABLE

Source of Variation	df	SS	MS	F	p
Between Groups (Treatment)	4	122.41	30.60	2.04	.10
Within Groups	45	675.43	15.01		
Total	49				

114

Questions:

1. The independent variable (treatment) had how many levels?
2. How many subjects were in each experimental group (level of the independent variable)?
3. What is the estimate of error variation in this experiment?
4. Was the effect of the independent variable statistically significant? Why or why not?
5. What conclusion may be made on the basis of this omnibus F-test?

4. Independent Groups Design: Calculation Problem

a. Perform an appropriate omnibus F-test on the data from the EAT measure presented in Table 6.1 on page 111. Be sure to state your conclusion both in terms of statistical significance (use alpha = .05) and in terms of the effect of the independent variable. Remember that higher numbers in Table 6.1 indicate more extreme responses on the EAT measure. [Note: You may wish to refer to the answers you gave to questions 1-3 on page 112 before stating your conclusions.]

b. Perform an analytical comparison testing whether the mean performance on the EAT measure for the recovered group differs from the mean of the acutely ill group. Prior to performing your calculations, state both the null hypothesis and alternative hypothesis for this comparison. Then, report your results both statistically and verbally.

c. Perform an additional analytical comparison testing whether the mean performance of the two anorexic groups (combined) differs from the mean of the (combined) normals and psychiatric controls. As you have been doing, first state the null hypothesis and the alternative hypothesis for this test. And again, report your results both statistically and verbally.

VI. REVIEW TESTS

These tests will be most helpful in preparing for your classroom tests if you test yourself under conditions that resemble those of your actual tests as closely as possible. We suggest, therefore, that you put away the book after completing the exercises in this unit and then return at a later study session to take the review tests.

A. Matching

In this unit we have introduced you to three different independent groups designs: (1) random groups (R); (2) matched groups (M); and (3) natural groups (N). Below are five brief descriptions of research procedures. Read each description carefully and use an R, M, or N to identify which type of independent groups design is illustrated.

_____1. A researcher asks for volunteers from a large psychology lecture class to participate in a psychology experiment involving two groups. He obtains 30 volunteers. Each person's name is put on an index card. The cards are shuffled and put into two piles of 15. Students whose names are in the first pile are placed in the experimental group and those in the other pile are assigned to the control group.

_____2. A researcher wishes to test a hypothesis about transfer of physical abilities between professional sports. Specifically, she believes that professional football players will have more difficulty hitting a baseball than will professional basketball players. From the rosters of two local professional teams she randomly selects 10 football players and 10 basketball players to compete in a baseball hitting contest.

_____3. A psychologist assigns 60 male schizophrenics to five different psychotherapy treatment groups. Only males who are under 60 years of age, have been on medication less than 10 years, and who are in good physical health are included in the study. Once the 60 patients were identified, they were assigned to treatment groups by using a random numbers table.

_____4. Twenty students with deficient study skills are assigned to two different training programs. Prior to assigning the students to the treatment groups a vocabulary test is given to all 20 students. Students with similar vocabulary test scores are paired and then members of each pair are randomly assigned to either the first or second treatment condition.

_____5. A researcher wishes to test the spelling abilities of 5th grade children from city and suburban schools. One hundred children from city schools and 100 children from suburban schools are randomly selected. Standardized test scores in the files of the students are used to find pairs of students (one from a city school and one from a suburban school) who have nearly identical reading comprehension scores. The investigator obtains 50 pairs of children in this way. The 50 children from the city schools and the 50 children from the suburban schools are then given a specially prepared spelling test.

B. Identification of Confoundings

The experiment described below contains a confounding that destroys the internal validity of the experiment. Read the description carefully and identify the nature of the confounding that is present.

A developmental psychologist wished to test the implications of a theory of cognitive development which states that children at an early stage of development are not capable of certain kinds of mental operations. The psychologist believed that young children's mental capacities have been underestimated because of the manner in which various cognitive tasks have been presented to them. The psychologist hypothesized that children are able to perform certain cognitive operations much earlier than predicted by the theory if tasks used to measure these processes are presented in a manner that is "developmentally sensitive." The psychologist decided to compare performance of children using both traditional tasks and the new developmentally sensitive tasks. Both the traditional and new tasks measure the same cognitive operations and differ only in terms of the method of presentation. The psychologist located two nursery schools, one associated with the college where he teaches (School A) and one in a nearby city (School B). Both nursery schools enroll children of approximately the same age. The two methods are assigned randomly to the different nursery schools. Children at School A use the new method while children enrolled at School B are tested using the traditional method. Results revealed that children tested with the new method did better than the children tested with the traditional method. The psychologist concluded that children are able to carry out certain cognitive operations earlier than expected on the basis of the theory if developmentally sensitive tasks are used.

C. Multiple Choice

1. In the independent groups design the only factor that should differentiate the separate groups at the start of the experiment is the
    a. dependent variable
    b. independent variable
    c. characteristics of the subjects
    d. conditions under which all subjects are tested

2. Which of the following terms describes the characteristic of an experiment that ensures there is an unambiguous interpretation for the outcome of the experiment?
   a. reliability
   b. external validity
   c. sensitivity
   d. internal validity

3. Which of the following is <u>NOT</u> one of the defining characteristics of selective subject loss?
   a. subjects are lost differentially across groups
   b. the number of subjects initially assigned to the groups is not the same
   c. the subject loss results from a characteristic of the subject
   d. the subject loss results from a characteristic important to the outcome of the experiment

4. The control technique that increases the sensitivity of an experiment (being able to detect an effect of an independent variable) is
   a. balancing using random assignment
   b. using intact groups
   c. holding conditions constant
   d. including extraneous factors

5. The matched groups design is used when separate groups are needed for the levels of the independent variable, when a good matching task is available, and when
   a. extreme groups need to be tested
   b. an adjustment needs to be made for nonequivalent groups
   c. a relatively small number of subjects is available
   d. a relatively large number of subjects is available

6. The matched groups design ensures that the groups in the experiment are equivalent
   a. on all subject variables
   b. only on the matching task variable
   c. on subject variables but not on context variables
   d. on context variables but not on nuisance variables

7. Which of the following types of variables is most likely to be an independent variable in a natural groups design?
   a. individual differences (subject) variables
   b. task variables
   c. nuisance variables
   d. environmental variables

8. The cues and other information that participants may use to guide their behavior in an experiment are called
   a. experimenter effects
   b. unobtrusive cues
   c. demand characteristics
   d. suggestive cues

9. The level of significance (e.g., alpha = .05) is equal to the probability of
   a. Type 1 error
   b. Type 2 error
   c. correct rejection of the null hypothesis
   d. correct acceptance of the null hypothesis

10. One of the most commonly used tests in the analysis of experiments is the
    a. analysis of variance
    b. chi-square test
    c. bivariate correlation
    d. multinomial test

11. An F-ratio reflects
    a. systematic variation only
    b. error variation only
    c. both systematic variation and error variation
    d. neither systematic variation nor error variation

12. The estimate of error variation in a random-groups design is based on variation
    a. within subjects
    b. between subjects
    c. within groups
    d. between groups

13. Which of the following represents an excellent complement to the information derived from a test of significance?
    a. measures of effect size
    b. measures of residual variation
    c. measures of treatment variation
    d. measures of complexity

14. One of the advantages of the measure of effect size is that it
    a. indicates statistical significance
    b. requires no calculations
    c. relies on clinical judgment to determine significance
    d. is independent of sample size

15. Which of the following provides a quantitative summary of the results of more than one experiment on an important research problem?
    a. quasi-analysis
    b. multi-analysis
    c. summa-analysis
    d. meta-analysis

ANSWERS TO EXERCISES AND REVIEW TESTS ARE FOUND

IN THE APPENDIX AT THE END OF THE BOOK

****

QUESTIONS/PROBLEMS FOR CLASS DISCUSSION

A. Terminology and Concepts

1. Using the independent variables in the Langer and Piper (1987) mindfulness study and the Clinton and McKinlay (1986) anorexia study, explain the difference between a random groups design and a natural groups design.
2. Specify the null and alternative hypotheses of the Langer and Piper (1987) mindfulness study.
3. Suppose that three different people served as experimenters in the Langer and Piper (1987) mindfulness study. Explain how you would keep this extraneous variable from being a source of confounding in the experiment.
4. Twelve former patients in the "Recovered" group in the Clinton and McKinlay (1986) study were "lost" (see summary on pp. 108-109). Speculate on whether this subject loss was mechanical subject loss or selective subject loss. What consequences would each type of loss have for the interpretation of their study?
5. Explain how demand characteristics may have been a factor in the Clinton and McKinlay (1986) anorexia study.

B. Critical Thinking: Analyzing Research

1. Although Langer and Piper's findings were statistically significant, explain why the alternative hypothesis is not "proven" to be correct (nor the null hypothesis "proven" to be wrong). Refer to your answer in part A.2. to identify the null and alternative hypotheses.

2. Langer and Piper suggested that giving information conditionally <u>caused</u> participants to think more flexibly about an object. Comment on whether this causal inference seems warranted given their procedure and results.

120

3. Identify three or more aspects of the Langer and Piper study that may limit the external validity of their findings regarding mindfulness.

4. What additional information about the Eating Attitudes Test (EAT) would you want to know in order to evaluate more fully the Clinton and McKinlay (1986) anorexia findings?

5. Outline the three conditions necessary to infer causation. Describe the extent to which these three conditions are met in the Langer and Piper study and in the Clinton and McKinlay study.

C.   Creative Thinking: Designing Research

1. Using only the "conditional information" condition developed by Langer and Piper (1987), design a study to examine the relationship between an individual differences variable (e.g., anxiety, intelligence) and "mindfulness." Identify clearly the independent and dependent variables, the levels of the independent variable, and level of measurement of your dependent variable. Outline the procedure of your study, giving particular attention to the methods of control you will use.

2. Based on the findings of the Clinton and McKinlay (1986) study on distorted attitudes of individuals who have "recovered" from anorexia nervosa, suppose that a researcher develops a treatment specifically designed to treat these distorted attitudes. Use a random groups design to evaluate the effectiveness of this new treatment in a sample of anorexics. Identify clearly the independent and dependent variables, the levels of the independent variable, and level of measurement of your dependent variable. Outline the procedure of your study, giving particular attention to the methods of control you will use and to the ethical issues you will need to address.

D.   Statistical Analysis

Suppose that a researcher conducts a study to test the hypothesis that when individuals are more "mindful" they are able to come up with more ideas for how an unknown object might be used. The same procedure is followed in this experiment as was used in the Langer and Piper (1987) study summarized on pages 106-107. Students are presented with an unknown black object in one of three conditions: Unconditionally ("This is a precision propel."); Conditionally ("This could be a precision propel."); and Conditionally Unknown ("I do not know what this is."). At the conclusion of the experiment, students are asked to come up with ideas for how the unfamiliar black object could be used. The dependent variable is the number of different ideas each student writes down on a sheet of paper. The researcher predicted that students in the conditional groups would identify more uses for the black object than students in the unconditional group.

Suppose the following data are observed:

Unconditional	Conditional	Conditional Unknown
1	7	5
4	5	7
3	3	4
3	6	5
2	4	7
5	7	8

1. Calculate the mean number of responses for each group. Does the pattern of means support the hypothesis that presenting information about the black object in a conditional manner will cause participants to identify more possible uses? By examining the differences among the means, are you willing to conclude that the independent variable had an effect? Why or why not?

2. Based on what you know about this study, complete the missing information in the ANOVA summary table:

Source	df	SS	MS	F	p
Between Groups (Treatment)	__	29.78	_____	_____	<.05
Within Groups	__	_____	_____		
Total	17	65.11			

3. How would you test the specific hypothesis that the two conditional groups identified more uses for the black object than the unconditional group?

4. Write a brief paragraph that describes these results using the style requirements of the American Psychological Association.

UNIT 7. REPEATED MEASURES DESIGNS

I. OVERVIEW

In Unit 6 we described experiments involving independent groups designs; these designs are also called between-subjects designs because different groups of subjects receive different treatments. Repeated measures designs (also called within-subjects designs) provide an effective and efficient alternative way to conduct an experiment by administering all the treatments in the experiment to each subject. For a repeated measures design experiment to be interpretable, however, practice effects must be balanced. Practice effects are changes that subjects undergo because of repeated testing. That is, with repeated testing subjects may tire, become bored, acquire more skill, become more or less motivated, or, most likely, experience some combination of these and other factors. Practice effects refer to the summation of both positive and negative factors that accrue with repeated tests. They can't be eliminated; practice effects must be controlled by balancing their effects across conditions of the experiment.

Two repeated measures designs can be distinguished: complete and incomplete. In the complete repeated measures design, each subject experiences each condition more than one time. Block randomization and ABBA counterbalancing can be used to balance practice effects in the complete within-subjects (repeated measures) design. When these counterbalancing techniques are used, practice effects are balanced for each subject. Block randomization was introduced in Unit 6 as a technique for assigning subjects randomly to conditions in a between-subjects design. It can also be used in a complete repeated measures design to balance practice effects by first constructing blocks of conditions. In each block all the conditions of the experiment are randomly arranged. The number of blocks depends on the number of times each subject will experience each condition. For example, if there are four conditions (A,B,C,D) and each subject is to be tested six times in each condition, then the experimenter needs to construct six blocks of four conditions. Each subject will be tested 24 times. The block randomization schedule might look like this: BCDA/ABDC/DCAB/ABCD/DABC/ADCB. A stage of practice in the complete within-subjects design is defined as the administration of each condition in the experiment once. Thus, each of the six blocks represents one stage of practice in this experiment. To compute the stage of practice effects in this experiment you would average the scores for the four conditions in each block, thereby ending up with one value for each of the six stages of practice.

ABBA counterbalancing can also be used to balance practice effects in a complete repeated measures design. It is generally used, however, when each subject experiences each condition only a few times. If each subject is going to experience two conditions (A and B), each four times, then an ABBA schedule would look like this: ABBAABBA. Practice effects can also be determined when ABBA counterbalancing has been used. If each condition is presented four times in an ABBA sequence

(ABBAABBA), then there are four stages of practice (each time the two conditions have been presented once, AB or BA). The average of the two conditions presented at each stage is used to describe the practice effects. The ABBA procedure should not be used, however, if practice effects are expected to be nonlinear or if anticipation effects are likely. Practice effects are linear if the effects of practice are approximately the same after each test. Anticipation effects can occur when ABBA counterbalancing is used if there are only a few conditions and each subject is tested in each condition many times. By repeating the ABBA pattern many times the subject may begin to anticipate what condition occurs next.

In the incomplete repeated measures design, each subject receives each treatment only once and the balancing is accomplished across subjects. Major techniques for balancing practice effects in the incomplete within-subjects (repeated measures) design involve either the use of all possible orders or selected orders (the Latin Square and rotation of a random starting order). The preferred technique is to use all possible orders of conditions. For example, if there are three conditions in the experiment (A,B,C), there is a total of six ways to arrange the order of these three conditions: ABC, ACB, BAC, BCA, CAB, CBA. Subjects would be assigned randomly to receive one of the six different orders. If there are four conditions then there are 24 possible orders; with five conditions there are 120 possible orders. Thus, when the number of conditions exceeds four, the experimenter typically must consider using selected orders rather than all possible orders. A single Latin Square can be used when the number of conditions is even. There will be as many orders as there are conditions in the experiment. In a Latin Square design, each condition appears at each ordinal position once, and each condition precedes and follows each other condition exactly once. An alternative counterbalancing technique in an incomplete repeated design is to randomly order the conditions and then systematically rotate the conditions. For example, if there are five conditions (A,B,C,D,E), the experimenter would first randomly order the five conditions (e.g., CEBDA). Then, the conditions would be rotated systematically so that each condition appears equally (once) at each ordinal position. Systematic rotation of the five conditions in the original random order (CEBDA) would result in a table like the following (each condition is moved one position to the left and the first condition loops around to the end of the next sequence).

Ordinal Position

1	2	3	4	5
C	E	B	D	A
E	B	D	A	C
B	D	A	C	E
D	A	C	E	B
A	C	E	B	D

Individuals would be randomly assigned to one of the five different orders. In the incomplete repeated measures design each ordinal position represents a stage of practice. Therefore, in the example illustrated in the table, there are five stages of practice. Practice effects are computed by determining the mean for each ordinal position (i.e., each column). To compute the effect of the independent variable you must average the scores that correspond to each condition (A,B,C,D,E) across all of the subjects who participated in each group.

An irreversible task is one that cannot be administered more than once to each subject. Consider, for example, an experiment investigating the effect of color background on learning associations between words. Let us assume that there are four different color backgrounds and that the experimenter wants each participant to be tested once with each color background (incomplete repeated measures design). The experimenter chooses a list of 20 word pairs for the participants to learn. Because only 16 people are available, the experimenter must use selected orders in order to counterbalance practice effects (all possible orders would require at least 24 participants to balance practice effects, one participant randomly assigned to each order). Whether a Latin Square or systematic rotation is used, there will be four selected orders of the four color backgrounds. Participants will be assigned randomly to the four orders and each participant tested four times, once with each color background. However, you should see a problem. Once a participant is presented the list of 20 word pairs to learn in the first condition, it is not possible to use the same list in subsequent conditions because the person will have begun to master the list. The solution to this problem is to use four different lists of words. However, if the same list is always used in the same ordinal position, then ordinal position and lists will be confounded. So, lists must also be balanced across ordinal position. When irreversible tasks are used, three independent variables must be balanced (the independent variable of interest, stage of practice, and the task variable). The balancing act is tricky, but it is essential for an interpretable experiment.

The most serious problem in any repeated measures design is differential transfer-- when performance in one condition differs depending on which other condition it follows. Procedures for detecting the presence of differential transfer are available, but there is little that can be done to salvage a study in which differential transfer occurs. In an incomplete repeated measures design, however, it is possible to analyze the results of the random groups design that is included at the first stage of practice (see the first ordinal position in the table on page 124). If the pattern of results obtained at the first stage of the experiment is not the same as that obtained in the experiment as a whole (after averaging across subjects to obtain means for each condition), differential transfer is the likely source of the discrepant results. If differential transfer does occur in an incomplete repeated measures design, the random groups design in the first stage is still interpretable. In general, however, if differential transfer is suspected, the repeated measures design should not be used (see, for example, Poulton, 1982).

Although the procedures for analyzing the results of experiments involving the repeated measures designs are basically the same as those used in the analysis of independent groups designs, there are a few salient differences and data reduction procedures are somewhat different for the repeated measures design. It is possible, for example, to assess practice effects in any repeated measures design.

One critical difference between independent groups designs and repeated measures designs involves the role of differences across subjects. For example, in a random groups design, individual differences among participants are balanced (through random assignment) and a measure of error variation is obtained based on these "within group" differences. In a repeated measures design, individual differences are held constant across conditions because each subject participates in every condition. However, the effect each treatment level has on subjects can vary (e.g., subject #1 could have a large response to condition A and a small response to condition B, whereas subject #2 could have the opposite responses). Thus, the source of error variation in the repeated measures design reflects the differences in the way the levels of the independent variable affect different subjects; in fact, it represents the interaction between the independent variable and subjects. It is what remains when variation due to subjects and that due to the independent variable are subtracted from the total variation. This estimate is called the residual and is an estimate of error variation alone just as variation within groups is an estimate of error variation alone in the random groups experiment. The residual is the denominator in the $\underline{F}$-ratios of within-subjects (repeated measures) designs in the same way that the within-groups variation is the denominator in the $\underline{F}$-ratios of random groups designs.

The estimate of error variation has important consequences for the sensitivity of the experiment. The likelihood of obtaining a statistically significant effect in an experiment is influenced by the sensitivity of the experiment and the power of the statistical test used to analyze the results. The sensitivity of an experiment is the likelihood that it will detect an effect of the independent variable if the independent variable does, indeed, have an effect. Experiments in which the effects of extraneous variables (e.g., room size, experimenter, form of test) are controlled by holding them constant generally have greater experimental sensitivity than do those controlling extraneous variables by balancing. In effect, repeated measures designs hold constant the subjects across conditions (because each subject participates in each condition); thus, repeated measures designs are also generally more sensitive than independent groups designs.

While an experiment is said to have sensitivity, a statistical test is said to have power. The power of a statistical test is the probability of rejecting a null hypothesis that is, in fact, false. A Type I error following a statistical test is concluding that the null hypothesis is false when it is true. A Type II error is failing to reject a false null hypothesis. The power of a test can be defined as: 1 minus the probability of a Type II error. Power of a statistical test is affected by three factors: the level of significance, the size of the treatment effect, and the sample size. For all practical purposes the sample size is what the researcher can use to control power (see Keppel, 1991). The larger the sample size the greater is the power of the test.

As you might suspect, the smaller the treatment effect the greater must be the sensitivity of an experiment and the power of the statistical test in order to "see" this effect. Thus, by knowing the size of an effect one is looking for, adjustments in the experimental procedure can be made, for example, by increasing the sample size when a small effect is likely to be present. In fact, so-called "power charts" exist to help guide the researcher in choosing sample sizes for a particular level of significance as a function of the size of the anticipated treatment effect (see Keppel, 1991). In general, measures of effect size reflect the differences between the means for the levels of the independent variable relative to the within-group standard deviation (see Unit 6).

References

Keppel, G. (1991). Design and analysis: A researcher's handbook. Englewood Cliffs, NJ: Prentice Hall.

Poulton, E. C. (1982). Influential companions: Effects of one strategy on another in the within-subjects designs of cognitive psychology. Psychological Bulletin, 66, 1-8.

II. KEY CONCEPTS

The following concepts are importantly related to the design and analysis of repeated-measures designs that are discussed in this unit. Use the information found in the **OVERVIEW,** as well as the definitions of the key concepts provided here, to complete the exercises in the following sections. [NOTE: Numbers in parentheses refer to pages in the fourth edition of Research Methods in Psychology by Shaughnessy and Zechmeister (1997), where these concepts are more fully defined.]

ABBA counterbalancing A technique for balancing practice effects in the complete repeated measures design that involves presenting the conditions in one sequence (e.g., AB) followed by the opposite of the same sequence (e.g., BA). (249)

counterbalancing Techniques for balancing practice effects across the conditions of an experiment. (245)

differential transfer Potential problem in repeated measures designs when performance in one condition differs depending on which of two other conditions precedes it. (258)

Latin Square Used in the incomplete repeated measures design to balance practice and order effects; a selection of orders in which each condition appears at each ordinal position once, and each condition precedes and follows each other condition exactly once. (254)

power The power of a statistical test is the probability that a false null hypothesis will be rejected; power is related to the level of significance selected, the size of the treatment effect, and the sample size. (259)

practice effects The changes subjects undergo across repeated testing in repeated measures designs; subjects may get better if a skill is being developed or worse due to factors such as fatigue or boredom. (243)

repeated measures design A design in which the independent variable is implemented by administering all the levels of the independent variable to each subject; also called within-subjects design. (240)

sensitivity The sensitivity of an experiment refers to the likelihood that the effect of an independent variable will be detected when that variable does, indeed, have an effect; sensitivity is increased to the extent that error variation is reduced (e.g., by holding variables constant rather than by balancing them). (259)

III. EXAMPLES OF EXPERIMENTAL STUDIES (Repeated Measures Designs)

Read the following two summaries of published research carefully. Answer the questions at the end of each summary. Answering these questions will require use of concepts introduced in this unit and in previous units.

A. Attention

Reference: Stroop, J. R. (1935). Studies of interference in serial verbal reactions. Journal of Experimental Psychology, 18, 643-662.

Article Summary: In this classic study, the author describes a phenomenon that would later bear his name: the Stroop effect. Three experiments investigated the effect of interfering color stimuli on reading names of colors (Exp. 1) and the effect of interfering word stimuli on naming colors (Exps. 2 & 3). Results of the second experiment have been given the most attention by cognitive psychologists, so this experiment will be described in more detail.

The stimuli were either color squares or color words. Both the colors and the words were: red, blue, green, brown, and purple. The color squares were arranged in a 10 X 10 array such that each color appeared twice in each row and column. The same color never appeared next to itself in a row or column. To construct the word array, each of the five color words was printed equally often in the four incongruent colors. For example, the word <u>blue</u> was printed five times in red, green, brown, and purple. A color word was never printed in the color named by the word (e.g., the word <u>red</u> never appeared in the color red). The 100 color words printed in incongruent colors were arranged in a 10 X 10 array similar to that used for the color squares; like the square array, the same color word did not appear next to itself in either the columns or the rows. After the color and word arrays were prepared, a second form was prepared for each set of stimuli that simply reversed the order of the original array. Thus, there were four 10 X 10 arrays of color stimuli: two forms of color squares (CS1 and CS2) and two forms of color words (CW1 and CW2).

One hundred college students (29 males and 71 females) were given the task of naming aloud the colors of the squares and the colors of the words. Participants were instructed to name the colors as quickly as possible and to leave no errors uncorrected. All participants attempted to name the colors in both conditions (CS and CW) and were tested on both forms in each condition. Thus, each participant made a total of 200 responses in each condition. Half the participants received the arrays in the order: CS, CW, CW, CS. The other half were tested in the order: CW, CS, CS, CW. Participants placed the sheets with the arrays face down in front of them and on a signal by the experimenter turned a sheet over and read aloud the color names. The experimenter used a stopwatch to measure the time taken to read each 10 X 10 array.

The dependent variable was each participant's time to name colors on the two 10 X 10 arrays in each condition. The mean time overall for 100 participants in the CS condition was 63.3 seconds; the mean time in the CW condition was 110.3. This difference was determined to be statistically reliable. In fact, Stroop showed that 99 percent of the participants took longer to name colors on the CW test than on the CS test, indicating that reading the incongruent color word interfered with students' ability to name the color.

Thus, the results revealed massive interference when students attempted to name colors of words printed in incongruent colors. There are many explanations given for the effect, but after more than 50 years no one explanation is accepted by all cognitive psychologists. (Interested readers are referred to a review of research on the Stroop phenomenon by C. M. MacLeod in <u>Psychological Bulletin</u>, 1991, <u>109</u>, 163-203: Half a century of research on the Stroop effect: An integrative review.)

<u>Questions</u>:

1. Identify (a) the independent variable and (b) the dependent variable in this study.
2. J. Ridley Stroop did several things in order to balance practice effects. For example, he made sure that in each 10 X 10 array the five different colors (words or color squares) appeared twice in each row and column. Also, he gave each

participant two different 10 X 10 arrays in each condition. One array was the reverse of the other. Finally, because each participant was tested on four arrays, the order of these four arrays was counterbalanced.

a) Would Stroop's experiment be classified as an incomplete repeated measures design or a complete repeated measures design?

b) What is the name of the specific counterbalancing technique used to present the four arrays?

c) How might Stroop show whether practice effects were present in his experiment? (Be specific. Explain how the relevant means would be obtained.)

3. Assume that you decide to conduct an experiment investigating the Stroop effect. More specifically, in order to test a theory you have about the nature of the Stroop effect, you construct four different 10 X 10 arrays. One array consists of 100 color squares arranged according to Stroop's procedure. The other three arrays each contain 100 color words printed in incongruent colors, again arranged according to Stroop's procedure. For purposes of testing your theory the words in the arrays are printed in three different sizes. Thus, you have four types of arrays, one with color squares and three with varying sizes of color words. To make things simple, let us refer to these four conditions as CS, CW1, CW2, CW3. Unlike Stroop, you decide to use only one form of each array. In your experiment, each participant is to be presented each of the four different stimulus arrays one time.

a) Assume that you have 16 participants available for testing. Identify two different counterbalancing techniques that might be used in your experiment to control for practice effects.

b) Explain how you would describe practice effects in your experiment.

c) A critical reviewer of your experiment suggests that there may be differential transfer present. Specifically, the critic argues that when participants move from the control condition (CS) to an experimental condition (CW1, CW2, or CW3) the effect may not be the same as when participants move from an experimental condition to the control condition. Suggest a way that you could investigate possible differential transfer effects in your experiment.

B. Memory

Reference: Landauer, T. K., & Bjork, R. A. (1978). Optimum rehearsal patterns and name learning. In M. M. Gruneberg, P. E. Morris, & R. N. Sykes (Eds.), Practical aspects of memory (pp. 625-632). New York: Academic Press.

Article Summary: When attempting to learn a list of items, such as new vocabulary words, a learner will usually study the items repeatedly until they are known well enough so that they can be recalled on a later test of retention. However, in some situations, such as when attempting to remember the last names of people we have just met, an "item" may be presented only one time for study with repetitions in the form of self-administered "tests." For example, suppose we are introduced to Kathleen O'Keane at a party. We might hear the name once and then attempt to rehearse it at varying intervals during the next few minutes, hours, or even days. Kathleen ?? ... Kathleen ?? What is the optimum schedule for such test trials? What is the optimum schedule in general for test trials following a study opportunity?

Consider the "behavior" that we wish to learn. Typically, our goal is to be able to recall something after a long interval. This behavior possibly can be "shaped" in a manner that is analogous to shaping a behavior by rewarding successive approximations to the desired response. Perhaps you have seen demonstrations of shaping by using food reinforcers to help an animal learn a response, such as teaching a rat to press a bar. First, the animal is rewarded for being close to the bar, then reinforcement is delivered only when the rat touches the bar, then only when pressure is placed on the bar, and then only when the bar is pressed. Such shaping procedures are used widely by animal trainers. Landauer and Bjork suggest that the behavior of recalling a fact after a lengthy interval might be acquired in an optimum manner by using a pattern of increasing intervals between successive tests. As the authors note, "A first test-trial at a short interval would be likely to succeed and strengthen an item sufficiently to survive a slightly longer interval that would yield a more effective second practice trial, etc." (p. 626).

Landauer and Bjork tested 468 students who were attending an introductory psychology lecture. Each student received a prearranged deck of cards with first and last names of fictitious people presented one time for study and then first names only presented for three test trials. The students "were told to imagine they were at a cocktail party, meeting people they wanted to remember." The students turned the cards at a 9-second rate in time to a signal. They were instructed that when only the first name appeared on a card, they should attempt to recall the last name and write it down on the card. Each student's deck of cards contained six kinds of items, with two instances of each kind. The first kind was a study-only item, that is, a first and last name appeared one time but were not viewed again until the final test. The remaining five kinds of items involved different schedules of test trials: Uniform short, Uniform moderate, Uniform long, Expanding, and Contracting. For example, a Uniform short might have only one intervening item between the three test trials (1,1,1), whereas a Uniform long might have 9-11 items between each of the three test trials following the study trial. The Expanding series had test trials spaced at 0,3,10 intervals or 1,4,10 intervals. Contracting was 10,3,0 or 10,4,1 spacing. After simply studying the names once or after studying them one time and then attempting to recall the last names three times according to the various practice schedules, the students were kept occupied for 30 minutes and then given a retention test for the 12 last names.

Results of the final retention test showed that the expanding schedule of tests produced nearly twice the level of recall of items presented for study only one time. Significantly greater recall was obtained for the Expanding series (.47) than for the Uniform series (.41) matched for average spacing interval. The Contracting intervals led to the poorest recall of the repeated items. The authors suggest that expanding

132

patterns of test-type rehearsal offer an effective technique for aiding "retention of information that cannot be conveniently recorded." Research investigating optimum patterns of testing also may provide clues to the best way to aid retention of other kinds of information.

EXPLANATORY NOTE: In order to understand completely the procedure used by Landauer and Bjork, it is helpful to try to imagine what a participant actually did in this experiment. Consider the fact that each student is tested using "six kinds of items, with two instances of each." Imagine a large deck of cards in front of the student. As was explained, the cards contain either the full name (first and last) or only the first name of fictitious individuals. Students turn the cards over, one at a time. If the full name is on the card, the students study it so that they can later remember both the first and last names. If only the first name is on the card, students try to recall the last name that was paired with it on an earlier card. Students always see both the first and last names at least once before they see test cards containing only the first name. A major variable is the spacing between the first presentation (when both first and last names are present) and the series of first-name-only cards when students are asked to practice retrieving the last name (if they can) that was paired with the first name. Consider, for example, what is called a 0,3,10 item. This is one that is presented once for study (full name) and then immediately following (0 spacing) is tested with only the first name present. Then, after 3 other cards are turned, the first name is presented again and the student tries to remember the last name; finally, 10 cards later only the first name is presented one more time and the student tries once again to recall the last name. After proceeding through the deck of cards, studying full names when present, and testing themselves when only the first name is present, the students are given (following a 30-minute delay) a memory test. Because students experienced two instances of six different item types, on the final test they saw 12 first names and tried to remember the specific last name that had been paired with each first name.

Questions:

1. Memory experiments such as that conducted by Landauer and Bjork illustrate how many different aspects of the experimental situation must be controlled. For instance, can you see a problem if the investigators always used the same names in each item category for all participants? That is, suppose Monty Python and George Bush were always the two instances of an expanding 0,3,10 item, and that John Smith and Mary Johnson were the two names used for the contracting 10,3,0 item. Clearly, if recall was better for the expanding items than for the contracting items we would not know whether the difference was due to the specific names that were used or to the way in which the items were tested. Speculate on how you think the researchers avoided confounding between the six item types and the specific names to be recalled. (Note: Exactly how the authors avoided this confounding is not explained in the description of the research; your task is to describe how they probably accomplished this.)

2. Practice effects could easily arise in the Landauer and Bjork study if participants changed with repeated test experiences. Remember that each student was tested two times on each of six types of items. This required that each student be given a relatively lengthy deck of cards. Students may find the task easier as they practice the task with different items in the deck, or they may become more bored with the task as they proceed through the deck. Or they may change in some other way. We must assume that practice effects are present. Again, exactly how Landauer and Bjork balanced practice effects in their experiment is not described in the summary of their research. However, how would you attempt to balance practice effects in this situation? (HINT: You will want to decide first whether this experiment is most similar to a complete repeated measures design or an incomplete repeated measures design.)

IV. PROBLEMS AND EXERCISES

A. Problem 1

Description: A psychologist believes that people are either "auditory learners" or "visual learners." Specifically, she thinks that some people remember information better when it is presented auditorily whereas others remember information better when it is presented visually. She decides to test her theory by asking undergraduate students to study and remember a list of words presented on a tape recorder (auditory) or on a sheet of paper (visual). To find out whether people are primarily auditory or visual learners, one week prior to the experiment a colleague asks students in a large introductory psychology class to fill out a long, involved questionnaire about attitudes, beliefs, etc. Buried in the questionnaire is a question asking about the student's most preferred mode of learning, that is, visual or auditory. When students come later for the memory experiment two different lists of 20 words are presented for study. Unknown to the students, the psychologist uses the information from the questionnaire to identify which mode of presentation is preferred by each student. Each student is tested first under his or her preferred mode of study and then under his or her nonpreferred mode. Although the manner in which the words are presented changes for each student, everything else is held constant. That is, the same 20 words are always used for the preferred mode of presentation and for the nonpreferred mode of presentation, the length of time the words are presented is the same, as is the retention interval, and so forth. The psychologist finds that the average recall in the preferred mode is significantly better than the average recall under the nonpreferred mode. She believes the results support her hypothesis.

Questions:

1. Identify the (a) independent variable and the (b) dependent variable in this experiment.

2. Would this experiment be classified as an incomplete repeated measures design or a complete repeated measures design?
3. (a) Identify <u>two</u> serious confoundings in this experiment.
   (b) Describe how the experiment should be conducted, that is, state specifically how the confoundings could be eliminated.

B. Problem 2

<u>Description</u>: A developmental psychologist believes that the more television violence children see, the less they are affected by it. To test his hypothesis he selects 24 two-minute cartoon episodes that vary in the amount of violence. He measures violence based on a formula using the number of "hits" and "kills." Each episode is scored according to the violence formula so that he is able to rank order the 24 episodes from most violent to least violent. He then selects the six most violent episodes. These six episodes are arranged in a random order and prepared for television viewing to 18 preschool children. The children are tested individually. After viewing each video episode, he asks the child several questions about the content of the video. From answers to these questions the psychologist computes a "comfort" index, purportedly revealing how comfortable the child was when viewing the video. The psychologist predicted that the children would become more comfortable as they viewed more of the violent videos. In fact, his results support his hypothesis. Average comfort ratings increased systematically as the number of episodes viewed increased.

<u>Questions</u>:

1. How is "violence" operationally defined in this experiment?
2. A critical reviewer of this study would likely want to know about the reliability of both the violence classification and the "comfort" index. Explain how reliability could be assessed for these two measures.
3. The same critical reviewer probably would raise questions about experimenter bias. (a) Suggest how experimenter bias could play a role in this experiment, and (b) describe what could be done to control experimenter bias.
4. Comment briefly on possible limitations on the external validity of this experiment in terms of the materials that were used.
5. Explain why the results of this experiment should not be considered seriously. Identify as specifically as you can what aspects of this study prevent an unambiguous interpretation of the researcher's findings.

V. DATA ANALYSIS

The following exercises ask you to describe the results obtained from repeated measures designs and to determine if practice effects appear to be present. As you will see, it can be time consuming to organize the data from a repeated measures experiment in order to obtain necessary descriptive statistics, such as means and standard deviations for the conditions. It is essential, however, before carrying out the appropriate inferential test.

A. Descriptive Statistics

1. Four individuals participated in a complete repeated measures design using an ABBA counterbalancing procedure. There were three conditions (C,S,W) in the experiment, and each individual participated in each condition four times. The dependent variable was measured on at least an interval scale (range 0-10). The following scores were obtained for each participant on each of 12 trials:

Trial:	1	2	3	4	5	6	7	8	9	10	11	12
Condition:	S	W	C	C	W	S	S	W	C	C	W	S
S#1	6	4	3	4	7	8	9	6	3	5	7	8
S#2	4	4	2	3	5	9	8	6	4	5	7	9
S#3	6	6	3	4	5	8	8	5	4	5	6	9
S#4	5	3	2	2	5	5	7	5	5	6	6	10

(a) Calculate the arithmetic mean for each of the three conditions (S, W, and C) by first finding the mean for each participant in each condition and then averaging these means.
(b) Provide a verbal description of the differences (or absence of differences) among the means of the three conditions.
(c) Calculate the means necessary to demonstrate whether there are practice effects in this experiment. Based on the means that you calculated would you suggest that practice effects are present?

2. The following data show hypothetical scores from eight individuals who participated in an incomplete repeated measures design using a Latin Square counterbalancing procedure. The dependent variable was measured on at least an interval scale (range 0-40). The experiment involved one independent variable with four levels (1-4). Levels are shown in parentheses in the following matrix.

Participant	Stage 1	Stage 2	Stage 3	Stage 4
1	34 (2)	26 (1)	36 (4)	29 (3)
2	29 (1)	30 (3)	35 (2)	35 (4)
3	28 (3)	34 (4)	22 (1)	36 (2)
4	33 (4)	31 (2)	25 (3)	22 (1)
5	35 (2)	22 (1)	34 (4)	24 (3)
6	31 (1)	32 (3)	35 (2)	37 (4)
7	24 (3)	35 (4)	24 (1)	35 (2)
8	34 (4)	30 (2)	29 (3)	25 (1)

(a) Calculate the means you would use to show whether there was an overall effect of the independent variable.

(b) Present the means you would use to describe practice effects in this experiment. Based on the means that you calculated, would you suggest that practice effects are present?

B. Inferential Statistics

The analysis of variance (ANOVA) for repeated measures designs is not always presented in introductory statistics books. Moreover, while the logic of hypothesis testing is the same for both independent groups designs (Unit 6) and repeated measures designs, the computation underlying the repeated measures ANOVA is sufficiently more detailed that it is best carried out using a computer. Typical computer output from a repeated measures ANOVA and its interpretation are discussed below. You also will be asked to carry out a repeated measures ANOVA for the data based on a Latin Square procedure that was presented above (Descriptive Statistics A.2).

1. Repeated Measures Design: Illustration of ANOVA Summary Table

As in Unit 6, we will use hypothetical results from a fictitious product commercial experiment. The experiment investigated people's interest ratings of a breakfast food after viewing four product commercials (A, B, C, and D). Thus, the independent variable, type of commercial, had four levels. Assume that the commercial product experiment was carried out using a repeated measures design in which 40 participants each viewed all four commercials and rated their interest in the product after seeing each commercial. Assume further that the mean interest ratings for the four experimental conditions were: A, 6.5; B, 6.0; C, 7.4; D, 6.5. Table 7.1 shows hypothetical results from an ANOVA following such an experiment.

TABLE 7.1 ANALYSIS OF VARIANCE SUMMARY TABLE

Source of Variation	df	SS	MS	F	p
Subjects	39	--	--	--	--
Commercial	3	46.26	15.42	3.01	.03
Residual	117	599.67	5.13		
Total	159				

Table 7.1 is somewhat different from Tables 6.2 or 6.3 which reported results of random groups designs. The differences arise due to the way that the estimate of error variation is calculated in the two types of design.

Because there were 40 participants in the experiment, the df for the Subjects effect are 39. The Subjects effect is not typically of interest in a repeated measures design and thus the SS and MS for this effect are not computed. There were four levels of the independent variable; thus, there are 3 df for this potential source of variation. The df for the residual variation are obtained by subtracting the df for Subjects and the df for the independent variable from the total df (159 - 39 - 3 = 117).

2. Repeated Measures Design: ANOVA Summary Table Problem

In order to evaluate your understanding of these concepts, first examine the following ANOVA Summary Table; then, answer the questions that follow.

TABLE 7.2 ANALYSIS OF VARIANCE SUMMARY TABLE

Source of Variation	df	SS	MS	F	p
Subjects	14	--	--	--	--
Treatment	2	26.44	13.22	10.75	.001
Residual	28	4.56	1.23		
Total	44				

Questions:

    a. How many subjects were in this experiment?
    b. The independent variable had how many levels?
    c. What is the numerator of the F-ratio for this analysis?
    d. Should the null hypothesis be rejected (use alpha = .05)? Why or why not?
    e. What conclusion may be made on the basis of this omnibus F-test?

3. Repeated Measures Design: Calculation Problem

a. Perform an ANOVA on the data found on page 135 wherein scores are reported for eight subjects in an incomplete repeated measures design. The purpose of this analysis is to determine the effect of the independent variable. Show the analysis of variance summary table; indicate whether the effect of the independent variable was statistically significant at the .05 level.

b. Perform an analytical comparison testing whether the performance of participants in the first two levels of the independent variable (1 and 2 combined) differed reliably from the mean performance in the third and fourth levels combined. Be sure to state clearly the null and alternative hypotheses for this analysis.

VI. REVIEW TESTS

These practice tests will be most helpful in preparing for your classroom tests if you test yourself under conditions that resemble those of your actual tests as closely as possible. We suggest, therefore, that you put away the book after completing the exercises in this unit and then return at a later study session to take the review tests.

A. Counterbalancing

For each of the following experimental scenarios you are to:
   (a) identify whether the experiment is a repeated measures experiment or an independent groups experiment.
If the experiment is a repeated measures experiment, then:
   (b) identify whether it is a complete repeated measures design or an incomplete repeated measures design; and,
   (c) describe how practice effects should be balanced. Be specific. Identify the kind of counterbalancing procedure that you would use and indicate how participants would be assigned to the orders. It is possible that for some scenarios two or more counterbalancing procedures could be appropriate. Identify what you believe would be the preferred counterbalancing technique for each experimental situation.

1. A researcher has five inkblots that he wishes to have 20 participants rate for their "sensuality." Assume that the researcher has a reliable and valid measure of sensuality. Each participant is to rate each inkblot one time.
   a. ?   b. ?   c. ?

2. An investigator wishes to test participants' ability to estimate time. She decides to present auditory tones for varying lengths of time and after presenting each tone she asks participants to estimate how long (in seconds) the tone was presented. She presents six different tones lasting 14, 21, 28, 35, 42, and 49 seconds. Twelve participants are available for testing. The investigator decides to present each of the six intervals four times to each participant.
   a. ?   b. ?   c. ?

3. A psychologist who is researching child abuse develops a questionnaire to help identify some of the antecedents of this problem. However, he also wishes to test a hypothesis that the ordering of certain critical questions will influence how participants respond on the questionnaire. He prepares two different forms of the questionnaire based on his analysis of the questions and of the possible effects that the order in which these questions appear might have on respondents' answers. The forms differ only in terms of the order in which certain critical questions are presented. Participants are randomly assigned to answer questions on one of the two forms.
   a. ?   b. ?   c. ?

4. A developmental psychologist wants to test children's reactions to four different "cereal creatures," that is, the creatures used by the cereal company to advertise their cereals (e.g., Tony the Tiger, Fred Flintstone, et al.). She decides to test 6th graders at a local elementary school. Each child will be asked to complete a brief response sheet about each of four cereal creatures. A total of 24 6th graders is available for testing.
a. ?   b. ?   c. ?

5. A researcher has devised a method to help stutterers. He wants to test the method against an alternative method. Eight stutterers volunteer for the experiment. The researcher decides that he can ask each stutterer to read a passage aloud to the group using both methods. In fact, he designs the experiment so that the participants read an experimental passage two times with each method.
a. ?   b. ?   c. ?

B. Multiple Choice

1. Which of the following must be balanced in order to have an interpretable repeated measures design experiment?
a. practice effects
b. individual differences
c. subject variables
d. task variability

2. Which of the following statements best describes the characteristics of the complete repeated measures design?
a. subjects are tested on each condition more than once
b. subjects are tested on each condition only once
c. subjects are tested on one condition more than once
d. subjects are tested on one condition only once

3. Which of the following is a balancing technique used in the incomplete repeated measures design?
a. block randomization
b. ABBA counterbalancing
c. all possible orders
d. ABAB counterbalancing

4. Under which of the following conditions should ABBA counterbalancing be used?
a. practice effects nonlinear and anticipation effects likely
b. practice effects nonlinear and anticipation effects unlikely
c. practice effects linear and anticipation effects unlikely
d. practice effects linear and anticipation effects likely

5. In an incomplete repeated measures design experiment each subject is tested in each condition
   a. once
   b. twice
   c. three times
   d. more than three times

6. In the context of the incomplete repeated measures design an irreversible task is one that
   a. can be done in only one order
   b. can be done in only one way
   c. can be done only at the end of a sequence
   d. can be done only once

7. The most serious problem in any repeated measures design experiment is
   a. nonlinear practice effects
   b. error variation
   c. irreversible tasks
   d. differential transfer

8. In the incomplete repeated measures design with four stages it is possible to test for differential transfer by comparing the results of the experiment as a whole with the results of the random groups design included in the experiment at the
   a. first stage
   b. second stage
   c. third stage
   d. fourth stage

9. Relative to an independent groups design, a repeated measures design is generally _____ sensitive in its ability to detect an effect of the independent variable.

   a. more
   b. less
   c. equally

10. In a repeated measures analysis of variance, the estimate of error variation is known as the
    a. subject variable
    b. residual
    c. interaction
    d. degrees of freedom

ANSWERS TO EXERCISES AND REVIEW TESTS ARE FOUND

IN THE APPENDIX AT THE END OF THIS BOOK

QUESTIONS/PROBLEMS FOR CLASS DISCUSSION

A. Terminology and Concepts

1. What is the major difference between a Latin square and a random starting order with rotation as techniques for counterbalancing?
2. Explain why the Landauer and Bjork (1978) study illustrates the problem of using an irreversible task.
3. How might anticipation effects influence behavior when using ABBA counterbalancing with many repetitions of conditions?
4. Why are repeated measures designs generally more sensitive than random groups designs?
5. Consider a problem solving experiment in which participants are given two types of clues to help them solve a problem about a person trapped in a cave. The clues differ in the kinds of information given to participants to help them identify a way for the trapped individual to exit the cave. Explain why it may not be a good idea to do this experiment using a repeated measures design.

B. Critical Thinking: Analyzing Research

1. Review the Stroop (1935) study summarized on pages 128-129. Consider your answer to question 3.a. on page 130. Identify how you might use block randomization to assign participants randomly to the orders of your experiment.

2. Again, consider your answer to question 3.a. on page 130. How would your answer change if there were 48 participants available rather than 16?

3. There is another way to assess differential transfer in an incomplete repeated measures design when all possible orders have been used. It involves comparing performance for a condition in the experiment when it was preceded by different conditions. For example, if we are worried that Condition A may have a different influence on Condition C than Condition B has on Condition C, then we might, when all possible orders have been used, examine performance on Condition C when immediately preceded by Condition A and when immediately preceded by Condition B.

a. If there are four conditions in the experiment (A,B,C,D), and all possible orders have been used with 48 participants, how many times does the order AC appear? How many times does B immediately precede C? (NOTE: You will need to list all possible ways to arrange A,B,C,D, in order to identify the number of instances when C follows A immediately, and when C follows B immediately.) How many times does each order of AC and BC appear at each stage of practice (i.e., each pair of ordinal positions--1 and 2, 2 and 3, 3 and 4)?

b. The logic behind this method of assessing differential transfer that we have been discussing is essentially the same as that associated with a random groups design. Assume that you were simply asked to answer the question: Does performance on Condition C differ depending on whether it was preceded by A or B? A reasonable way to answer this question would be to perform a random groups design with two conditions: AC and BC. Half of the participants would participate in Condition A then C, and the remaining participants would participate in Condition C then A. In addition to randomly assigning participants to your two conditions, you would want to balance and/or hold constant other extraneous factors so that the only difference between your two groups is whether A comes before C or B comes before C. Of course, you will need an appropriate measure on C to serve as your dependent variable. In the repeated measures design involving all possible orders, you essentially have already done this random groups experiment. That is, by "collecting" the AC pairs and the BC pairs from your design, and then finding the mean performance on C as a function of which condition (A or B) preceded it, you have, in essence, identified a mini random groups experiment inside your repeated measures design because different participants were randomly assigned to receive different orders in your repeated measures design. However, can you explain why this little experiment (and method of assessing differential transfer) is valid only when all possible orders have been used (and not, for instance, when only selected orders have been used)? [Note: To answer this question you may wish to construct a Latin square or a set of orders using a random starting order with rotation. Compare the occurrence of AC and BC orders in the selected orders to what you obtained using all possible orders.]

C. Creative Thinking: Designing Research

1. Use the general procedure for the Stroop task outlined in question A.3 on page 130 to design your own incomplete repeated measures design experiment investigating how a characteristic of the stimulus display (associated with either the colors or the words) might influence performance on the Stroop task. In the example on page 130, the size of the words was manipulated. Other researchers have investigated the content of the words, whether all of the letters were printed, and so forth. Choose some aspect of the stimulus to manipulate using a repeated measures design. Assume that there are 32 people willing to participate in your experiment. Identify your independent variable, the dependent variable, and the methods of control and counterbalancing you will use.

2. The testing procedure used by Landauer and Bjork (1978) to investigate optimum patterns of study is somewhat similar to the "flashcard" method used by students to study terms and their definitions. When using the flashcard method, a

student will typically look at a term and attempt to remember the definition; the student then usually "looks" to see if his or her definition was correct. (The correct definition is often on the other side of the card that has the critical term.) Landauer and Bjork (1978) did not provide students with the opportunity to get feedback as to whether their answers were correct; that is, the investigators used only test trials in which the correct answer was never provided.

Design a study similar to the Landauer and Bjork study in which you manipulate whether students receive feedback about their answers. One way to do this is to put the last name on the back of the card for half of the cards (similar to a flashcard), and for the other half of the cards leave the back of the card blank. Rather than manipulating the spacing between cards, as Landauer and Bjork (1978) did, hold constant the spacing by making sure that all cards are tested three times, with 0, 3, and 10 spaces between the presentation of the first and last name card and each test card. Assume that 12 names will be presented. An incomplete repeated measures design should be used in which participants get feedback for 6 of the names and do not get feedback for 6 of the names. The first presentation of each name will include the first and last names. The next card (0 spaces) will be the first name and a space to write in the last name. When participants turn over this card, half of the participants will see the correct answer and half will not. The procedure for this name will be repeated following 3 and 10 spaces. After all of the cards are presented, students will take a written test for all 12 items in which the first name is presented and they are asked to write down the last name. Scores on this test represent the dependent variable. Each student will have two scores: the number correct for the feedback names and the number correct for the no-feedback names. The hypothesis is that students will have more correct answers for the feedback names relative to the no-feedback names.

O.K., now that we have the basics described, what needs to be counterbalanced and how should counterbalancing be accomplished? Consider in your answer for which names participants will receive feedback, whether all participants will receive feedback for the same 6 names, and the order in which feedback is given (e.g., would you want to present all 6 feedback names then all 6 no-feedback names?). Don't worry about the final test; assume that the 12 first names are presented in a random order on this test.
[Note: To help think through this problem, you may wish to come up with the names of 12 people you know, and think about how some participants would get feedback for half of them, and others would not, etc.]

144

D. Statistical Analysis

Assume that 24 students participated in your "flashcard" study and the following data were observed for the feedback and no-feedback conditions. These numbers represent the number of last names correctly identified on the test at the conclusion of the experiment:

Participant	Feedback	No Feedback	Participant	Feedback	No Feedback
1	5	3	13	4	3
2	6	2	14	5	3
3	6	3	15	5	1
4	5	5	16	6	3
5	5	2	17	5	4
6	4	3	18	4	1
7	5	2	19	5	0
8	6	3	20	5	2
9	4	1	21	6	2
10	5	3	22	6	0
11	6	2	23	5	4
12	5	3	24	5	2

Questions:

1. What statistical tests could be used to analyze whether there is an effect of the independent variable? Explain.
2. Perform the calculations necessary to determine whether the difference between the mean for the feedback group is different from the mean for the no-feedback group. Is this result statistically significant?
3. Write a paragraph that describes these results that follows the style requirements of the American Psychological Association.

UNIT 8. COMPLEX DESIGNS

I. OVERVIEW

A complex design is one in which two or more independent variables are studied in the same experiment. This is usually done by combining variables factorially. Factorial combination occurs when each level of one independent variable is combined with each level of a second independent variable. A complex design is a very efficient way to do an experiment. An experiment involving two independent variables, for instance, allows the researcher to determine the overall effect of each independent variable (the main effect of each variable) as well as the interaction between the independent variables. An interaction exists when the effect of one independent variable differs depending on the level of the other independent variable. The smallest possible complex design is the 2 X 2 design, in which two independent variables are both studied at two levels.

Variables in a complex design can be investigated using an independent groups design, a repeated measures design, or both. A mixed design refers to a complex design wherein different designs are used for the different independent variables. For example, the overall design would be a mixed design if an individual differences variable (natural groups design) were studied with a manipulated independent variable using the incomplete repeated measures design.

Consider a complex design involving two independent variables: (a) difficulty of task and (b) amount of distraction. Assume that the first factor, difficulty of task, has two levels: low and high. Assume that the second factor, amount of distraction, also has two levels: small and large. A factorial design would require four different conditions, each representing a combination of levels of the two independent variables: a low difficulty task with a small amount of distraction, a low difficulty task with a large amount of distraction, a high difficulty task with a small amount of distraction, and a high difficulty task with a large amount of distraction. Thus, the design is a 2 X 2 factorial design.

The analysis of complex designs with two independent variables involves three potential sources of systematic variation. Each independent variable can produce a significant main effect, and there can be an interaction between the two variables. Results of a complex design involving at least an interval level of measurement can be described efficiently by reporting the mean performance in each of the conditions defined by the combinations of levels of the independent variables (called the cells of the design). Consider the following hypothetical means from the example 2 X 2 experiment involving difficulty of task and amount of distraction. Let us assume that the higher the score on the dependent variable the better is performance.

146

Difficulty		Distraction	
		Small	Large
	Low	40	30
	High	55	15

The most important effect and the one to be checked first in the analysis of a complex design is to see if the two independent variables have combined to produce a significant interaction. If one or both of the independent variables has two levels, interactions can be initially identified by using the subtraction method. To use the subtraction method, determine the difference between the means for the two-level variable at each level of the second variable. Then compare these differences to see if they are different from each other. For a 2 X 2 design, determine the differences between the column means in each row of the design or determine the differences between the row means in each column. The subtraction method can be illustrated by applying it to the distraction/difficulty example. The difference between the two column means in the first row is: 40 - 30 = 10. The difference between the levels of the distraction factor in the second row is: 55 - 15 = 40. A difference between the differences calculated by the subtraction method suggests an interaction between the two variables. [NOTE: It is important always to subtract in the same direction across columns or rows and to pay attention to the sign (positive or negative) of the difference when using the subtraction method.]

Remember, an interaction arises when the effect of one independent variable differs depending on the level or setting of a second independent variable. A difference revealed by the subtraction method shows that the effect of one independent variable (defined by the difference between the means for the levels of that variable) depends on the level of a second independent variable that you are considering. In the above example, there was a relatively small difference between the levels of distraction when difficulty of the task was low, but there was a much larger difference between these two levels when the difficulty of the task was high. In other words, the effect of distraction was less when the task was low in difficulty than when the task was high in difficulty. The presence of an interaction also can be shown by graphing the means of the experiment. Nonparallel lines in the graph suggest that an interaction is present; parallel lines indicate no interaction. Inferential statistic tests, however, are required to confirm the presence of an interaction.

Main effects (the independent effects of each independent variable) are also revealed in a complex design. Specifically, the main effect for the difficulty variable can be examined by comparing the means for the two rows representing the two levels of difficulty (collapsing across the distraction variable): Low (40 + 30)/2 = 35; High (55 + 15)/2 = 35. In this particular example, there is no difference between the row means;

thus, no main effect is present for the factor of task difficulty. A main effect for the distraction factor is examined by calculating the means for the two columns (collapsing across the difficulty variable): Small (40 + 55)/2 = 47.5; Large (30 + 15)/2 = 22.5. There is a large difference between the column means when averaging over the difficulty variable, suggesting a main effect for the distraction variable. Again, inferential tests are needed to confirm the presence of main effects.

The analytical power of complex designs increases when additional levels of one or both of the independent variables are included in the design, yielding designs such as the 3 X 2, the 3 X 3, the 4 X 2, the 4 X 3, and so on. Additional independent variables can also be included to yield designs such as the 2 X 2 X 2, the 3 X 3 X 3, and so on. Experiments involving three independent variables are remarkably efficient. They allow determination of the main effects of each of the three independent variables, the three two-way interactions of the three independent variables, and the simultaneous interaction of all three independent variables.

When a complex design is used and no interaction occurs, we know that the effects of each independent variable can be generalized across the levels of the other independent variable(s). When an interaction does occur, however, limits on the generality of a finding can be clearly specified. For some interactions, the effects of the independent variable are in the same direction at each level of the other independent variable but the effects differ in size. For example, the hypothetical means found in the example above reveal such an interaction; performance is worse with large distraction for both the low and high difficulty tasks, but the effect of distraction is much greater for the high difficulty task. Other interactions place even greater limits on the generality of a finding. For these interactions the effects of one independent variable are opposite in direction at different levels of the second independent variable. Referring again to our example of a 2 X 2 design, we can see that the effects of the difficulty variable are in opposite directions at the two levels of the distraction variable: Small, 40 - 55 = -15; Large, 30 - 15 = +15. Here, performance is better on the high difficulty task with small distraction, but performance is worse on the high difficulty task with large distraction. [Note: There is only one possible interaction in a two-factor design. The description of this interaction can differ, however, depending upon which independent variable's effect is being emphasized.]

The possibility of interactions requires that we expand the definition of a relevant independent variable to include those that influence behavior directly (produce main effects) and those that produce an interaction when studied in combination with another independent variable. Interactions that may arise because of measurement problems such as ceiling or basement effects must not be confused with interactions that reflect the true combined effect of two independent variables.

Complex designs are essential to resolve contradictions that arise when two experiments involving the same independent variable result in different findings.

Investigators can trace the source of the contradictory findings by using a complex design in which both the original independent variable and the independent variable that is presumed to be responsible for the discrepant findings are manipulated in the same experiment. Assume, for example, that investigator A tests female students on variable X, while investigator B tests male students on variable X. If the effect of variable X differs between the two experiments, it may be useful to investigate variable X and the variable of gender (male and female) simultaneously in a single experiment with a complex design. If gender is responsible for the discrepant findings, then an interaction in the complex design will be found and limits on the generality of variable X will be established. Complex designs also play a critical role in the testing of predictions derived from psychological theories and can be most helpful in solving the problem of drawing causal inferences based on the natural groups design.

The computational procedures associated with the ANOVA for a complex design depend on the type of complex design that is used (see, for example, Keppel, 1991). Whatever type of complex design is used, however, an investigator will at times be required to report more than main effects and interactions. For example, if the interaction in a complex design proves to be statistically significant, its source can be located by analyzing the simple main effects and then the simple comparisons. When no interaction arises, the main effects of each independent variable can be analyzed further using analytical comparisons. In the exercises following this Overview, we discuss more fully the analysis of complex designs.

Reference

Keppel, G. (1991). <u>Design and analysis: A researcher's handbook</u> (3rd ed.). Englewood Cliffs, NJ: Prentice-Hall.

II. KEY CONCEPTS

The following concepts are importantly related to the experimental methods that are discussed in this unit. Use the information found in the **OVERVIEW,** as well as the definitions of the key concepts provided here, to complete the exercises in the following sections. [NOTE: Numbers in parentheses refer to pages in the fourth edition of <u>Research</u> <u>Methods</u> <u>in</u> <u>Psychology</u> by Shaughnessy and Zechmeister (1997), where these concepts are more fully defined.]

ceiling (basement) effect A measurement problem whereby the researcher cannot measure the effects of an independent variable or a possible interaction because performance has reached a maximum (minimum) in any condition of the experiment. (295)

complex design An experiment in which two or more independent variables are studied simultaneously. (269)

interaction Occurs when the effect of one independent variable differs depending upon the level of a second independent variable. (270)

main effect The overall effect of an independent variable in a complex design. (274)

relevant independent variable An independent variable that has been shown to influence behavior, either directly by producing a main effect, or indirectly by resulting in an interaction in combination with a second independent variable. (293)

simple main effect The effect of one independent variable at one level of a second independent variable in a complex design. (287)

III. EXAMPLES OF COMPLEX DESIGNS

Read the following two summaries of published research carefully. Answer the questions found at the end of each summary. Answering these questions will require use of concepts introduced in this unit and previous units.

A. Human Decision Making

Reference: Arkes, H. R., Christensen, C., Lai, C., & Blumer, C. (1987). Two methods of reducing overconfidence. <u>Organizational Behavior and Human Decision Processes, 39</u>, 133-144.

Article Summary: "Who has won more National League championships? A. The Chicago Cubs. B. The Cincinnati Reds." "How confident are you that the answer you have selected is correct?" Research has shown that people typically are overconfident in their answers to general knowledge questions. This has been demonstrated by experiments which present a large number of questions to participants with the request that they (a) attempt to answer each question and (b) rate their confidence in each answer. Results of such research show that the probability of a correct answer is generally lower than participants predict. For example, answers that are given a 90% chance of being correct are often answered correctly with a likelihood that is much less than 90%. Research also has shown that attempts to reduce people's overconfidence frequently have failed. Ironically, people who are overconfident may resist such attempts because they believe (mistakenly) that they are doing well!

In the first experiment reported in this article, 58 college undergraduates were asked to answer five general knowledge questions prior to being given a final 30 questions to answer. Each question involved a two-alternative forced choice.

Participants also rated confidence in having chosen the right answers by writing a percentage between 50% (guessing) and 100% next to each item. For half the participants, the first five questions were difficult but looked easy; for the other half the first five questions looked difficult and were difficult. The question given at the beginning of this summary is an example of an item that the experimenters judged was hard but looks easy. (The answer is "The Cubs.") An example of a difficult question that looked difficult was: "The highest mountain in South America is: A. Aconcagua. B. Tormando." (The correct answer is "Aconcagua.") Within each question group, half the participants were given feedback regarding their answers to the first five questions ("so that you can get an idea of the difficulty level of these questions") and half were not given feedback. All participants answered the same final 30 questions.

Two separate 2 X 2 ANOVAs were carried out on the results from the <u>first five</u> questions. The first ANOVA examined number correct on the first five questions; the second ANOVA examined average confidence expressed in the first five questions. There were no significant sources of variation in the first ANOVA; the four means were very close to one another. The second ANOVA revealed that average confidence was significantly higher for groups given the easy-looking items than groups with the difficult-looking items. Two separate ANOVAs were performed on the data from the final 30 questions. The first ANOVA tested number correct and found no significant differences. For the second ANOVA, the dependent measure was the average confidence expressed on the final 30 items <u>minus</u> the proportion correct on these items. (A positive difference indicates overconfidence; a negative difference indicates underconfidence.) This ANOVA revealed a significant main effect for the feedback vs. no feedback variable, $\underline{F}$ (1, 54) = 8.43, $\underline{p}$ < .01, and a significant interaction between the feedback/no feedback and question type, $\underline{F}$ (1,54) = 4.58, $\underline{p}$ <.05. The mean over/underconfidence score for the participants having easy-looking items and feedback was -4.67; that of the group having easy-looking items and no feedback, +9.13. The mean over/underconfidence score for the group having hard items and feedback was +4.36; that of the group with hard items and no feedback, +6.29.

The significant interaction had been predicted by the researchers. They suggested that giving people feedback in the easy-looking item condition was a "humbling" experience for these individuals and caused them to adjust their confidence levels downward on the final 30 questions. The authors note that this debiasing technique possibly could be used to introduce material in textbooks to show readers that forthcoming material is "not as intuitively obvious" as they might think.

Questions:

1. Identify (a) the major independent variables and (b) the dependent variables in the experiment performed by Arkes et al. (1987). HINT: Two major independent variables and three different dependent variables are mentioned.

2. The participants in this study were randomly assigned to the four major conditions and were tested in small groups. Materials were presented to participants in booklets. Describe how the three major methods of control, that is, manipulation, balancing, and holding conditions constant, were used to ensure the internal validity of this experiment.

3. The results of the two ANOVAs carried out on the participants' responses to the first five questions do not bear directly on the major goals of the study; rather, they represent what is called a "manipulation check." What do you think that means in terms of the present study? Specifically, what did the researchers hope to see (and not see) (a) in the results of the ANOVA for number correct on the first five questions, and (b) in the results of the ANOVA for mean confidence on the first five questions?

4. The rationale behind the over/underconfidence measure is that if participants' average confidence (over all items) is higher than their proportion correct, then the subject is overconfident. For example, if for every one of 30 answers you indicated that you were 80% sure the answer is right, then we might expect that when we look at proportion correct over all of these items that you would average about 80% correct. If your proportion correct is lower than 80%, however, then we might judge you to be overconfident, indicating that you think you know more than you actually do.
    (a) Summarize the results of the Arkes et al. (1987) experiment by drawing a line graph showing the mean performance of the four groups based on the over/underconfidence measure obtained on the final 30 items. NOTE: The dependent variable can take on negative values; thus, the vertical axis of your graph will need to include both positive and negative values.
    (b) Describe verbally what you have graphed in terms of the variables in this study. NOTE: Your verbal description should describe how the figure shows that an interaction is present.

5. What two specific means would you use to describe the overall main effect of feedback vs. no feedback in terms of over/underconfidence? HINT: You will need to calculate these two means using cell means reported in the article summary.

B. Depression and Causal Attribution

Reference: Rodman, J. L., & Burger, J. M. (1985). The influence of depression on the attribution of responsibility for an accident. Cognitive Therapy and Research, 9, 651-657.

Article Summary: Results of research studies indicate that depressed individuals do not make causal attributions for events in the same way as do nondepressed individuals. For instance, depressed people apparently do not exhibit certain cognitive biases that would protect them from perceiving various events as depressing. Rodman and Burger investigated whether depressed individuals would exhibit a "defensive attribution" bias. This bias is revealed when people are asked to assign responsibility for an accident that has either severe or mild consequences for a victim. Nondepressed individuals tend not to attribute the cause of a severe accident to chance, thereby, it is assumed, "reducing the perceived possibility that such an accident is uncontrollable and that it might someday happen to them." The researchers presented nondepressed, slightly depressed, and depressed college students with a description of an accident that had either mild or severe consequences. They predicted that "the strength of the defensive attribution effect would decrease as level of subject depression increased."

Initially, 120 individuals were given the Beck Depression Inventory (BDI) to assess level of depression; 56 people (30 males and 26 females) were selected for the study on the basis of their BDI scores. They were assigned to one of three groups: nondepressed, slightly depressed, depressed. Then participants were asked to read a description of a three-car accident as if they were members of a jury. The accident description "was written to give all three drivers a role in the accident, yet still allow for the perception of some uncontrollable variables." Half the participants in each depression group were randomly given a description of an accident with mild consequences (e.g., "driver received minor cuts and abrasions") and half were assigned to read a description with severe consequences (e.g., "driver in critical condition with head injuries"). After reading the accident description, participants were asked to divide responsibility (100%) for the accident among four categories: each of the three drivers and "uncontrollable circumstances." A 2 X 3 ANOVA revealed a significant interaction between accident severity and depression level for the key dependent variable of amount of responsibility assigned to uncontrollable factors. A series of analytical comparisons showed that nondepressed individuals assigned significantly less responsibility to uncontrollable factors for the severe than for the nonsevere accident (the defensive attribution effect), slightly depressed individuals did not differ in their degree of assignment, while depressed individuals assigned more responsibility to uncontrollable factors for severe than for mild accidents ($p < .10$). These findings are consistent with results of earlier research showing that depressed and nondepressed individuals differ in the manner in which they make causal attributions.

Questions:

1. The BDI was originally designed for use with clinical populations but has been used extensively with college populations. It asks people to indicate the degree to which they currently experience 21 different symptoms of depression. In order to find enough depressed individuals in the college population, Rodman and Burger had to give the BDI to many more students (120) than they actually tested in the experiment (56). Only 16 students met the criterion of "depression" on the BDI; the 20 students with the lowest BDI scores were assigned to the nondepressed group and 20 students with scores between those of the depressed and nondepressed participants were assigned to the "slightly depressed" group. Given these considerations, comment critically on the <u>external</u> <u>validity</u> of the results.

2. Based on your reading of the article summary, identify at least three factors that were held constant across conditions.

3. The experiment was a complex design involving two factors. Classify each of the two independent variables as a manipulated variable or a nonmanipulated (i.e., individual differences or subject) variable and explain your classification.

4. The data in Table 8-1 are fictitious but closely resemble the actual data obtained by Rodman and Burger. Draw a bar graph (with level of depression on the horizontal axis) displaying these results.

Table 8-1

<u>Mean Percentage of Accident Responsibility Attributed to Uncontrollable Factors</u>

<u>Level of Depression</u>

<u>Accident</u>	<u>Nondepressed</u>	<u>Slightly Depressed</u>	<u>Depressed</u>
Severe	7.00	14.00	17.00
Nonsevere	30.50	16.50	4.00

5. Complex designs involving both a manipulated variable and a natural groups variable can help an investigator draw appropriate causal inferences regarding the natural groups variable. Causal inferences regarding natural groups variables can be strengthened by a three-stage process of theory development and experimentation: (1) Outline a theory stating why performance among the natural groups will vary; that is, identify what <u>process</u> or processes are involved. (2) Identify an independent variable that can be manipulated and that is presumed to influence the likelihood that this theoretical process will occur. (3) Test for an interaction between the manipulated variable and the natural groups variable. A reliable interaction provides evidence that your thinking about why the natural

groups differ is correct (although it does <u>not</u> necessarily <u>prove</u> your theory correct). (a) Show how Steps 1 and 2 in this approach apply to the study by Rodman and Burger. Specifically (Step 1), what "process" did Rodman and Burger identify that they believe distinguishes the thinking of nondepressed individuals from that of depressed individuals? And (Step 2), how was the manipulated variable in their study predicted to influence the likelihood of that process?

(b) Step 3 of this approach requires a test for an interaction between the natural groups variable and the manipulated variable. Explain how the interaction obtained by Rodman and Burger supports their idea about the nature of the difference between depressed and nondepressed individuals. That is, how was the theory about the nature of thinking among depressed individuals relative to nondepressed individuals strengthened by the results of this complex design in a way that it could not have been if there had been no interaction present?

IV. PROBLEMS AND EXERCISES

Read the following descriptions of psychological research carefully and then answer the questions that follow.

A. Problem 1

<u>Description</u>: A developmental psychologist investigates memory performance among 2nd and 6th graders as a function of story coherence. Specifically, two types of stories are prepared that are identical except that events in one story are logically ordered according to a theory of memory organization whereas events in the second type of story are arranged such that the natural order of the story is disrupted. The investigator believes that younger children will remember less overall than will older children, and that the logically disrupted story will be harder overall to recall than will the logically ordered story. However, an interaction is also predicted. The investigator believes that the effect of the story variable will be less among older children than among younger children. Forty 2nd graders and 40 6th graders are randomly assigned in equal numbers to the two story conditions. Thus, there are 20 children tested in each cell of the complex design. The children are tested individually with the stories presented auditorily using a tape recorder. Recordings are made by a trained story teller. Children are asked to recall the story orally when it is completed and retention is scored on at least an interval scale of measurement in a way that we will assume is reliable and valid. Scores can vary from 0 to 100.

<u>Questions</u>:

1. Answer the following True or False:

(a) The experiment is appropriately described as a 2 X 2 complex design.

(b) One of the independent variables is an individual differences variable.

(c) One of the independent variables is manipulated as repeated measures.

(d) Two main effects are predicted by the experimenter.

2. Using hypothetical means that you make up, construct a design matrix showing main effects for each of the independent variables and an interaction as predicted by the experimenter.

3. Assume that the investigator obtains both main effects and the interaction as predicted; however, assume also that on close examination a critical reviewer of this study suggests that the interaction was due to ceiling effects in the retention scores of the 6th graders. Construct a design matrix using hypothetical means that shows the predicted results and also suggests that ceiling effects may be responsible for the obtained interaction effect.

B. Problem 2

Description: A researcher sets out to replicate the experiment described in Problem 1. However, the investigator adds a third variable to the complex design: length of story. Specifically, the investigator uses stories of the same length as in the original experiment, but also prepares stories that are similar in content but are one-third longer. By doing this, the researcher hopes to avoid any ceiling effects in the recall of the 6th graders. In order to test children efficiently, half the participants in this experiment are tested on both the nondisrupted and disrupted story using the original story length, and half are tested on both types of stories using the longer length. The investigator tests 80 children (40 2nd graders and 40 6th graders) who were not in the previous experiment. Other procedures and measures are the same as those used in the original experiment.

Questions:

1. Identify the three independent variables and the levels of each.
2. Does this replication represent a mixed design? Explain.
3. Why would the type of story variable need to be counterbalanced?
4. How many children will be tested on each length of story?
5. How many children will be tested at each level of story type (disrupted and nondisrupted)?

V. DATA ANALYSIS

A. Descriptive Statistics

A clinical psychologist prepares three types of communications to test the degree of anxiety among groups of patients being treated for various anxious tendencies. The communications differ in the degree of affect elicited and in the number of vivid details of a traumatic event. The dependent variable is a paper and pencil anxiety test that can be assumed to represent at least an interval level of measurement. Scores can vary from 0 to 40; the higher the score, the greater the measured anxiety. Two categories of anxious individuals are identified based on their symptomatology. For our purposes we will simply refer to these categories as A1 and A2. Twenty-four individuals from each of the two patient groups are assigned randomly in equal numbers (8) to listen to one of the three types of communications prior to completing the anxiety test. The scores on the anxiety test for the 48 individuals in this experiment are shown below:

A1 Participants

Communication A	Communication B	Communication C
39	16	20
36	26	10
28	23	13
31	18	21
26	11	13
35	11	6
30	13	5
38	8	11

A2 Participants

Communication A	Communication B	Communication C
25	11	7
20	15	3
10	12	3
16	14	1
14	12	7
9	20	1
3	12	1
12	19	1

1. Find the means for each of the six cells of the complex design.
2. Report the means in a table prepared according to the stylistic rules of the American Psychological Association.
3. Describe the results verbally in terms of the two variables.

B. Inferential Statistics

The data presented above (Descriptive Statistics 8.A.) can be appropriately analyzed using an ANOVA for a complex random groups design (2 X 3). The logic and computational procedures underlying this type of ANOVA will be discussed more completely below. Depending on the nature of the results for the omnibus-F test, one or more "follow-up" tests may be in order. Answer the following questions regarding these possible additional analyses:

Questions:
1. Following a complex analysis of variance, what is the major consideration in deciding whether simple main effects or analytical comparisons are to be carried out?
2. When an independent variable has only two levels, neither simple comparisons nor analytical comparisons are called for (although simple main effects may be). Explain.

1. Complex Design: Illustration of ANOVA Summary Table

A complex design involves more than one independent variable. A factorial design is one in which all levels of one independent variable are combined with each level of another independent variable. Thus, a 2 X 3 factorial design has two independent variables, one with 2 levels and one with 3 levels. There are a total of six conditions in this design represented by the combination of the levels of the independent variables. A complex design may be carried out as an independent groups design, a repeated measures design, or what is called a mixed design. We will consider only the ANOVA for an independent groups design involving two independent variables.

Let us consider a hypothetical commercial product experiment. There are two variables, namely, gender of the participants, and type of commercial. Participants are randomly assigned to view one of four commercials. After seeing the commercial, participants provide ratings for how interested they are in the product using a 10-point rating scale (1 = not interested in trying this product, 10 = very interested in trying this product). The design can be designated as 4 X 2. The first independent variable, type of commercial, has four levels (A,B,C,D); the second independent variable, gender, has two levels (male and female). You should recognize that type of commercial is a random groups variable and gender is an individual differences variable. Assume that 20 males and 20 females viewed and rated their interest in the product after viewing one of the four commercials. Therefore, there are 160 total participants in the fictitious experiment.

Let us also assume that the mean interest ratings produced by male and female participants after viewing the four product commercials in this experiment were as follows:

Commercial

	A	B	C	D
Male	6.7	5.9	7.9	6.7
Female	6.5	5.3	7.4	6.2

Gender

Table 8.2 presents an ANOVA summary table for this hypothetical 4 X 2 experiment involving commercial and gender.

TABLE 8.2 ANALYSIS OF VARIANCE SUMMARY TABLE

Source of Variation	df	SS	MS	F	p
Commercial	3	34.10	11.37	4.21	.007
Gender	1	12.22	12.22	4.53	.03
Commercial X Gender	3	15.16	5.05	1.87	.14
Within Groups	152	410.96	2.70		
Total	159				

There are three sources of systematic variation in this experiment: the main effect of commercial, the main effect of gender, and the interaction between commercial and gender. For the main effects, the df are equal to the number of levels of the independent variable minus one. The df for the interaction are obtained by multiplying the df for each of the main effects (3 X 1 = 3). The within groups df are obtained by multiplying the number of df for each group times the number of groups. Because there are eight groups, each with 20 participants, the within groups df are 152 (8 X 19). The three F-tests entered in the summary table are each computed by dividing the MS within groups into the MS for each main effect and for the interaction. The probabilities for each of the F-tests were determined using the value of F and the appropriate df for each effect (3 and 152 for commercial main effect and for the interaction; 1 and 152 for the gender main effect). The three F-tests in the summary table represent the counterpart of an omnibus F-test in a single factor design. As is true in a single factor design, analyses to follow up the initial omnibus tests are needed to interpret the results.

Based on the outcome of the omnibus F-test for the interaction, either simple main effects or simple comparisons can be analyzed. The decision to perform these analyses depends on whether or not the interaction effect is significant. A significant interaction suggests that the investigator should track down the source of the interaction, analyzing the simple main effects and then performing simple comparisons. If the interaction is not significant, then the main effects of each independent variable can be further examined using analytical comparisons similar to those used with only one independent variable. Of course, if the independent variable producing the main effect in a complex design has only two levels there is no need for additional comparisons. The main effect associated with an independent variable with two levels tells you that the two means differ significantly; no further analyses are necessary.

2. Complex Design: ANOVA Summary Table Problem

In order to evaluate your understanding of these concepts, first examine the following ANOVA Summary Table; then, answer the questions that follow.

TABLE 8.3 ANALYSIS OF VARIANCE SUMMARY TABLE

Source of Variation	df	SS	MS	F	p
Type of Problem	2	96.00	48.00	3.70	.03
Presentation Rate	1	16.50	16.50	1.27	.26
Type X Rate	2	14.00	7.00	.54	.41
Within Groups	42	545.00	12.98		
Total	47				

Questions:

1. How many independent variables were in this experiment?
2. How many levels did each variable have?
3. How many participants were in the experiment?
4. How many participants were in each condition of the experiment (assuming cell sizes are equal)?
5. Was either main effect statistically significant?
6. Was there a statistically significant interaction?

3. Complex Design: Calculation Problem

The following exercises give you practice with some of the statistical procedures common to using ANOVA and performing analyses to follow up on initial omnibus tests. It is suggested that you use a computer with appropriate statistical software to perform these analyses. You will need to refer to Appendix A (Statistical Methods) of the Shaughnessy and Zechmeister (1997) textbook or to an introductory-level statistics books in order to do the analyses that follow up the results of the omnibus test.

a. Carry out the appropriate ANOVA for the data presented on page 156 (Section V.A., Descriptive Statistics). Report your results in an analysis of variance summary table.

b. Describe the appropriate decision concerning the statistical significance of each source of variation in the experiment (use .05 level of significance).

c. Based on the outcome of the omnibus F-test for the interaction, either simple main effects or simple comparisons can be analyzed. Given the results of your omnibus ANOVA do you need to test the simple main effects? If yes, which simple main effects would you test and what would you expect to learn from these tests?

VI. REVIEW TESTS

These practice tests will be most helpful in preparing for your classroom tests if you test yourself under conditions that resemble those of your actual tests as closely as possible. We suggest, therefore, that you put away the book after completing the exercises in this unit and then return at a later study session to take the review tests.

A. Main Effects and Interactions

1. The following design matrix shows cell means for a 2 X 3 complex design. Based on an examination of the cell means would you suggest that a main effect is present for factor A? For factor B? Is there an interaction between A and B? (Assume that any difference between means is significant. However, keep in mind that main effects and interactions can be confirmed only through the appropriate inferential statistical tests.)

Factor A

		a_1	a_2	a_3
	b_1	10	15	40
Factor B				
	b_2	20	25	30

2. The following design matrix shows three cell means for a 2 X 2 complex design. Assume that the analysis of the experiment showed a main effect of factor A, no main effect of factor B, and an interaction between A and B. What value should be placed in the missing cell for this pattern of results to be obtained? (Again, assume that any difference between means is significant.)

Factor A

		a_1	a_2
	b_1	20	30
Factor B			
	b_2	40	?

3. Assume that the analysis of the means in the previous problem had revealed two main effects but no interaction. What value should be placed in the missing cell for this pattern of results to be obtained?

4. The following graphs show results of two different complex designs involving two variables. For each graph, decide if there is a main effect of variable A, a main effect of variable B, and whether or not an interaction between variables A and B is present.

(a)   (b)

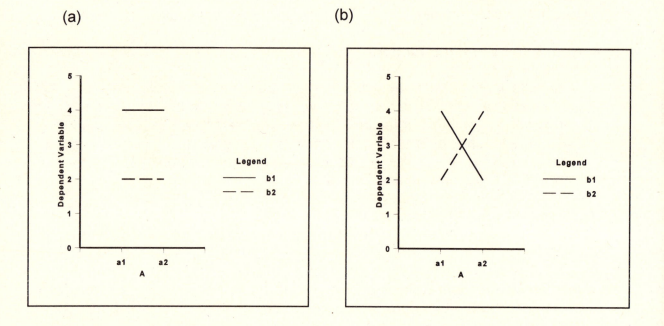

B. Multiple Choice

1. A complex design always involves
   a. only one independent variable
   b. two or more independent variables
   c. two or more different research designs
   d. two or more dependent variables

2. Which of the following occurs when the effect of one independent variable differs depending on the level of a second independent variable?
   a. main effect
   b. interaction
   c. differential effect
   d. bilevel effect

3. The overall effect of one independent variable in a complex design is called a(n)
   a. omnibus effect
   b. main effect
   c. singular effect
   d. independent effect

4. When each level of one independent variable is combined with each level of a second independent variable the combination of these two variables is called
   a. factorial combination
   b. complete combination
   c. counterbalanced combination
   d. successive combination

5. The absence of an interaction in a complex design can be seen in a graph when the lines in the graph are
   a. intersecting
   b. nonparallel
   c. converging
   d. parallel

6. An experiment that is described as a 3 X 3 X 2 is one that has
   a. one independent variable with a total of 18 levels
   b. two independent variables, each with 3 levels
   c. three independent variables, two with 3 levels and one with 2 levels
   d. two independent variables with 3 levels and one dependent variable with 2 levels

7. When an independent variable such as task difficulty has been shown to interact with a second independent variable such as age, the generality of the effect of the task difficulty variable is
   a. increased
   b. unaffected
   c. decreased

8. Which of the following is not an advantage of using a complex design?
   a. resolving contradictions when two experiments involving the same independent variable result in different findings
   b. expanding the definition of relevant independent variables to include those that produce an interaction
   c. testing of predictions derived from psychological theories
   d. increasing the effectiveness of matching procedures in the matched groups design

9. The interpretation of an interaction may be limited when this problem in measurement occurs:
   a. ceiling or basement effect
   b. nonparallel lines
   c. simple main effect
   d. highly reliable measurement of the dependent variable

10. Which of the following types of analyses is used to locate the source of a statistically significant interaction in a complex design?
    a. main effect
    b. marginal effect
    c. simple main effect
    d. internal effect

ANSWERS TO EXERCISES AND REVIEW TESTS ARE FOUND

IN THE APPENDIX AT THE END OF THIS BOOK

****

QUESTIONS/PROBLEMS FOR CLASS DISCUSSION

A. Terminology and Concepts

1. Use the "subtraction method" outlined in the Overview to describe the interaction obtained by Arkes et al. (1987) when they analyzed over/underconfidence scores as a function of feedback and question type (see pp. 149-150). NOTE: Because one of the means is a negative number you must be careful to subtract correctly.

2. Examine the means found in Table 8.1 (p. 153) that describe results similar to those found by Rodman and Burger (1985) in their study of depressive attribution. Let us assume that the mean percentage of accident responsibility attributed to uncontrollable factors was 1.50 for nondepressed individuals who read the serious accident scenario (rather than 7.00). Would you consider a mean of 1.50 a "basement effect"? If so, discuss how this result might influence your interpretation of a significant interaction based on an analysis of the means in Table 8.1.

3. Explain how findings from a complex design experiment with two independent variables can set "limits" on generalizing the results obtained from a different experiment involving a single independent variable.

4. Demonstrate the difference between main effects and interactions by calculating the values for the main effects of Accident Type and Level of Depression for the data presented in Table 8-1. What values would you use to interpret the interaction between these two independent variables?

5. Suppose that Rodman and Burger performed their experiment not with two independent variables but with three. Let us assume further that the third variable was gender of the participants and it was factorially combined with the original two variables. How many different groups of individuals would be represented in the new design? Identify all of the groups in this complex design.

B. Critical Thinking: Analyzing Research

1. Arkes et al. (1987) obtained a significant interaction between the variables of feedback/no feedback and question type when the dependent measure was over/underconfidence (see section III.A., pp. 149-150). The interaction had been predicted by the researchers. The same analysis also revealed a main effect of feedback/no feedback. Let us assume that another researcher repeated the Arkes et al. study and obtained mean over/underconfidence scores that were exactly five units greater in all conditions. That is, the mean over/underconfidence scores for participants having easy-looking items and feedback was +.33, that of the group having easy items and no feedback was +14.13, and so on for the other two means. (Such a result may occur if the second researcher used easier items.)
   a. Would you still expect to see an interaction and a main effect as found by Arkes et al.?
   b. Would these new results be supportive of the explanation given by Arkes et al. for their findings?

2. Rodman and Burger (1985) performed a series of comparisons (specifically, simple main effects and simple comparisons) to analyze further the nature of the interaction they obtained and to determine whether their results were consistent with those of past studies (see section III.B., p. 152). Three particular comparisons were made, each within a level of the depression variable.
   a. Explain why these specific comparisons make more sense than performing two comparisons, one within each level of the severity of accident variable.
   b. If simple main effects had been carried out within each level of the severity variable, what would each comparison tell us? Would you need to do more analyses within each severity level? What additional analyses might you suggest?

C. Creative Thinking: Designing Research

1. Suppose a researcher takes seriously the suggestion by Arkes et al. (1987) that a "debiasing technique" could be used to reduce students' overconfidence when learning material for class examinations (see p. 150). Specifically, the researcher wishes to design an experiment to find out whether reducing students' overconfidence will affect their preparation for a test. That is, the researcher predicts that reducing students' overconfidence will make them study harder for an exam. However, before trying this in a real classroom situation, the researcher decides to do a laboratory experiment. The debiasing technique is based on the Arkes et al. finding that attempting to answer easy looking (but hard) items and receiving feedback about the correctness of their (often wrong) answers leaves students "humbled" and reduces their overconfidence. The experiment asks students to participate in an experiment "investigating student study methods."

When participants arrive for the experiment, they are asked to read a 5-page article on world geography in preparation for a test.

a. Based on the general outline provided above, design a 2 X 2 experiment that will (hopefully) show that students' preparation for a test is affected by the nature of questions (and feedback) that they experience prior to study. You will have to fill-in many missing details. Feel free to modify the general procedure as presented. Identify your independent variables, the conditions of the experiment, the dependent variable(s), your hypotheses and how you would conduct the study.

b. Provide hypothetical results consistent with your predictions and draw a graph showing the results of your 2 X 2 experiment.

2. As you learned in this Unit (see especially the discussion associated with Question B.5. on pp. 153-154), complex designs involving both a manipulated variable and a natural groups (individual differences) variable can help researchers draw appropriate causal inferences regarding the natural groups variable. Complex designs are also used to identify relevant variables and to test competing theories. That is, when two or more theories make contrasting predictions about a behavior, a complex design can be used to determine which theory receives more support.

Another theory about depression suggests that depressives tend to feel hopeless about the events that affect them personally. Based on this theory, one could predict that depressed individuals would be more likely to state that <u>all</u> events in their life, serious and not-so-serious, are due to uncontrollable factors relative to nondepressed individuals. In contrast, events that do not affect them are less likely to be rated as uncontrollable.

Assume that you wish to test these ideas using a slightly different scenario with two natural groups of college students: depressed and nondepressed. As in the Rodman and Burger (1985) study, your scenario involves a three-car accident. However, instead of manipulating whether the accident is serious or not-so-serious, suppose you manipulate whether the accident personally involves the participant. Assume that, as in the Rodman and Burger study, there are three individuals involved, and that you will hold constant the seriousness of the accident at the "serious" level. However, in one condition, an important modification of their study will be to write the scenario in the "first-person." That is, one of the individuals in the car accident will be described as "you." For example, one sentence might read, "You were approaching the intersection when you saw the red car." This modification is needed because the hopelessness theory states that depressed individuals are hopeless about events that affect them personally. This condition is identified as the "personal condition." The second condition will be "impersonal," and will use the Rodman and Burger scenario with three unnamed individuals.

As in the Rodman and Burger study, the scenario will be ambiguous so that it is not clear who is responsible for the accident. Participants will be asked to rate the percentage responsibility for the three people in the accident (including themselves in the personal condition) and "uncontrollable factors." The critical dependent variable will be the percentage of responsibility attributed to "uncontrollable factors."

a. Outline an experiment based on these conditions. Identify your independent variables and the conditions of the experiment. Describe how you would conduct the study.

b. Considering what you know about defensive attribution bias and hopelessness, what are your predictions for the results of this 2 X 2 experiment? What might the pattern of means look like? [Note: You may wish to draw a figure.]

D. Statistical Analysis

Suppose the following hypothetical data were observed for the dependent measure identified in problem C.2. Recall that the dependent variable is the percentage responsibility assigned to uncontrollable factors. Ten depressed and ten nondepressed participants were randomly assigned to the "personal" or "impersonal" conditions (i.e., five in each cell).

Depressed

Personal	Impersonal
25	30
35	25
25	10
40	15
50	25

Nondepressed

Personal	Impersonal
0	15
5	10
5	10
10	5
5	15

1. Calculate the means for each cell and the 2 X 2 Analysis of Variance. Create an ANOVA summary table for these data.
2. Using the style requirements of the American Psychological Association, write a brief paragraph that describes these data.
3. Do any of these data replicate the findings of the Rodman and Burger (1985) study? Explain.
4. Do these data support the defensive attribution theory, hopelessness theory, neither, or both? Explain.

UNIT 9. SINGLE-CASE RESEARCH DESIGNS

I. OVERVIEW

Yet another important alternative to studying behavior is the case study method. The intensive study of individuals that is the hallmark of the case study method is called idiographic research, and it can be viewed as complementary to the nomothetic inquiry (seeking general laws or principles) that is also characteristic of psychology and which is often the goal of observational or survey research (see Allport, 1961). There are a number of advantages to using the case study method to learn about behavior. It can (a) be an important source of hypotheses about behavior, (b) provide an opportunity for clinical innovation (for example, trying out new approaches to therapy), (c) permit the intensive study of rare phenomena, (d) challenge theoretical assumptions, and (e) provide tentative support for a psychological theory (see Bolgar, 1965; Hersen & Barlow, 1976; Kazdin, 1980b). There are, however, a number of disadvantages associated with the case study method. It is difficult to draw cause and effect conclusions on the basis of a case study due to the fact that many factors often are left uncontrolled. Moreover, biases can arise if the observer (for example, a therapist in charge of a person's treatment) allows subjective impressions to enter into reports of the study's outcome (Hersen & Barlow, 1976). Biases in data collection also can arise when self-report measures constitute the data. Is the client, for instance, purposely distorting a self-report in order to look good in the therapist's eyes? Another problem often associated with the case study is generalizability: how to generalize on the basis of studying a single individual (Bolgar, 1965). Though the "dramatic" results obtained from some case studies may offer important insights to scientific investigators, the problems associated with this method suggest that the outcome of a case study be treated tentatively, waiting until further data, perhaps based on other methods, have been obtained (Kazdin, 1980b). Unfortunately, members of the general public, who often are not aware of the limitations of this method, frequently accept the results of a case study as sufficient evidence for the success of a treatment.

Behaviorism is an approach to the study of psychology that emphasizes the study of observable behavior under strictly controlled conditions. The behaviorism of B. F. Skinner is called an experimental analysis of behavior. Researchers associated with this approach typically investigate how behavior changes as a function of various schedules of reinforcement and punishment. Principles derived from an experimental analysis of behavior have been applied successfully to a wide variety of socially relevant problems, including those related to the treatment of clinical populations (e.g., individuals diagnosed as psychotic, retarded children and adults, stutterers, and autistic children) and the education of both normal and learning disabled students, as well as many other areas. The application to real-world problems of the principles derived from the experimental analysis of behavior is also known as applied behavior analysis.

The major methodology of applied behavior analysis is the single-case or $\underline{N}$ = 1 experimental design. Although there are many kinds of $\underline{N}$ = 1 designs, the most common are the ABAB design and the multiple-baseline design (Kazdin, 1978). An ABAB design allows a researcher to confirm a treatment effect by showing that behavior changes systematically with conditions of No Treatment (A) and Treatment (B). The no treatment stage is a baseline stage. During the baseline period, a specific behavior is observed without any intervention by the experimenter. The most common measure of behavior is frequency of occurrence of the target behavior, but other measures such as duration of the behavior are sometimes used. Following the first no treatment or baseline stage, an intervention is introduced with the goal of changing the target behavior (e.g., its frequency). Behavior is continuously monitored; then, the treatment variable is withdrawn. Finally, following a second baseline stage, the treatment is again introduced. The researcher using the ABAB design focuses on the way behavior changes with the systematic introduction and withdrawal of the treatment. Behavior is expected to change immediately upon introduction of the treatment (first B stage), when treatment is withdrawn (second A stage), and, again when treatment is reintroduced (second B stage). Because any improvement in behavior observed during the first treatment stage is likely to be reversed when treatment is withdrawn in the second baseline stage, the ABAB design is also called a reversal design.

Methodological problems arise in the ABAB design when behavior that changed during the first treatment (B) stage does not reverse when treatment is withdrawn during the second baseline (A) stage. When this occurs, it is difficult to establish that the treatment, rather than some other factor, was responsible for the initial change (see Hersen & Barlow, 1976; Kazdin, 1980a). Also, ethical problems can arise when using the ABAB design if a treatment that has been shown to be beneficial is withdrawn during the second baseline stage. Fortunately, there exists another $\underline{N}$ = 1 design for the researcher to use in this situation, one that does not require that a successful treatment be removed.

A multiple-baseline design demonstrates the effectiveness of a treatment by showing that behaviors across more than one baseline change as a consequence of the introduction of a treatment. Baselines are first established across different subjects, across different behaviors in the same subject, or across different situations for the same subject. A minimum of two baselines must be used; however, three or four baselines typically are recommended (Hersen & Barlow, 1976). Once behavior in the multiple baselines has stabilized, the treatment variable is introduced for one subject, behavior, or situation. Behavior is monitored continuously across all conditions (subjects, behaviors, or situations). Then, the treatment is introduced after another baseline and behavior is again monitored. This procedure is repeated for all baselines. Confirmation of a treatment's effectiveness rests on the demonstration that behavior changes after each baseline stage when the experimental variable is introduced.

Methodological problems arise when behavior does not change immediately with the introduction of a treatment or when a treatment effect generalizes to other subjects, other behaviors, or other situations. If, for example, behavior changes following one baseline stage when a treatment is introduced but not after another baseline when a treatment is introduced, evidence for the effectiveness of the treatment is seriously threatened. Similarly, if a treatment is introduced for one subject, behavior, or situation, and changes are observed in more than one baseline, the evidence for a specific effect of the treatment variable is weakened (see Kazdin, 1980a).

Problems of increasing or decreasing baselines, as well as excessive baseline variability, sometimes make it difficult to interpret the outcome of single-case designs. The problem of excessive baseline variability can be approached by seeking out and removing sources of variability, by extending the time during which baseline observations are made, or by averaging data points to remove the "appearance" of variability (Kazdin, 1978). Increasing or decreasing baselines may require the researcher to obtain other kinds of evidence for the effectiveness of a treatment. For example, an important consideration in applied behavior analysis is obtaining evidence for the clinical significance of a treatment. That is, evidence is sought showing that the treatment actually works to modify the behavior of a client in a real world setting. Evidence sometimes can be obtained by comparing the client's behavior after treatment with that of a normal group of subjects (social comparison approach) or by asking people familiar with the client to judge whether the behavior of the individual after treatment differs significantly from that before treatment (subjective evaluation approach) (Kazdin, 1977).

The $\underline{N}$ = 1 design is often criticized for its lack of external validity. However, because treatments typically produce substantial changes in behavior, these changes can often be easily replicated in different individuals (Kazdin, 1978). Moreover, by using "single groups" of subjects in an $\underline{N}$ = 1 design, rather than "single subjects," a researcher can also provide immediate evidence of generality across subjects. The fact that the $\underline{N}$ = 1 design usually is not appropriate for testing the possible interactions of variables emphasizes the importance of selecting the research methodology that is most relevant to answering the particular question under investigation.

References

Allport, G. W. (1961). Pattern in growth and personality. New York: Holt, Rinehart, and Winston.

Bolgar, H. (1965). The case study method. In B. B. Wolman (Ed.), Handbook of clinical psychology (pp. 28-39). New York: McGraw-Hill.

Hersen, M., & Barlow, D. H. (1976). Single-case experimental designs: Strategies for studying behavior change. New York: Pergamon Press.

Kazdin, A. E. (1977). Assessing the clinical or applied significance of behavior change through social validation. Behavior Modification, 1, 427-452.

Kazdin, A. E. (1978). Methodological and interpretive problems of single-case experimental designs. Journal of Consulting and Clinical Psychology, 46, 629-642.

Kazdin, A. E. (1980a). Behavior modification in applied settings. Homewood, IL: Dorsey Press.

Kazdin, A. E. (1980b). Research design in clinical psychology. New York: Harper & Row.

II. KEY CONCEPTS

The following concepts are importantly related to the applied research methods that are discussed in this unit. Use the information found in the **OVERVIEW,** as well as the definitions of the key concepts provided here, to complete the exercises in the following sections. [NOTE: Numbers in parentheses refer to pages in the fourth edition of Research Methods in Psychology by Shaughnessy and Zechmeister (1997), where these concepts are more fully defined.]

ABAB design (reversal design) A single-case experimental design in which an initial baseline stage (A) is followed by a treatment stage (B), a return to baseline (A), and then another treatment stage (B); the researcher observes whether behavior changes on introduction of the treatment, reverses when the treatment is withdrawn, and improves again when the treatment is reintroduced. (322-323)

baseline stage The first stage of a single-case experiment in which a record is made of the individual's behavior prior to any intervention. (321)

behaviorism An approach to the study of psychology that emphasizes observable behavior as the only legitimate source of scientific evidence and that defines psychology's goal as the prediction and control of behavior. (318)

behavior modification The application of learning-conditioning principles in order to change behavior; first used synonymously with behavior therapy. (320)

behavior therapy The application of learning-conditioning principles to clinical populations; first used synonymously with behavior modification. (320)

case study An intensive description and analysis of a single individual. (308)

clinical significance A measure of the strength of a treatment as indicated by the extent to which it has improved the life of a client in a real-world setting; usually assessed using either subjective evaluation or social comparison. (322)

idiographic approach The intensive study of an individual, with an emphasis on both individual uniqueness and lawfulness. (315)

multiple-baseline design (across subjects, across behaviors, across situations)
A single-case experimental design in which the effect of a treatment is demonstrated by showing that behaviors in more than one baseline change as a consequence of the introduction of a treatment; multiple baselines are established for different individuals, for different behaviors in the same individual, or for the same individual in different situations. (325-328)

nomothetic approach An approach to research that seeks to establish broad generalizations or laws that apply to large groups (populations) of individuals; the average or typical performance of a group is emphasized. (314)

single-case experiment A procedure that focuses on behavior change in one individual by systematically contrasting conditions within that individual while continuously monitoring behavior. (321)

social comparison A measure of clinical significance of a treatment in which the researcher compares the behavior of a client after treatment with the behavior of a "normal" group of subjects. (322)

subjective evaluation A measure of clinical significance of a treatment in which the judgments of people who have contact with the client are used to assess whether the behavior of the client is perceptibly different after treatment from what it was before treatment. (322)

III. EXAMPLES OF SINGLE-CASE RESEARCH

Read the following three summaries of published research carefully. Answer the questions at the end of each summary. Answering these questions will require use of concepts introduced in this unit and in previous units.

A. Kleptomania

Reference: Glover, J. H. (1985). A case of kleptomania treated by covert sensitization. British Journal of Clinical Psychology, 24, 213-214.

Article Summary: Kleptomania is an uncontrollable urge to steal things without any motive for profit or gain. In this case study, a therapist describes the successful treatment of a 56-year-old married woman who had been "shoplifting every day for the previous 14 years." She generally would shoplift on her lunch hour, obtaining objects with no apparent purpose. For example, she might steal a pair of baby shoes but there would be no baby to whom she might give the shoes. The woman told the therapist that on awakening each day "she would have a compulsive thought that she must shoplift later that day." She expressed "repugnance" at the thought but found that she invariably would give in to it.

This individual's compulsion to shoplift apparently began about a year after her husband had been convicted of embezzlement and heavily fined. She was very upset by that experience and still found it hard to forgive him. Because her husband could find only poor paying jobs she was forced to work full-time, which she resented. She lost many of her friends following the husband's criminal conviction and over the years she had been on antidepressant medication. Only a few weeks prior to seeing the therapist she had told her husband for the first time about the shoplifting. She also had confided in her general practitioner at this time. She told the therapist that she finally could no longer deal with the problem alone.

The woman agreed to be treated by covert sensitization. This process involved pairing imagery of nausea and vomiting with the act of stealing. She was treated during a total of four sessions, one session every two weeks. In the first three sessions, the therapist asked her to imagine "increasing nausea as she approached an article" she was attempting to steal, to imagine vomiting in front of other shoppers as she took the article, then to reduce the degree of imagined nausea as she returned the article and left the store. In the final session, she was asked to imagine increasing nausea as she approached an object but then to imagine the nausea "dissipating" as she turned away without taking the object. Hypnosis was also used in the last two sessions. Between sessions she was asked to rehearse thinking about nausea and vomiting several times daily, and to leave at home a particular bag she had used when shoplifting.

During the 8-week period of therapy her compulsion to shoplift diminished. She stole only four objects during the treatment period. Nineteen months after the completion of covert sensitization therapy, she had lapsed and shoplifted only one time. She reported feeling better about herself and had begun to seek out social contacts. The thought of shoplifting when it did occur was usually accompanied by an "unwell" feeling that she could remove "by walking away from any tempting article."

Questions:

1. One problem often associated with the case study method is that a "treatment" has many components. Thus, several components are present simultaneously. This makes it difficult if not impossible to draw cause and effect conclusions about the effect of a specific component. Identify two components of the treatment in this study other than the covert sensitization procedure per se that also were present and that may have contributed to the woman's recovery.
2. Not only are treatments in a case study frequently multifaceted, but many variables often are left uncontrolled. Identify two factors other than the treatment that may have contributed to a change in this woman's behavior.

3. Results of a case study can be biased both by the observer and by the client. There is no evidence that bias was actually present in the Glover (1985) study. Nevertheless, to demonstrate your understanding of potential sources of bias in the case study method: (a) Show with an example how the therapist in this study could have biased the results. (b) Explain how the client could have biased the results.

4. Review the five advantages (a through e) to using the case study method mentioned in the **OVERVIEW**. Which of these five advantages are illustrated by this particular case study? Explain your answer.

B. Infantile Autism

Reference: Matson, J. L., Sevin, J. A., Fridley, D., & Love, S. R. (1990). Increasing spontaneous language in three autistic children. Journal of Applied Behavior Analysis, 23, 227-233.

Article Summary: Early infantile autism is a childhood psychosis, apparently inborn, characterized by an inability to relate to others, obsession with sameness or repetition, and impaired language development. The present study investigated ways to increase the "spontaneous verbalizations" of three autistic children with "moderate mental retardation" (ages 11, 11, and 9). Language use was minimal in all cases. A multiple-baseline across behaviors design was used for each child. Two spontaneous responses ("please" and "thank you") and one verbally prompted response ("you're welcome") were the behaviors selected. The procedure consisted of baseline and treatment sessions which took place two afternoons each week in an experimental room. The experimenter sat facing the child across a table; training periods lasted about 1 hour and consisted of 15 to 25 trials. Each child participated in approximately 50 sessions.

The three target responses were trained in the same order for each child. During the baseline period a child was shown one of five desirable objects (e.g., stuffed animal) by the experimenter for 10 seconds. For the first target behavior, the "please" response, records were made of whether the child responded with "(Item), please" when shown an object. If the child did not, the correct response was modeled and the next object shown. For the "thank-you" response, each of the objects was handed one at a time to the child with the requirement that the child respond correctly within 10 seconds. Again, if the correct response was not made, the experimenter modeled the appropriate response. Finally, for the third behavior, the experimenter requested each of the objects which had been given to the child, said "thank you" upon receiving the object, and then required the child to respond "you're welcome" within 10 seconds.

The treatment consisted of a combination of edible reinforcers (e.g., candy and popcorn) and verbal praise for correct imitation of the target response or for spontaneous use (defined initially as a response within 2 seconds). However, only spontaneous responses were recorded as correct; verbal responses of any other kind were not scored. The time delay was gradually increased by 2-second intervals (up to 10 seconds) as the child responded correctly according to set criteria (e.g., four out of five correct consecutive responses). When a response was mastered, training was instituted for the next target behavior in accord with the multiple-baseline across behaviors design. Following training, additional sessions were conducted to determine whether the children responded appropriately to five objects (toys) not used in training. Follow-up sessions also were conducted at 1- to 6-month intervals. For each child, spontaneous use of target responses increased rapidly (from near zero rates) when the treatment was applied. Each child also responded appropriately when the novel objects were used at the follow-up sessions.

Behavior change also was evaluated using social validation procedures. Ten community members were shown videotapes of pre- and post-training behaviors and asked to rate the children on overall social appearance and on the use of specific target responses. All three children showed significant improvement in use of target responses, and two of the three children were rated significantly better in overall social appearance following training. Informal data collected from parents and teachers indicated that the spontaneous use of the target behaviors generalized to the home and other situations.

Questions:

1. Describe briefly the pattern of results you would expect during the baseline and treatment stages for one child in this study. The dependent variable used by Matson et al. (1990) was percentage of target behaviors for trials during each session.
2. Identify two characteristics of the Matson et al. study that serve to increase the external validity of their results.
3. Explain why the results of this multiple-baseline design study would be difficult to interpret if changes in frequency of the "thank you" response were observed immediately following the application of the treatment to the "please" response.
4. The authors assessed the clinical significance of the treatment by using a "social validation" procedure. This also could be labeled a "subjective evaluation" procedure. (a) Comment on the general difference between this approach to assessing clinical significance and that associated with a "social comparison" procedure. (b) Explain how Matson et al. might have used a social comparison approach in their study.

C. Facial Screening

Reference: Horton, S. V. (1987). Reduction of disruptive mealtime behavior by facial screening. Behavior Modification, 11, 53-64.

Article Summary: The application of learning-conditioning principles with the goal of changing an individual's behavior is called behavior modification. In this particular study, the goal was to control the repetitive spoon banging at mealtime by "an 8-year-old, severely mentally retarded girl." The girl had been placed in a group home at age 3. She exhibited a number of stereotypical behaviors, such as repetitive hand clapping while walking, and her speech was mainly "echolalic" (repeating simple phrases spoken to her). She had been isolated from her classmates during lunch because her spoon banging was disruptive, being noisy and frequently causing food to be flung at others, and sometimes leading to the spoon's being dropped on the floor.

The behavioral technique chosen to modify her maladaptive behavior was facial screening: a form of punishment involving the application of a face cover contingent on the target response. An ABAB single-case experimental design was used to assess the effects of this mildly aversive stimulus on frequency of spoon banging. During a baseline period a frequency count was made to determine the extent of spoon banging during each 15-minute eating session. A spoon banging response was "operationalized as two or more consecutive movements in which the subject held the spoon and rapidly turned her wrist causing an audible sound of metal hitting either the dish or table" (p. 56). Sessions were videotaped and used to obtain a measure of observer reliability. Average reliability across the experimental sessions using a percent agreement measure was 96 percent. During the 16-day baseline stage, a paraprofessional sat next to the child and said "no bang" each time a spoon banging response was made, then gently grasped the child's wrist and returned her hand to her dish.

During the first treatment stage, the paraprofessional continued to say "no bang" but now pulled a soft terry-cloth bib over the child's face each time a response was made. The bib was removed contingent on 5 seconds without spoon banging. This first treatment also lasted 16 days. Then, another 16-day baseline period was initiated, and finally another 16-day treatment stage followed. A series of follow-up observations were made beginning 6 months later. Visual inspection of the behavioral record showed that the first treatment phase resulted in an abrupt reduction in response frequency, that response frequency began to increase during the second baseline stage, but then reversed (decreased) during the last treatment stage. Spoon banging was not observed during any of the follow-up sessions.

Following the final treatment phase the child no longer required direct supervision during mealtime and was able to eat with the other children. Facial screening was judged to be a relatively efficient technique for behavior control, which should be considered "after less intrusive strategies have failed."

Questions:

1. Draw a figure showing the results of this study. Be sure to identify correctly the dependent variable and to show the general pattern of behavior change in baseline and treatment stages as described in the article summary. (NOTE: To simplify your figure you can report only four portions of each 16-day stage representing the average of behavior over 4 days. This procedure will result in 16 data points along the x-axis of your figure.)

2. Assume that instead of using an ABAB design to assess the effect of facial screening, Horton had used a multiple-baseline design across situations: breakfast, lunch, dinner. Describe how the results might have looked if facial screening worked to reduce spoon banging behavior in the multiple-baseline design across situations.

3. To what other situations, responses, and populations, in general, do you think the results obtained by Horton (1987) can be generalized?

4. In the original article, Horton (1987) provided information based on social comparison and subjective evaluation procedures that gave evidence for the clinical significance of this treatment. What general type of information can we assume that Horton used in gathering social comparison and subjective evaluation measures?

IV. PROBLEMS AND EXERCISES

A. Problem 1

Description: A behavior therapist seeks to reduce the frequency of hitting behavior exhibited by a 6-year-old child in a classroom for emotionally disturbed children. The child frequently strikes other children and even the teacher when they are nearby. The therapist trains one of the teacher's aides to reward the child with small candy reinforcers when the child has not struck anyone for a period of 5 minutes. The experiment is conducted during two 1-hour sessions each weekday for a period of 4 weeks. An ABAB design is used, each week comprising a different stage. The results of this behavioral intervention are shown below:

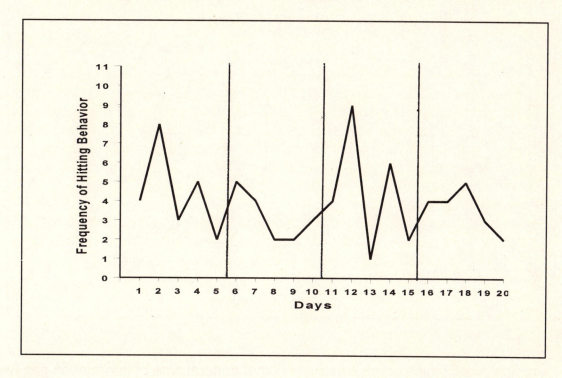

Questions:

1. Does visual inspection of the data obtained in this hypothetical study provide evidence for the effectiveness of the treatment? Why or why not?
2. Provide two suggestions for improving the quality of the evidence for the effectiveness of the treatment in this situation.

B. Problem 2

Description: A sports psychologist is hired by a college to help its basketball team get back on a winning track. The psychologist meets with the coach to plan a series of treatments designed to improve the players' performance and the team's morale. One of the behaviors selected for improvement is frequency of taking "good shots." Specifically, the coach thinks that a major problem with her team is the tendency of the players to take low percentage shots rather than show patience in waiting for a higher percentage shot opportunity. The psychologist decides to work with the three starting players with the lowest overall field goal percentages: Beth, Carol, and Arlene. The dependent variable is the proportion of high percentage shots taken during practice scrimmages during a 3-week period prior to the beginning of the season. The psychologist decides that the reinforcer for behavior change will be a visual record of a player's performance posted on the door of a player's locker after each practice session. The psychologist uses a multiple-baseline across subjects design to assess the effectiveness of this motivational technique. Results are shown below:

180

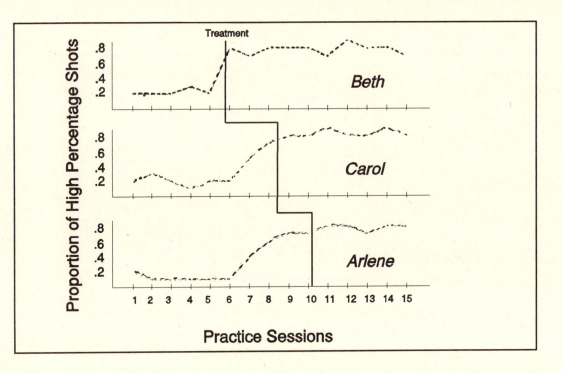

Questions:

1. Does visual inspection of the data obtained in this hypothetical study provide evidence for the effectiveness of the treatment? Why or why not?
2. Based on your reading of the brief outline of this study, what is one reasonable explanation for why changes in the baselines might be observed prior to the introduction of treatment?
3. A critical reviewer of this study would likely want information regarding degree of observer reliability. (a) What are two suggestions you might make in order to help ensure observer reliability in this situation? (b) How specifically might information about observer reliability be obtained using a percent agreement measure?

V. DATA ANALYSIS

The "analysis" of results of a single-case experimental design typically consists of (a) charting the frequency or some other measure of the target behavior across the various stages of the design, and (b) "visual inspection" of the graph. By doing the above exercises and problems, you already have had some practice with this type of analysis. Moreover, you have been introduced to some of the problems associated with an analysis that relies simply on visual inspection of the pattern of changes revealed in a graph (e.g., excessive variability). To some, this aspect of applied behavior analysis is seen as a clear and simple technique for assessing the effectiveness of a treatment; to others, basing a conclusion about a treatment's effectiveness simply on the inspection of the visual record is somewhat disquieting, to say the least. Obviously, this particular approach to assessing the effect of a psychological treatment differs substantially from approaches involving the use of a large N and a combination of descriptive and inferential statistics to help make a decision regarding whether the independent variable "worked" to change behavior. But, as you are also aware, all research methods have both strengths and limitations; thus, perhaps once again, you can see the value of a multimethod approach to investigating behavior.

VI. REVIEW TESTS

These practice tests will be most helpful in preparing for your classroom tests if you test yourself under conditions that resemble those of your actual test as closely as possible. We suggest, therefore, that you put away the book after completing the exercises in this unit and return at a later study session to take the review tests.

A. True-False

1. Research emphasizing the lawfulness of an individual's behavior is characterized as nomothetic.

2. A definite obstacle to drawing cause and effect inferences based on results of a case study is the frequent use of multicomponent treatments.

3. The first stage of a single-case experimental design is usually the treatment stage.

4. A limitation of the ABAB single-case experimental design is that it ends on a baseline stage.

5. The ABAB single-case experimental design generally should not be used when it might be considered unethical to withdraw a treatment from an individual.

6. A multiple-baseline design typically is used across subjects, across behaviors, or across dependent variables.

7. An ABAB single-case experimental design is also called a reversal design.

8. The interpretation of results from single-case experimental designs is always made problematic by steadily decreasing baselines.

9. Excessive variability in a baseline stage of a single-case experimental design can make it difficult to determine whether the treatment had an effect.

10. A major limitation of the $\underline{N} = 1$ design is that it is difficult to assess interactions between variables.

B. Multiple Choice

1. Which of the following is <u>not</u> one of the <u>advantages</u> of the case study method?
    a. provides opportunity for clinical innovation
    b. challenges theoretical assumptions
    c. provides tentative support for a theory
    d. permits intensive study of common phenomena

2. Which of the following is <u>not</u> one of the <u>disadvantages</u> of the case study method?
    a. difficulty in drawing cause and effect conclusions
    b. bias can arise due to distortions in patient's self-reports
    c. poor source of hypotheses about behavior
    d. difficult to generalize from a single case

3. Which of the following designs is used when the researcher focuses on the way behavior changes with the systematic introduction and withdrawal of the treatment?
    a. successive treatment design
    b. ABAB design
    c. alternating baseline design
    d. repeating pattern design

4. Which of the following raises ethical concerns peculiar to the ABAB design?
    a. the use of aversive stimuli in treatment
    b. the excessive length of time it takes to complete a study
    c. the withdrawal of a beneficial treatment
    d. the deception required to establish a control group

5. In a multiple-baseline design the target behavior should change
    a. just before the onset of the treatment
    b. long before the onset of the treatment
    c. just after the onset of the treatment
    d. long after the onset of the treatment

6. In the multiple-baseline design across subjects the treatment is administered
    a. to all subjects at the same time
    b. many times to each subject
    c. during the common baseline period for all subjects
    d. successively to one subject at a time

7. Which of the following patterns represents an ideal baseline in an $\underline{N}$=1 design?
   a. line with a positive slope (diagonal from lower left to upper right)
   b. line with zero slope (horizontal line)
   c. line with a negative slope (diagonal from upper left to lower right)
   d. jagged line with several peaks and valleys

8. Which of the following is <u>not</u> an acceptable approach to dealing with the problem of excessive baseline variability?
   a. seeking out and removing sources of variability
   b. selecting only the last data point in the baseline for analysis
   c. extending the time during which baseline observations are made
   d. averaging data points to remove the "appearance" of variability

9. The method of determining clinical significance by asking people familiar with the client to judge whether the behavior of the individual after treatment differs significantly from that before treatment is called
   a. subjective evaluation
   b. expert judgment
   c. purposive evaluation
   d. clinical judgment

10. Which of the following statements concerning the external validity of the results of $\underline{N}$=1 designs is generally true?
    a. $\underline{N}$=1 designs yield results with less external validity than those from case studies.
    b. $\underline{N}$=1 designs yield results with about the same external validity as those from case studies.
    c. $\underline{N}$=1 designs yield results with greater external validity than those from case studies.

ANSWERS TO EXERCISES AND REVIEW TESTS ARE FOUND

IN THE APPENDIX AT THE END OF THIS BOOK

****

QUESTIONS/PROBLEMS FOR CLASS DISCUSSION

A. **Terminology and Concepts**

1. Explain how subjective evaluation and social comparison approaches to assessing clinical significance could be used to evaluate the improvement of the woman suffering from kleptomania in the Glover (1985) study.

2. Explain why Glover's (1985) treatment of the woman with kleptomania could not be described as a single-case experiment.

3. How does the baseline stage differ in the ABAB design from the baseline stage in the multiple-baseline design?

4. Would the research on infantile autism by Matson et al. (1990) be considered idiographic or nomothetic? Explain your answer.

5. What features of the research by Matson et al. (1990) indicate that the theoretical approach of behaviorism may be used to understand the treatment?

B. Critical Thinking: Analyzing Research

1. Glover (1985) presented a case study describing the treatment of a woman with kleptomania using covert sensitization. What evidence provided in the summary (pp. 173-174) indicates that the treatment caused the woman's improvement? What evidence is lacking that would convince you that the cause of the woman's improvement was covert sensitization? Explain how a single-case experiment might provide this evidence.

2. Is there any reason to believe that a single-case experiment would be unethical in treating kleptomania? Explain.

3. Explain why it is difficult to identify what particular aspect of the treatment caused autistic children's improvement in the Matson et al. (1990) study. How might a researcher determine which aspect of the treatment was critical?

4. Re-read the description of the dependent variable in the Matson et al. (1990) study (pp. 175-176). The goal of the study was to increase specific (target) verbalizations of autistic children . How might a researcher determine whether all verbalizations increased with the reinforcement? What data would the researcher have to present to demonstrate that only the target behaviors were influenced?

5. Suppose that when performing a study similar to the Horton (1987) facial screening study (summarized on pages 177-178), a researcher observed the following pattern of spoon-banging behavior:

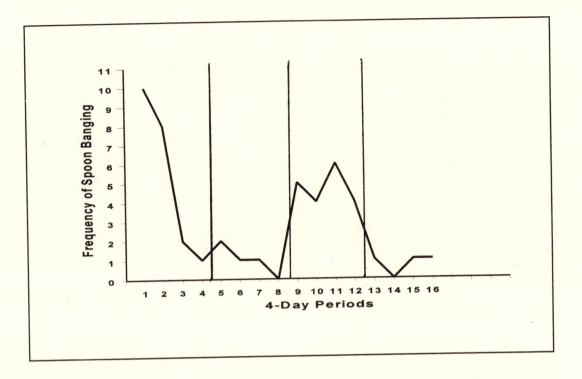

(a) How do the observations during the initial baseline affect the interpretation of whether subsequent treatment was effective?

(b) Do the observations during the second baseline stage change your interpretation of the treatment effectiveness? Would you conclude that the facial screening treatment was effective? Explain.

C. Creative Thinking: Designing Research

1. Building on the work of Glover (1985) and your ideas in response to B.1. and B.2. above, design a single-case experiment to determine whether covert sensitization is an effective treatment for shoplifting. Specify which design you will use, what observations will be made, and how the experiment will be conducted. Draw a figure with a pattern of data that would support the hypothesis that covert sensitization is an effective treatment.

2. Using either a case study method or a single-case experiment, design a study to examine the treatment effectiveness of relaxation training for someone who is highly test anxious. Assume that the test anxiety is related to the student's poor test performance in a number of different classes and feelings of dissatisfaction with school. There is no need to provide details about relaxation training; simply describe how relaxation training would be implemented in the design of the study. What would you use as your dependent variable(s)? What methods would you use to assess the clinical significance of your treatment?

D. **Statistical Analysis**

Suppose the following data were observed in an ABAB design that examined the effectiveness of nicotine patches to help a person stop smoking. Each baseline stage and each treatment stage represent 5 consecutive days of observation. Number of cigarettes smoked on each day is plotted along the y-axis. Calculate the descriptive statistics that would demonstrate that although the average number of cigarettes smoked decreased with the nicotine patches, the variability of smoking behavior increased when the nicotine patches were used.

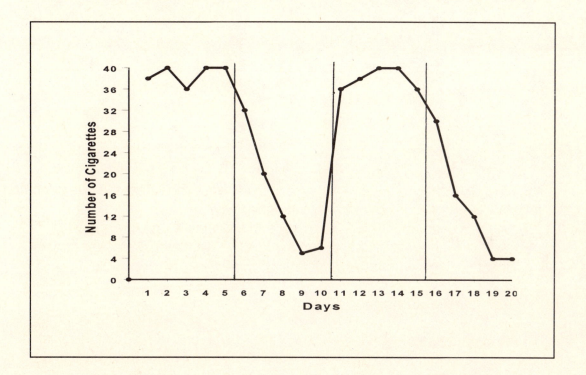

UNIT 10. QUASI-EXPERIMENTAL DESIGNS AND PROGRAM EVALUATION

I. OVERVIEW

Experiments done in natural settings differ in many ways from those done in psychological laboratories. There are likely to be more problems in exerting experimental control in a natural setting, for instance, than in a psychology laboratory. The stated goals of the research and its possible consequences also differ when research is conducted in natural settings. The psychology laboratory typically is an appropriate setting for basic research: seeking knowledge about nature simply for the sake of understanding it better. Natural settings are often more appropriate for applied research: seeking knowledge that will improve conditions under which people work and live. Another important goal of research in natural settings is to assess the external validity of laboratory findings.

The late Donald Campbell, past president of APA and one of America's foremost social psychologists, and others have argued that society must be willing to take an experimental approach to social reform--one that will allow the clearest evaluation of the effectiveness of new programs (see Campbell, 1969). Whenever possible (and especially when available resources are scarce), true experiments involving randomization of individuals to Treatment and No Treatment conditions are recommended. Because true experiments provide a comparison between two or more groups that have been treated alike except for the treatment variable of interest, it can be logically argued that any differences in a dependent variable are due to the treatment variable. True experiments, in other words, are free of confoundings. The major threats to internal validity (such as confoundings) that are controlled by a true experiment can be described using the terminology of Campbell and Stanley (1966; see also Cook & Campbell, 1979) as follows:

a) history--the occurrence of an event other than the treatment which produces a change in subjects' behavior; for example, an experimenter who behaves differently toward experimental and control subjects may affect subjects differentially in addition to any differences due to the presence or absence of a treatment.

b) maturation--changes in subjects associated with the passage of time; for example, subjects may become more experienced or more emotionally mature as they grow older.

c) testing--the effect of testing on subsequent tests; for example, familiarity with a particular test gained during initial testing may influence subjects' performance on subsequent testing.

d) instrumentation--changes over time in the instruments used to measure behavior; for example, human observers performing a rating task may become bored or fatigued with the passage of time.

e) regression--because some component of a test score is due to error, there is a tendency for subjects with either extremely high or extremely low scores on an initial test (presumably due in part to a larger than average error component) to perform closer to the mean of the group on a second test; for example, subjects who are selected for treatment because they score particularly low on a test likely will score higher on the same test when it is administered again simply due to regression effects.

f) selection--differences that exist between different groups of subjects from the outset of the experiment; for example, if students in a treatment group are selected from one school and students in a control group are selected from another school, it is possible that one group may be brighter or more motivated than the other.

g) subject mortality--when subjects are lost differentially across conditions of an experiment due to some aspect of the subject that is related to the experimental procedure; for example, if students must be tested twice at a 24-hour interval in one condition and only once in another condition, subjects who do not return for a second test in the 24-hour condition may differ in important ways from those who do return, thus threatening the equivalence of the groups.

h) interactions between selection and history, between selection and maturation, or between selection and instrumentation--one or more groups of subjects may respond differentially to effects associated with history, maturation, or instrumentation; for example, an event occurring in time may have a greater effect on subjects in one group than on those in another (interaction with history), subjects in one group may mature at a faster rate than subjects in another group (interaction with maturation), or test instruments may be less sensitive (e.g., due to ceiling or floor effects) to changes in performance of one group than to those of another (interaction with instrumentation).

In addition to these major threats to internal validity, an experimenter must be sensitive to possible contamination effects that result when there is communication between groups of participants (see Cook & Campbell, 1979). For example, if participants in a treatment group tell participants in a control group about the "good" treatment they are receiving, the individuals in the control group may become upset or demoralized and perform more poorly than they normally would. Problems of observer or experimenter bias, questions of external validity, and Hawthorne effects are potential problems in all experiments, whether conducted in the laboratory or in the field. Hawthorne effects arise when participants respond simply to the attention they receive from significant others. Because the application of a treatment variable often involves substantial contact between an experimenter and participants, to control for a potential Hawthorne effect an experimenter must try to provide the same amount of attention to participants in all conditions of the experiment.

In many situations, a true experiment is not feasible. In these cases, quasi-experimental procedures are the best alternative. Quasi-experiments differ from true experiments in that fewer threats to the internal validity of an experiment are controlled; thus, plausible rival hypotheses for an experimental outcome can arise. When this occurs, the experimenter, by logically examining the situation and perhaps by collecting additional evidence, must seek to rule out alternative rival explanations for the obtained effect (Cook & Campbell, 1979).

A particularly strong quasi-experimental procedure is the nonequivalent control group design (see Campbell & Stanley, 1966). This design involves a comparison between control and experimental groups that have been established on some basis other than by random assignment of subjects to conditions. It is important that the groups be as similar as possible and that there be an opportunity for both a pretest and posttest in both the treatment and control groups. This particular quasi-experimental procedure generally controls for all major threats to internal validity except those associated with interactions of (a) selection and history, (b) selection and maturation, (c) selection and instrumentation, and (d) threats due to differential statistical regression (Cook & Campbell, 1979).

When it is possible to observe changes in a dependent variable before and after a treatment is administered, one can carry out a simple interrupted time-series design (Cook & Campbell, 1979). Typically, a dependent variable is measured repeatedly over time before and after treatment. The researcher using this design looks for an abrupt change in the time series that coincides with the introduction of treatment (Campbell, 1969). The major threat to internal validity in this design is that of history -- some event other than the treatment may have been responsible for the change in the time series (Cook & Campbell, 1979). Instrumentation also can be a problem, especially when the treatment represents a type of social reform that may lead to changes in the way records are kept or data collected (Cook & Campbell, 1979). By including a control group that is as similar as possible to the experimental group, one can strengthen the internal validity of a simple time-series design. A time series with nonequivalent control group, for example, controls for many possible history threats (Cook & Campbell, 1979).

The logic and methodology associated with single-case experimental designs (see Unit 9) can be applied to experimentation in natural settings. For instance, an ABAB design may be used when a researcher can control the application and withdrawal of a treatment. The "single case" may be an intact group (e.g., residents of an institution or members of a community) that is scheduled to receive a treatment designed to improve the lives of the individuals involved. In such cases the internal validity of the experiment can approach that of a true experiment (see Horn & Heerboth, 1982).

A particularly important goal of research in natural settings is program evaluation (see Posavac & Carey, 1997). Many organizations and institutions, including hospitals, schools, charities, and government agencies, are engaged in human service activities. The goal of program evaluation is to provide feedback regarding these human service activities. Types of program evaluation include assessment of needs (What are the unmet needs of people who might be served by an agency?), process (How is a program actually being carried out?), outcome (Is a program effective in meeting its stated goals?), and efficiency (What is the cost of the program?). Observational and survey methods are useful in carrying out an assessment of needs and a process evaluation. Both experimental and quasi-experimental methods are especially helpful in doing outcome evaluations.

Perhaps the most serious constraints on program evaluation are the political and social realities that surround it. The reluctance of public officials, for instance, to seek an evaluation of social reforms is often an obstacle to overcome. Nevertheless, social scientists have called on individuals who are knowledgeable about the procedures of program evaluation to make themselves available to those who are responsible for the delivery of social services. Should you choose to answer this call, perhaps you can help change society in a way that brings the most effective services to those most in need.

References

Campbell, D. T. (1969). Reforms as experiments. American Psychologist, 24, 409-429.

Campbell, D. T., & Stanley, J. C. (1966). Experimental and quasi-experimental designs for research. Chicago: Rand McNally.

Cook, T. D., & Campbell, D. T. (1979). Quasi-experimentation: Design and analysis issues for field settings. Chicago: Rand McNally.

Horn, W. F., & Heerboth, J. (1982). Single-case experimental designs and program evaluation. Evaluation Review, 6, 403-424.

Posavac, E. J., & Carey, R. G. (1997). Program evaluation. Englewood Cliffs, NJ: Prentice Hall.

II. KEY CONCEPTS

The following concepts are importantly related to the quasi-experimental methods that are discussed in this unit. Use the information found in the **OVERVIEW,** as well as the definitions of the key concepts provided here, to complete the exercises in the following sections. [NOTE: Numbers in parentheses refer to pages in the fourth edition of Research Methods in Psychology, by Shaughnessy and Zechmeister (1997), where these concepts are more fully defined.]

applied research (see basic vs. applied research)

basic vs. applied research Whereas basic research mainly seeks knowledge about nature simply for the sake of understanding it better, applied research seeks knowledge that will modify or improve the present situation; however, basic and applied research are considered to have a reciprocal relationship, for example, when basic research is used to identify abstract principles that can be applied in "real-world" settings, and when applied research is used to help reveal possible limitations or extensions of these principles. (342)

contamination When there is communication of information about the experiment between groups of participants. (350)

Hawthorne effect Refers to changes in a person's behavior brought about by the interest shown in that person by significant others. (351)

nonequivalent control group design A quasi-experimental procedure in which a comparison is made between control and treatment groups that have been established on some basis other than through random assignment of subjects to groups. (353-354)

program evaluation Research that seeks to determine whether a change proposed by an institution, government agency, or other unit of society is needed and likely to have an effect as planned, or, when implemented, to actually have an effect. (371)

quasi-experiments Procedures that resemble the characteristics of true experiments, for example, that some type of intervention or treatment is used and a comparison is provided, but are lacking in the degree of control that is found in true experiments. (352)

regression to the mean Because some component of a test score is due to error (as opposed to true score), extreme scores on one test are likely to be closer to the mean on a second test, thus posing a threat to the validity of an experiment in which extreme scores are selected; the amount of regression will be greater for less reliable tests. (347)

simple interrupted time-series design A quasi-experimental procedure in which changes in a dependent variable are observed for some period of time both before and after a treatment is introduced. (362)

threats to internal validity Possible causes of a phenomenon which must be controlled so that a clear cause-effect inference can be made. (345)

time series with nonequivalent control group (see also **simple interrupted time-series design**) A quasi-experimental procedure that improves on the validity of a simple time-series design by including a nonequivalent control group; both treatment and comparison groups are observed for a period of time both before and after the treatment. (366)

III. EXAMPLES OF QUASI-EXPERIMENTAL STUDIES

A. Environmental Psychology

Reference: Levitt, L., & Leventhal, G. (1986). Litter reduction: How effective is the New York State Bottle Bill? Environment and Behavior, 18, 467-479.

Article Summary: The authors of this article review evidence showing that Americans produce as much as 140 million tons of litter each year and that the annual cost of cleaning it up may be as much as one billion dollars. A significant portion of this litter is in the form of nonreturnable cans and bottles. This has prompted many approaches to the littering problem, including those using monetary rewards for picking up litter and for recycling. As the authors note, monetary rewards need to be easily obtainable and continuously available to be effective. On September 12, 1983, the state of New York enacted a "Bottle Bill" which required a "5-cent deposit on every bottle and can of beer and soda" sold in New York. The goal was to provide a positive incentive for people to return these containers rather than discard them, as well as to encourage people to pick up those that had been discarded.

To evaluate the effectiveness of this anti-littering measure a quasi-experimental design was used. Specifically, measures of littering were obtained before and after the bill was put into law, both in New York State and in neighboring New Jersey, which did not have such a law. Following a survey to determine where litter was prevalent, two specific sites (highways ramps and railroad tracks) in the general metropolitan areas of New York and New Jersey were chosen for observation. Litter was operationally defined as "all bottles and cans, returnable and nonreturnable, of which at least one-half of the container was visibly present or intact" (p. 471). Experimenters counted the litter in the designated areas at 2-week intervals for 14 weeks both prior to and after the implementation of the bill.

Results showed that there was a significant decrease in returnable litter following the enactment of the bottle bill at highway sites, but not at railroad sites (although littering did decrease), in New York. There was no decrease in returnable litter at the New Jersey sites; neither were there any significant differences found for nonreturnable litter.

Questions:

1. (a) What specific quasi-experimental design was used by the researchers to assess the effects of the bottle bill?
   (b) Explain why you classified it as you did.
2. What is the operational definition of "litter" used in this study?

3. Identify two (plausible) threats <u>in general</u> to the internal validity of this type of design; then, indicate how these two threats to internal validity might operate <u>in this particular experiment</u> (i.e., speculate on ways that these threats might operate given the particular operations and procedures of the Levitt and Leventhal design).
4. Discuss two specific threats to the <u>external</u> validity of this study. You might consider the problem from the point of view of legislators in another state as they try to decide whether or not to enact a similar bill based on this evaluation of the New York bottle bill.

B. Vocational Psychology

Reference: Taylor, M. S. (1988). Effects of college internships on individual participants. <u>Journal of Applied Psychology, 73</u>, 393-401.

Article Summary: Many colleges and universities provide opportunities for advanced students to combine work and academic experiences in the form of internships. These structured work experiences are sponsored by a variety of academic programs, such as departments of business, industrial relations, nursing, and communications. The benefits of internships are generally assumed to be many, although there has been little empirical work done to evaluate these experiences. It was hypothesized that internships: (1) assist students in the "crystallization of vocational self-concept" (e.g., perceived job interests); (2) make the transition from school to work easier; (3) result in greater employment opportunities for students with these experiences than those without. Specific predictions based on various objective criteria were associated with each hypothesis. For example, Hypothesis #3 was tested by looking at number of job offers, accepted salary, ratings of job satisfaction, and ratings by employers of intern performance.

A quasi-experimental design was used in the first of two studies. A total of 67 students (32 interns and 35 noninterns) from a large Midwestern university participated; they were paid $5 to $8 for completing each of four questionnaires. Participation in an internship was operationalized in terms of college degree requirements and number of hours spent working in an established organization during the academic year. Both interns and control participants were recommended by college advisors in five departments offering optional internship programs (e.g., interior design, industrial relations). Experimental and control participants were shown <u>not</u> to differ in terms of age, average grade point average, credits toward major, part-time work experience, and marital status. Males and females were represented approximately equally in each group. Questionnaires were administered to participants in both groups before beginning the internship and at the end of the internship. More than a dozen variables were measured to test the several hypotheses.

In general, the results partially supported Hypothesis #1. Specifically, a measure of "vocational self-concept" differed significantly between the two groups; however, there was no significant difference in terms of a measure of work values. Initial results revealed no support for Hypothesis #2. It had been expected that interns would experience less "reality shock" when starting new jobs than would other students. Measures of anxiety, conflict, confidence in preparation for work, and job assessment did not reveal significant differences between the two groups. Hypothesis #3 was also partially supported in that the groups differed significantly in terms of starting salary; however, the groups did not differ significantly in terms of number of job offers received or in their satisfaction with an accepted position. The percentage of students accepting jobs at time of graduation was approximately equal for the two groups. Additional analyses provided some support for all three hypotheses. A second study using a true experimental design showed that recruiters said they would more likely hire interns and rated them as significantly more qualified than students without internship experience. The author suggested that the time and effort spent on an internship may be cost effective in the long run.

Questions:

1. (a) What specific quasi-experimental design was used in this study?
   (b) Explain why you classified it as you did.
2. (a) Identify two (plausible) threats in general to the internal validity of this type of design. (b) Then, indicate how these two threats might operate in this particular situation. That is, speculate on ways that the two threats which you have identified might operate given what you know about the method and measures used by Taylor (1988). (Keep in mind that the two groups were shown not to differ initially on certain relevant characteristics.)
3. The author points out in her discussion of results that the study did not identify all the particular mechanisms through which interns could benefit from work experience. For example, she indicated that interns may sharpen social skills that will aid them when interviewing. Can you identify at least one other mechanism by which an intern could benefit from work experience (and hence have an edge in the job market) compared with someone not having an internship?
4. The author did not find a significant difference overall between the two groups for measures of "reality shock" (e.g., confidence in work preparation or anxiety). Identify one possible reason no difference was found in terms of both the measures used and the nature of the participants tested.
5. Identify two questions of external validity which an investigator might want to address in future research.

IV. PROBLEMS AND EXERCISES

A. Problem 1

Description: At one large university, a group of education specialists wanted to test the effectiveness of a newly designed academic improvement course. Students seeking academic help at the university counseling center were asked to participate in this 6-week program. Only students who were judged to have deficiencies in reading comprehension and other study-related skills were chosen for the program. That is, students whose academic problems were judged to be the result of emotional difficulties of one sort or another were not enrolled in the program but were counseled in a manner more appropriate to their problem. A group of 30 students completed the program at the counseling center. A review of grades and teachers' comments revealed that a large majority of the students were doing better in school after completing the program than before. The difference between preprogram and postprogram performance measures was statistically significant.

Questions:

1. Identify three major threats to the internal validity of this study as it has been described. That is, show why there are at least three plausible hypotheses for the obtained effect other than that based on the effectiveness of the academic improvement course.
2. Explain how a nonequivalent control group design could be used to strengthen the internal validity of this investigation of the effect of the academic improvement program. Be sure to identify how you would obtain a control group and what measures would have to be obtained to carry out this type of design.
3. Identify two issues of external validity that might concern an administrator of another university who is considering implementing this program at her institution.

B. Problem 2

Description: A social scientist was hired by a local police department to evaluate the effectiveness of a program aimed at reducing juvenile delinquency in the community. When the psychologist arrived on the scene, the program had already begun. It included a three-pronged educational campaign directed at parents, community residents, and adolescents attending local schools. Public service messages appeared on television and radio; police officers and social workers made personal appearances in school classrooms; police officers went door to door in the highest crime areas to help educate residents about community resources for troubled teens. The program lasted 6 weeks.

1. What <u>type</u> of program evaluation has the social scientist been asked to conduct?
2. Describe how a quasi-experimental design, specifically a simple time-series design, might be used by the scientist as part of the program evaluation. Be sure to provide details regarding relevant procedures and measures for this type of design.
3. Discuss the major threats to internal validity associated with the design that you have outlined.
4. The internal validity of a simple time-series design can be strengthened by including a nonequivalent control group. (a) Suggest a possible control group that the social scientist might consider in this situation. (b) Identify what measures must be obtained from the control group.

V. DATA ANALYSIS

The analysis of data obtained from quasi-experimental procedures begins with the calculation of descriptive measures (e.g., means, proportions) similar to those used in most psychological studies. Inferences regarding the effect of a treatment sometimes rest on a combination of results from inferential statistical tests (e.g., ANOVA, t test) and visual inspection of trends in the data. For example, evidence for the effect of a treatment in the simple interrupted time-series design depends on evidence showing a clear discontinuity in the time series. Often this evidence comes from visual inspection of the time-series measures when plotted in a graph; however, inferential tests on the data may also be used. Because quasi-experimental designs typically do not involve random assignment of subjects to conditions, an experimenter must be aware that important assumptions of some inferential tests may not be met in these situations. Rather sophisticated statistical techniques may be required to analyze the results from a quasi-experimental design. Students planning a quasi-experiment should discuss with an expert the best way to analyze the data from a proposed design.

VI. REVIEW TESTS

These practice tests will be most helpful in preparing for your classroom tests if you test yourself under conditions that resemble those of your actual tests as closely as possible. We suggest, therefore, that you put away the book after completing the exercises in this unit and then return at a later study session to take the review tests.

A. Matching

Each of the 10 brief descriptions of psychological research found below has a serious methodological weakness which threatens the internal validity of the research. No doubt there is more than one serious problem in the research, but the descriptions are written such that one particular problem is highlighted. Each of these major problems is also listed below. You are asked to match the name of the problem with its description by placing the letter associated with the problem name next to the appropriate problem description. Any one problem is used only once. Some problems were introduced in previous units.

Research problems:

(a) regression toward the mean
(b) Hawthorne effect
(c) contamination effect
(d) maturation
(e) history
(f) interaction of selection and history
(g) reactivity
(h) testing
(i) observer bias
(j) subject mortality

_____ 1. In order to find out how much alcohol is consumed by residents of a small town, a researcher prepares a brief survey and then obtains a random sample of 30 households from the telephone book. He goes to each household and personally interviews the first adult who answers the door. Questions include how much the person drinks each week, whether the person drinks alone, etc.

_____ 2. To improve the morale of inmates in a federal prison the warden implements a new program of "group dynamics." The program is accompanied by much publicity; thus, details regarding program costs and the amount of time spent by prison officials in implementing the program are known to the inmates. An analysis of results shows that the program worked to lift inmate morale.

_____ 3. A nonequivalent control group design is used in a study comparing two different teaching methods. One method is used at School A and the other method is used at School B. During the course of the study, the principal at School B is fired and replaced by a new principal.

_____ 4. Children recently enrolled at a nursery school are having trouble adjusting to the teacher and the scheduled activities. The head teacher designs a program of story telling that is intended to help them adjust. Four weeks later, observations are made and the children are found to be better adjusted than they were before the program began.

_____ 5. A researcher uses a simple interrupted time-series design to assess the effect of a college energy conservation program. Amount of energy use is determined from archival sources for 2 years prior to the program and for 2 years following the end of the program. There is a definite discontinuity in the time series showing a decrease in energy use at about the time when the program was initiated.

_____ 6. A researcher randomly assigns workers in a factory to two different groups. The workers in one group are given bonuses for particularly good production; workers in the other group do not receive extra compensation. Workers in the no-bonus group find out that other workers are receiving extra pay for the same work that they are doing.

_____ 7. A clinical psychologist conducts a study to evaluate the effects of a program aimed at increasing patients' compliance with rules in an inpatient facility for the mentally disabled. The psychologist designed the program herself and she personally selects the 10 individuals who will participate. She guides them through 10 sessions. Based on the psychologist's observations made before and after the treatment, she concludes that her program is very effective.

_____ 8. An educational psychologist designs a demanding but fair spelling test that can be administered to grade school children. The test is found to be valid and reliable. A researcher selects the test to help evaluate a "cognitive" approach to teaching spelling. A 5th grade class is tested prior to being taught the new method and then again after the new method is taught. The children show improvement on their spelling scores from the first to the second test administration, suggesting that the program was effective in helping children to learn to spell.

_____ 9. All students planning to enroll in a small Midwest college are given math aptitude tests prior to registration for classes. Students scoring the lowest are selected for a 1-week math enrichment program to be taken prior to registration for classes. Following participation, students are tested again. Scores on the math aptitude test following the enrichment program show that students have improved. Credit for this change is given to the program.

_____10. A social scientist is hired by a large company to assess the effect of an employee training program. Volunteers are sought from the employees and a modest bonus offered for participation. Thirty-six employees agree to participate and are randomly assigned to the program condition (n = 18) or to a waiting list control group (n = 18). The employees on the waiting list are scheduled to receive the training program following the first group's training; meanwhile, these employees serve as a control group for the group trained first. Training requires that the employees attend sessions after normal work hours and also that they complete brief written assignments at home. Twelve of the employees finish the training program, and an analysis of appropriate job performance measures reveals that their scores are better than those of the employees in the control group.

B. Multiple Choice

1. As compared with experiments done in psychological laboratories, experiments done in natural settings are likely to have
    a. fewer problems in exerting experimental control
    b. about the same number of problems in exerting experimental control
    c. more problems in exerting experimental control

2. Research done in natural settings is
    a. more likely to involve applied research than basic research
    b. equally likely to involve applied research or basic research
    c. more likely to involve basic research than applied research

3. Which of the following threats to internal validity arises when an event other than the treatment produces a change in subjects' behavior?
    a. maturation
    b. history
    c. testing
    d. coincidence

4. Which of the following threats to internal validity arises when subjects are selected for treatment because they score particularly high on a less than perfectly reliable test?
    a. instrumentation
    b. testing
    c. convergence
    d. regression

5. Which of the following threats to internal validity arises when subjects in one group develop at a faster rate in one group than in another group?
   a. interaction between selection and testing
   b. interaction between selection and history
   c. interaction between selection and maturation
   d. interaction between selection and instrumentation

6. When there is communication between the groups in a true experiment or in a quasi-experiment, which of the following threats to internal validity could occur?
   a. Hawthorne effects
   b. demand characteristics
   c. regression effects
   d. contamination effects

7. Which of the following quasi-experimental designs involves the comparison of a control and a treatment group that have been established on some basis other than random assignment with both groups given only a pretest and a posttest?
   a. simple time-series design
   b. nonequivalent control group design
   c. time-series design with a nonequivalent control group
   d. pre-post nonmatched groups design

8. Process evaluation is done in a program evaluation to determine
   a. if a service is actually offered as it was planned and how it can be improved
   b. if a specific service is needed
   c. how, when, and where a program should be implemented
   d. if the program has been effective

9. Which type of program evaluation is most likely to make use of experimental and quasi-experimental methods?
   a. assessment of needs
   b. outcome evaluation
   c. process evaluation
   d. program planning

10. Perhaps the most serious constraints on the effective use of program evaluation are those that arise because of the
    a. threats to internal validity
    b. threats to external validity
    c. inapplicability of program evaluation to social reform
    d. political and social influences that affect programs and evaluators

ANSWERS TO EXERCISES AND REVIEW TESTS ARE FOUND

IN THE APPENDIX AT THE END OF THIS BOOK

****

QUESTIONS/PROBLEMS FOR CLASS DISCUSSION

A. **Terminology and Concepts**

1. Explain why the Levitt and Leventhal (1986) study summarized on page 194 would be described as applied research rather than basic research.
2. Identify why the Levitt and Leventhal (1986) study is characterized as a quasi-experiment, and not a true experiment.
3. What type of program evaluation is employed in the Levitt and Leventhal (1986) study? Explain.
4. Explain why the threats to internal validity in the Taylor (1988) study on college internships (pp. 195-196) involve interactions with selection (e.g., selection X history).
5. What is the main difference between the quasi-experimental design used in the Levitt and Leventhal (1986) study and the quasi-experimental design used in the Taylor (1988) study?

B. **Critical Thinking: Analyzing Research**

1. Suppose that advertisements about the New York "Bottle Bill," as described in the summary of Levitt and Leventhal's (1986) study, were widely presented on television and in print. How could contamination be a problem in this study? If contamination were a problem, what effects of these advertisements would you expect to see in New Jersey?

2. Why do you think Levitt and Leventhal believed it important to conduct a time series with nonequivalent control group quasi-experiment rather than a less expensive nonequivalent control group quasi-experiment?

3. One could argue that Levitt and Leventhal's (1986) dependent variable assessed the effect of New York's "Bottle Bill" on littering but not recycling. What measures could researchers use to evaluate whether the New York "Bottle Bill" influenced people's <u>recycling</u> behavior (i.e., returning the bottles and cans). Explain why your dependent variable(s) might be better measures of recycling than the dependent measure used by Levitt and Leventhal (1986).

4. Quasi-experimental designs may frequently be identified by the lack of random assignment of participants to conditions. Instead, participants choose (or "select") whether they are in the treatment or control condition. With respect to the Taylor (1988) study on the benefits of internships, describe some ways in which the students who selected an internship experience may differ from students who did not. Make sure you do not identify ways that students were shown <u>not</u> to differ in Taylor's study (described in the summary).

5. Choose one of the ways that students may have differed that you identified in question B.4. Based on this difference, are there any events or other experiences (other than the internship) that internship students may have experienced that could have produced the results Taylor observed? Be sure to demonstrate how this "selection X history" interaction could have influenced the results.

6. An alternative selection X history interaction would involve events or experiences that occurred to the students who did not participate in the internship program (control participants). Suppose that these students did not complete an internship because they were employed at a part-time or full-time job and did not have time to participate in the internship program. Explain how this is a selection X history interaction, and identify how this could have had an impact on the results that Taylor (1988) observed.

C. Creative Thinking: Designing Research

1. Similar to the Levitt and Leventhal (1986) quasi-experimental research on the New York "Bottle Bill," many researchers are trying to evaluate the effectiveness of community recycling programs. Is there recycling in your community? Describe how residents in your community are asked to recycle their waste.
    Design a quasi-experiment that could be used to evaluate the effectiveness of a recycling program in your community (i.e., asking residents to place their glass, cans, plastic, and print material in a separate container next to their garbage for regular pick-up). Specify the type of quasi-experiment you would conduct, the observations you would make (i.e., your dependent variable), and the evidence you would need to demonstrate that the recycling program is effective. Explain how you would rule out threats to the internal validity of your study.

2. It was suggested in question B.6. that one reason students may not participate in an internship program is because they are employed while attending school. Are there benefits of an internship program in which work experiences are tied to classroom experiences that do not occur with "outside" employment? Identify some advantages and disadvantages that internships may have compared to employment that is not part of students' formal education program.

Develop a quasi-experiment to examine the differences between internships and "outside employment." Refer to the advantages and disadvantages you identified, and choose at least one advantage and one disadvantage to evaluate. Develop one dependent variable to assess each. What are your hypotheses? Explain the type of quasi-experiment you would use, and how your study would be conducted. How will you rule out threats to internal validity?

D. Statistical Analysis

1. Draw a figure to illustrate hypothetical data that would indicate that the recycling program evaluated in your study (see C.1.) is effective. Write a brief paragraph that describes the pattern of data, and why it indicates that the recycling program is effective.

2. For each dependent variable you described to evaluate internship programs (see C.2.), draw a figure with hypothetical data that would support your hypothesis regarding that variable. (It may be easier to draw two figures, one for each dependent variable, rather than to put all of the data in one figure). Write a brief paragraph that describes the pattern of data, and why the data demonstrate support for your hypotheses.

APPENDIX

Answers to Problems, Exercises, and Review Tests

Unit 1 INTRODUCTION

III. QUESTIONS ABOUT EXAMPLE STUDIES

A.   The Krumhansl and Jusczyk (1990) study:

1. The authors are attempting "to find out" what effects music with natural and unnatural pauses have on infants' attention to music. The suggestion that this experiment provides evidence for young children's sensitivity to natural acoustic cues indicates that this experiment is part of a research program intended to understand children's perception of acoustic cues. Understanding is achieved when the causes of a phenomenon are identified. Because the authors employed the experimental method, wherein an independent variable is manipulated, evidence supporting a causal inference has been obtained.

2. (a) The independent variable in this study was the type of music played and the dependent variable was the length of time the child oriented to the speaker. (b) The specific levels of the independent variable were natural pauses and unnatural pauses in the music.

3. The experimenter manipulated the two levels of the independent variable as indicated by the infants listening to music with either natural or unnatural pauses.

B.   The Colangelo and Kerr (1990) study:

1. The primary goal of this study appears to be to describe the prevalence of perfect scores on different types of standardized tests for boys and girls. As indicated in the summary, however, obtaining this description is one step in trying to understand whether intelligence is better conceived of as a general ability or as a set of relatively independent specific abilities.

2. The operational definition of giftedness in this study was scoring perfectly on at least one subtest of the American College Testing Assessment Program.

3. If a perfect score on the ACT subtest in mathematics is a valid measure of giftedness in mathematics then it should correlate with other reasonable measures of mathematical giftedness like grades in high school math courses and scores on other standardized tests measuring mathematical aptitude.

4. The reliability of the ACT test as a measure of giftedness would be established if students scored consistently on comparable, but independent, forms of the ACT test.

C. The Skowronski and Thompson (1990) study:

1. On one level this study can be seen as testing a rather specific implication (hypothesis) from a stereotype about differences between men and women in reconstructing dates. Viewed in this way the study could be seen as having a primary goal of understanding a gender difference. With the information available in the summary, however, there is no theoretical basis for explaining the gender difference. Moreover, it is inadvisable to draw causal inferences when an individual difference variable is the only independent variable (see answer #4 below). The experiment does, however, describe a slight difference between males and females. Knowing this relationship between gender and memory for events permits us to predict better memory for dating events in women than in men (at least in the specific situation detailed in this study).

2. (a) The independent variable in this study is gender, and the dependent variable is the median error made in estimating the date of a given event.
(b) The specific levels of the independent variable are male and female.

3. The independent variable, gender, is an individual difference variable (subject variable) and so its levels have been selected rather than manipulated by the researchers.

4. (a) Covariation has been established in the study--women were slightly better than men at reconstructing dates. A time-order relationship also seems to have been established in that the gender differences preceded the differences in reconstructing dates rather than the reverse. (b) The third condition for establishing a causal relationship, however, has not been established. The differences between men and women in reconstructing dates may not be due solely to gender differences in dating events. The idea that men and women may have kept different types of diaries of the events is one such plausible alternative; that women simply have better memories than men is another. In general, when the independent variable is an individual difference variable, and levels of the variable are selected rather than manipulated, we must be aware that other factors associated with the independent variable are not controlled.

D. The Cunningham et al. (1991) study:

1. The researchers are trying to identify personality characteristics that predict prejudicial attitudes toward individuals with AIDS. The use of survey research and the correlational analyses are strong indicators that the primary purpose of the study is prediction.

2. With a positive correlation, a person with a low authoritarianism score would be predicted to have a relatively low prejudice score.

3. Before these results can be interpreted as representing two different relationships we need to know how the dependent variables were scored in the two studies. For example, if self-righteousness were scored in one study with 1 indicating a low score and 7 indicating a high score while in the other study the reverse was true (1 indicating a high score and 7 a low score), then this scoring difference would yield opposite signs for the resulting correlations. The way to avoid this problem is to be sure variables are being scored in the same way across studies.

IV. PROBLEMS AND EXERCISES

A. The intended independent variable in this problem is the presence or absence of the chemical RTQX. A confounding is present, however, because the experimental rats were separated from their mothers and the control rats were not. Mental development may have been affected by this second, unintended independent variable. We cannot conclude that the RTQX does not cause mental retardation (the opposite of the investigator's conclusion). All we can conclude when a confounding is present is that we do not know whether or not the intended independent variable had an effect.

B. The intended independent variable in this problem is an individual differences variable with two selected levels, musicians and non-musicians. We need to be careful whenever this type of variable is the only independent variable in a study. Individual differences variables are complex independent variables and are naturally confounded. The psychologist tested participants only on similar musical tones. When the musician group did better she concluded that the musicians had a naturally (i.e., innate) better ear for music. It is clearly the case that the musicians here had more experience (practice) with musical instruments than the non-musicians. Musical training and experience may have produced the difference, rather than an innate difference between musicians and non-musicians. In general, be wary of potential confoundings and causal inferences whenever individual differences variables are involved in a study.

V. REVIEW TESTS

A. Matching

   1. d
   2. e
   3. c
   4. b
   5. a

B. Identification

   1. IV = conversing in pairs or in groups of three (selected)
      DV = distance between a speaker and a listener

   2. IV = grade levels (1st, 3rd, 5th) (selected)
      DV = moral reasoning ability as measured from child's response to the moral dilemma

   3. IV = two different "prompting methods" (manipulated)
      DV = degree to which memories of childhood abuse are elicited from patients

   4. IV = three different levels of illumination (manipulated)
      DV = worker productivity

C. Multiple Choice

Numbers in parentheses following each answer refer to pages in the fourth edition of <u>Research Methods in Psychology</u> (1997), by Shaughnessy and Zechmeister, which contains discussion of these concepts.

   1. c (8)   6. c (23)
   2. d (10)   7. c (25)
   3. c (11)   8. b (26)
   4. b (16)   9. b (26)
   5. a (17)   10. d (30)

Unit 2   ETHICAL ISSUES IN THE CONDUCT OF PSYCHOLOGICAL RESEARCH

IV. APPLYING THE ETHICAL PRINCIPLES

A.   Research Proposal 1

This study involves two types of risk. The participants could be placed at a social risk if their responses in the study were to be made public in a way in which individual respondents could be identified. The participants could also be placed at psychological risk because describing their sexual activity to the investigator could be stressful. The possibility of social risk means that the ethical issue of privacy is also relevant to this study. The investigator must ensure that the data she obtains remain confidential. There may be an issue with informed consent in this study if the five-dollar payment is considered a potentially excessive inducement for participating in the study. Informed consent requires that the participant not be unfairly induced to participate. In this case, however, it is likely that the relatively small offer of five dollars does not represent an unfair inducement. Nothing in the description of the research indicates that deception is involved in this study. The risk/benefit ratio that is the basis of a final decision by an Institutional Review Board would be computed in this case using the risks outlined above along with the possible benefits of the findings of this study for what is stated in the description as the important problem of date rape.

B.   Research Proposal 2

The ethical principle that would require the most careful review in this study is deception. The participants were given different information about the relation between the anagram task and intelligence. And they were not told that the pair working in the anagram task were given anagrams of differing difficulty such that the control participant would win most of the points. These deceptive procedures were intended by the researchers to result in stress reactions on the part of the experimental participants (these reactions were monitored by measuring blood pressure of both the control and experimental participants). It is unlikely that these manipulations would put typical college students under physical stress, but some psychological stress is likely. The use of deception also raises the issue of informed consent. Telling the students about the deception mitigates against the effective manipulation of stress, but not telling the students about the deceptive procedures means the students are not fully informed. Thus, it is important that students be debriefed following their participation; this should be a precondition for approval of this study. Nothing in the description of the research suggests that privacy is at issue in this study. The general principle of keeping data confidential would, however, apply to this study. The stress and the deception contribute to the risk component of the risk/benefit ratio. Your judgment of the potential benefits to be gained from this research determine whether or not those benefits outweigh the risks.

C. Research Proposal 3

Subjecting female rats to toxins over a lengthy period of time raises the ethical issue of subjecting animals to potential pain or stress. The female rats were sacrificed and this raises the ethical issue of whether a rapid and painless procedure was used. No surgical procedures were used and so this ethical issue does not apply to this study. The ethical issue of ensuring the comfort, health, and humane treatment of the animals applies to every study testing animals, but there is no information in the description of the study which would allow an assessment of this issue. There may be potential scientific or applied benefit from learning about the effects of this toxin on rats' reproductive behavior, but your decision, as always, is whether the potential benefit outweighs the risks to the welfare of the animals tested in this study.

V. REVIEW TEST

Numbers in parentheses following each answer refer to pages in the fourth edition of <u>Research Methods in Psychology</u> (1997), by Shaughnessy and Zechmeister, which contains discussion of these concepts.

Multiple-choice

1. a (40)	6. b (52)
2. d (47)	7. c (51)
3. a (46)	8. a (57)
4. a (58)	9. b (65)
5. d (65)	10. b (64)

Unit 3 OBSERVATION

III. QUESTIONS ABOUT OBSERVATIONAL STUDIES

A. The Latané and Bidwell (1977) need for affiliation study:

1. This study should be classified as naturalistic observation. There is no indication that the observers systematically set up the situation in which the observations were made, so it is not structured observation. No independent variables were manipulated in the situation, so it is not a field experiment. The naturally occurring independent variables of gender and whether the students were entering or sitting in the cafeteria and the high likelihood that the observations were made unobtrusively indicate that this is naturalistic observation.

2. The operational definition of "affiliation" used in this study is whether the student was observed in the presence of other people in a public setting (as compared with being alone).

3. A nominal scale of measurement was used to measure affiliation because the observers recorded only whether the students were or were not with other people.

4. Evidence for the external validity of the findings given in the summary is that females were more likely than males to be in the presence of another person: (1) both when entering and when sitting in the cafeteria; and (2) on both campuses. The large number of students observed (6,300) also increases the likelihood that the findings will be both reliable and externally valid.

5. One alternative explanation for the major finding is that men actively avoid being with others in public places. This tendency would lead to the same outcome as women having a greater need for affiliation. An important constraint on any alternative explanation is that it must be consistent with the obtained finding, namely that females were more likely than males to be in the presence of another person in a public place.

B. The Crusco and Wetzel (1984) interpersonal touch study:

1. Because there was active intervention in this study through the manipulation of the independent variable of the type of touch and because the study was done in a natural setting this study would be classified as a field experiment.

2. (a) The first main independent variable was the type of touch manipulated at three levels (no touch, shoulder touch, and hand touch). The second main

independent variable was a nonmanipulated (naturally occurring) independent variable of gender of the diner with two levels (male and female). (b) The first major dependent variable was the mean tip percentage, and the second major dependent variable was the survey rating of the customers' dining experience.

3. Specifying the measurement scale used for a dependent variable is not always an exact process. (a) The percentage tip measure represents either an interval or a ratio scale. One indication that the tip measure is at least interval data is that the mean was used to describe the results for this variable. If one were to consider that a tip of 10 percent represents twice as large a tip as a tip of 5 percent, then the percentage tip measure could represent a ratio scale. (b) It is not clear from the summary what scale was used in rating the customers' dining experience. If the survey had asked only for a rating of whether the experience had been good/bad or pleasant/unpleasant, then the rating would represent a nominal scale. If, on the other hand, the customer had been asked to rate the experience on a scale from 1 to 100 with 50 being an average dining experience, then the rating would represent an interval scale.

4. The external validity of the study may have been limited because "most of the data" were collected by only one waitress working in only one restaurant. The waitress may not be typical, and the clientele of the restaurant may not be representative of restaurants in general. Notice that holding these two factors relatively constant represents a type of control that enhances the internal validity (interpretability) of the study while at the same time potentially limiting the external validity of the study.

IV. PROBLEMS AND EXERCISES

A. Problem 1

1. Because the investigator is interested in studying certain behaviors of coaches at soccer games she has used event sampling--she is recording events that meet her definition, namely soccer games.

2. The investigator was likely to be able to avoid reactivity because she could have mingled with other spectators at the games. Most instructions to players on the field would be shouted by the coaches so she would not need to be close to the coaches to observe them. She could stay behind the coach on one side of the field and across the field from the other coach--her presence would be unlikely to influence the behavior of either coach.

3. (a) The relationship observed between the time coaches spent directing the players on the field and the probability of winning indicates that as the amount of time coaches direct their players increases, the probability of winning the

game decreases. (b) The investigator is trying to draw a causal inference based only on a correlation. She has found evidence for covariation (correlation) between the coaches' directing the players and the probability of winning. Before she could draw a causal inference she would need to confirm the time-order relationship for these two measures. She is presuming that the coaches' comments cause the players to not play well; however, perhaps teams with players who do not play well cause their coaches to direct them more. Her interpretation also presumes that the coaches' comments have a negative effect because the players are distracted. Perhaps the players are irritated by the coaches' comments and are thereby less motivated to play well. Plausible alternative hypotheses such as this one need to be eliminated before the investigator's causal inference can be accepted. Note that in this situation we do not know that the investigator's causal inference is incorrect. All we know is that her evidence is insufficient to support her causal inference.

B.   Problem 2

1.   Reactivity may be a problem in this study. The investigator "positioned herself so that she had a clear view of the door and the people entering the buildings." It is not clear whether the investigator's position was such that the people entering the building could see her recording her observations. If the people could not see her, reactivity is unlikely. If they could see her, then reactivity could have affected the people's behavior.

2.   One problem with these observations is that the investigator observed different kinds of settings at the different schools--a student cafeteria at School A and a main classroom building at School B. The investigator also made all her observations at School A for two weeks before she made her observations at School B the next two weeks. Also, the morning and evening time periods may have been times of higher student traffic at the student cafeteria than at the main classroom building.

3.   The researcher's results are uninterpretable because any differences between School A and School B could as easily be due to differences between a student cafeteria building and a main classroom building or to the different time periods during which the researcher observed the two schools. In addition to these problems of interpretation, the researcher's results are meaningless because she has reported the results only in terms of the number of people who held open the door. If, for example, 1,284 people had had the opportunity to hold open the door at School A, then the 642 who did hold the door open represent 50 percent of the total number observed. Continuing the example, if 400 people at School B had had a chance to hold open the door, then the 352 people who did hold the door open represent 88 percent of the total number observed. The example illustrates how the data reported by the researcher

could actually have supported a conclusion exactly opposite to the one drawn by the researcher. In general, proportions or percentages should be used to adjust frequency counts for the number of possible opportunities for an event to occur.

V. DATA ANALYSIS

A. Descriptive Statistics

1. Measures of relative frequency

(a) The overall proportion of males was .56 and the overall proportion of females was .44.

(b) The proportion of males with others when outside was .40 and the proportion of males with others when inside was .625.

(c) The proportion of females with others when outside was .61 and the proportion of females with others when inside was .77.

(d) The difference between the proportions of women and men being with others is slightly smaller in inside settings (.77-.625=.145) than in outside settings (.61-.40=.21), but both differences show a greater tendency for females to be with others.

2. Measures of central tendency and dispersion (variability)

	Mean	Standard Deviation
Hand Touch	15.7	3.5 (3.6)
No Touch	12.4	2.0 (2.1)

The means above show that the mean tip percentage was lower for the No Touch condition. Note: There are two entries for both groups under the column for the standard deviation. That is because there are two ways to compute the standard deviation. The sample mean is an unbiased estimate of the population mean and so a single value can be used to describe the sample mean and the estimate of the population mean. For the standard deviation, however, the sample standard deviation is a biased estimate of the population standard deviation--the sample value consistently underestimates the population value. The standard deviation of the sample is computed using the square root of n (the sample size) as the denominator. To adjust for the bias in estimating the population standard deviation, the computation of the population estimate of the standard deviation based on the sample data uses the square root of n-1 as the denominator of the formula. Hand calculators and computer printouts don't always specify which formula is used in computing the standard deviation and so we have provided both. The smaller value is the sample standard deviation, and the larger value in parentheses is the estimate of the population standard deviation. These two formulas are not interchangeable and so it is essential that you know which formula you are using when you compute a standard deviation using a set of sample data.

3. Interobserver reliability

(a) Time spent playing is at least interval data so interobserver reliability can be measured using a Pearson r computed on the time estimates for two different observers who both observed a number of coaches. (The observers should be making their observations at the same game, but they should make them independently.)

(b) To assess interobserver reliability for the classification of comments as positive or negative a percent agreement measure should be used because the classifications represent a nominal scale.

(c) The interobserver reliability will likely be lower for the classification of positive and negative comments than for the time spent directing players. Measuring time using an instrument like a stopwatch is likely to be more consistent across observers than is measuring the coaches' positive and negative comments. Good operational definitions, however, will increase the reliability of the classification judgments.

4. Measures of interobserver reliability

(a) The observers agreed on 13 of the 15 observations so their percent agreement is 86.67.

(b) The measure of time (in seconds) represents at least an interval scale and so the appropriate measure of interobserver reliability is the Pearson product-moment correlation coefficient (r). The correlation for the two observers measuring the time taken by 10 students to walk between two points on campus was $r(8)=.94$.

220

5. Graphing

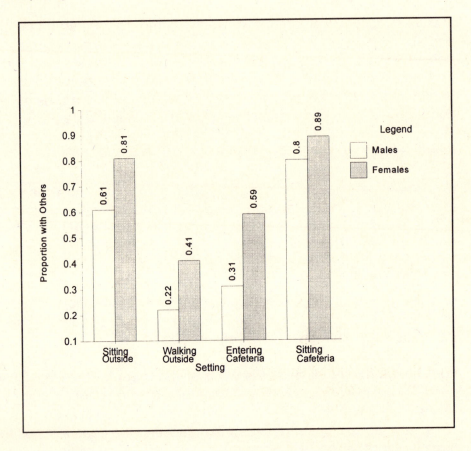

B. Inferential Statistics

1. Chi-square test of association (contingency test)

The computed chi-square value for this contingency table is $X^2(2)=195.99$. The critical value for a chi-square test with 2 df at the conventional level of significance of .05 is 5.99. Therefore, the chi-square test has a probability less than .05 and is statistically significant, indicating that there is an association or contingency between the three different meals and whether the students ate together or alone. The data in Table 3-2 show that the students were just as likely to eat alone as together at breakfast; somewhat more likely to eat together at lunch; and much more likely to eat together at dinner. The result of the chi-square test confirms that this is a statistically significant pattern.

2. <u>Test for difference between two means</u>

The computed value for this independent-groups $\underline{t}$-test is $\underline{t}(22)=2.68$. The critical value for a $\underline{t}$-test with 22 $\underline{df}$ at the .05 level of significance is 2.07. Therefore, the $\underline{t}(22)=2.68$ has a $\underline{p}$ value less than .05 (i.e., $\underline{p}<.05$) and is statistically significant. The mean for the Hand Touch group (15.7) was thus statistically significantly larger than that of the No Touch group (12.4). These data support the conclusion that touching the customers caused them to leave a larger percentage tip. (This conclusion is valid only if the field experiment from which these data come is internally valid.)

VI. REVIEW TESTS

A. Matching

1. Type of observational study (Column A): a
Concepts from Column B: a, f, h, j, k, l, p

2. Type of observational study (Column A): d
Concepts from Column B: c, h

3. Type of observational study (Column A): a
Concepts from Column B: g, m, p

4. Type of observational study (Column A): c
Concepts from Column B: d, p

5. Type of observational study (Column A): a
Concepts from Column B: i, n, q

B. Classification

1. R
2. R
3. O-I
4. N
5. I
6. O
7. N

NOTE: Specifying the measurement scale used for a dependent variable is not always an exact process. Classifying nominal scale measures is usually straightforward because separate categories define the scale (e.g., "ugly toy" or "pretty toy"). Ordinal scales are also usually easily identifiable when they involve rankings (e.g., see number 6). Rating scales, however, like the self-reported level of frustration in number 3, are harder to classify. Typically these scales are considered interval scales as indicated by the use of descriptive statistics like the mean and standard deviation to summarize the results obtained using such scales. Examining these scales more stringently, however, may indicate that participants can use the scale only as an ordinal scale. A rating of 1 would indicate a lower rating than a rating of 2, but the difference between ratings of 1 and 2 and that between ratings of 3 and 4 may not be equal as would be required if the ratings represented an interval scale. Similarly, it is not always easy to distinguish interval and ratio scales. Procedures that allow for more definitive distinctions between types of scales than those described in this unit have been developed in the advanced area of psychology known as psychometrics. For now, if you have questions concerning discrepancies between your answers and those listed here, be sure to ask your instructor for clarification.

C. Multiple Choice

Numbers in parentheses following each answer refer to pages in the fourth edition of Research Methods in Psychology (1997), by Shaughnessy and Zechmeister, which contains discussion of these concepts.

1. b (106)	6. c (90)
2. d (82)	7. a (91)
3. a (107)	8. c (104)
4. b (103)	9. d (109)
5. b (106)	10. b (102)

Unit 4 CORRELATIONAL RESEARCH: SURVEYS

III. QUESTIONS ABOUT SURVEY STUDIES

   A.   The Snyderman and Rothman (1987) intelligence test study:

      1. The respondents were surveyed only once and so this is a cross-sectional design and not a successive independent samples design or a longitudinal design.

      2. (a) The researchers developed a sampling frame from the membership directories of several national societies. The elements of their sample were drawn randomly from this sampling frame. This random selection from a well-defined sampling frame represents the key characteristic of probability sampling. (b) The researchers could have used purposive sampling by identifying 100 or so national experts on intelligence testing. It would be essential in developing this sample that the researchers include experts representing different views of intelligence testing since the research is intended to examine the controversy regarding the use of IQ tests.

      3. When there is the possibility of a response like "not qualified" it is also possible for a larger percentage value on one question to reflect fewer actual respondents. For example, the 90 percent who identified the small set of specific traits associated with intelligence were from that set of respondents who responded to this specific question (those who did not choose the alternative "not qualified"). The 53 percent agreeing that there was a consensus about "intelligent" behaviors was based on the total set of respondents who answered this specific question. If only 300 of the respondents answered the question on specific traits, then the 90 percent agreeing represents only 270 respondents. If all those who responded to the survey (661) answered the specific questions about a consensus on intelligent behaviors, then the 53 percent agreeing about the consensus represents 350 of the total 661 respondents.

      4. (a) The value that serves as the denominator when computing a proportion for "more than two-thirds of those surveyed" is the size of the original sample; the value that serves as the denominator when computing a proportion for "more than three-fourths of those responding" is the number indicating the number of respondents who returned the survey. These two numbers are essential so that the response rate can be computed to determine if there is a potential problem of response bias. The sample size and the number of respondents also are essential in determining just how many respondents are represented by a reported percentage (see Problem 3). (b) The researchers gave respondents the option of indicating that they were "not qualified" to

respond to certain questions. Such a procedure almost ensures that the number of respondents to a given question will not equal the total number of respondents to the survey as a whole. Thus, the number of respondents to each question needs to be reported.

5. The researchers used a phone survey to reach a sample of 40 nonrespondents in order to determine whether there was a problem of response bias in their original sample of respondents. If the questionnaire responses from the sample of nonrespondents are similar to those from the original sample, then response bias is unlikely. If, on the other hand, the responses from the nonrespondents are systematically different from those from the original sample, then response bias is likely. This direct test of response bias is a better procedure than basing a decision about the likelihood of response bias solely on the response rate.

B.   The Simpson et al. (1986) love and marriage study:

1. The samples in this study are most likely nonprobability samples, specifically, accidental samples. There is no mention in the summary of a sampling frame or of a random procedure for selecting students--both necessary characteristics of probability sampling. The students who were surveyed may have been members of large introductory psychology classes at the university or they may have been volunteers who participated to fulfill a research participation option in an introductory course.

2. It is unlikely that the present sample is representative of the population of U.S. college students. The population is likely to be less than 90 percent "white," is likely to include an age range greater than 18-24, and likely includes students from many different geographical areas in the U.S. The current sample may be representative of college students who are "white" and between the ages of 18 and 24 and who attend college in the Midwest. The key issue in determining the representativeness of a sample is the extent to which the distribution of characteristics in the sample corresponds to those of the population of interest.

3. The comparison of the Kephart 1967 survey with the 1976 and 1984 surveys of Simpson et al. involves asking basically the same question of three different samples of college students. These characteristics (asking the same questions of successive samples of respondents) meet the specifications of the successive independent samples design. The intent of the successive independent samples design (as in the Simpson et al. study) is to assess changes in response patterns over time. Because the people in the successive samples are different it is harder to assess change over time than in the longitudinal study in which the same individuals are tested over time.

4. Researchers use the successive independent samples design to determine if changes have occurred over time. In the current study the researchers expected that the attitudes of college students toward romantic love had changed since the 1967 survey. The successive independent samples are supposed to be equally representative of the general population of interest, in this case, college students. If, for example, researchers had surveyed university students in 1967 and community college students in 1976, then changes in attitudes across time would not be interpretable because the two samples of college students are not likely to be from the same underlying population and so the samples would be noncomparable.

5. The statement that one-fourth of the women who agreed with a position in 1976 no longer agreed with it in 1984 implies that the same women were tested in the two years. The same individuals are not tested each time in the successive independent samples design like that used by Simpson et al. The extent to which individuals' attitudes change over time can be determined only by testing the same individuals in a longitudinal study.

IV. PROBLEMS AND EXERCISES

A.   Problem 1

1. (a) The sampling frame used in this study was the graduates who appeared on the graduation rolls in the last two years. (b) The survey procedure used in this study was exhaustive sampling--a survey was sent to all those on the sampling frame. Because the probability of each element's being included in the sample is known (namely, 1.0), exhaustive sampling qualifies as a type of probability sampling, albeit a somewhat unusual type.

2. (a) The survey research problem illustrated in this problem is the potential for response bias because only 504 of the original 682 surveys were returned. Response bias is a problem if those who returned the surveys are systematically different from those who did not. (b) It is possible that those who did not return the surveys were the graduates who were unemployed or underemployed. If that happened, then the estimate of 9 of 10 graduates having jobs is an overestimate.

3. The actual percentage of graduates holding jobs could be as low as 65 percent-- 444 (88% of 504) out of 682. This estimate assumes that all nonrespondents do not have a job. Perhaps the best estimate is the range from a lower boundary of 65 percent to an upper boundary of 88 percent.

B. Problem 2

1. The sampling frame was a list of all the physicians working at the five hospitals in the researcher's community.

2. Selection bias arises when the sample (or the sampling frame) systematically excludes elements such that the sample is not representative of the population. Response bias arises when fewer than all of the elements selected for the sample return the survey. If those who do not respond are systematically different from those who do, then the sample is no longer representative of the population of interest. In this problem it is likely that selection bias has occurred. The sampling frame of physicians in a single community is unlikely to be representative of the population of professionals that would be the basis of a national estimate of the incidence of child abuse.

V. DATA ANALYSIS

A. Survey Results

1.

		Type of Response		
		Agree	Disagree	Neutral
Gender	Men	.462 (78)	.267 (45)	.272 (46)
	Women	.443 (73)	.333 (55)	.224 (37)

2. n = 169 for men and n = 165 for women (see parentheses in Part 1 for computed frequencies, rounded to whole numbers).

3.

Table 1

Proportion of Men and Women in Each of Three Response-Type Categories

	Type of Response		
Gender	Agree	Disagree	Neutral
Men	.462 (78)	.267 (45)	.272 (46)
Women	.443 (73)	.333 (55)	.224 (37)

Note. The corresponding absolute frequency is reported in parentheses next to each proportion. The n was 173 for the men and 166 for the women.

B. Test Results

A Pearson product-moment correlation coefficient, r, was used to determine the test-retest reliability of the ESP test. [See an introductory statistics textbook or Appendix A of the fourth edition of Research Methods in Psychology by Shaughnessy and Zechmeister (1997) for a description of r.] The obtained correlation was r (13) = .93. Because this correlation of .93 is greater than the .80 value that researchers like to see for coefficients of test-retest reliability, the ESP test would be considered to have acceptable test-retest reliability.

VI. REVIEW TESTS

A. Matching

1a. C (cross-sectional)
1b. S (successive independent samples)
1c. C (cross-sectional)
1d. L (longitudinal)
1e. C (cross-sectional)

2a. 2 (stratified random sample)
2b. 4 (accidental sample)
2c. 3 (purposive sample)
2d. 1 (simple random sample)

B. True-False

1. F
2. F
3. T
4. T
5. F
6. F
7. T
8. F

C. Multiple Choice

Numbers in parentheses following each answer refer to pages in the fourth edition of <u>Research Methods in Psychology</u> (1997), by Shaughnessy and Zechmeister, which contains discussion of these concepts.

1. b (136)   6. a (146-147)
2. a (135)   7. c (150)
3. d (138)   8. a (152)
4. c (141)   9. d (136-137)
5. b (141)   10. b (120)

Unit 5 UNOBTRUSIVE MEASURES OF BEHAVIOR

III. QUESTIONS ABOUT STUDIES USING UNOBTRUSIVE MEASURES

A. The Frank and Gilovich (1988) dark side study:

1. The authors operationally defined "black" as a uniform in which the colored part was at least 50 percent black. They operationally defined "aggression" as yards penalized for NFL teams and minutes in the penalty box for NHL teams.

2. The investigators tested the hypothesis that if there is an association between black and aggression then teams wearing black should be penalized more than would be expected by chance.

3. (a) The summary includes results from archival studies and from laboratory experiments; all these studies are directed at testing the same basic hypothesis concerning the relation between black and aggression. The use of the two different types of studies testing the same hypothesis illustrates the multimethod approach. (b) A multimethod approach is especially recommended because it reduces the chance that results are due to some artifact of the measurement process peculiar to one method.

4. (a) The editing of the teams' records illustrates the problem of selective survival. (b) The differences in which serious injuries were recorded for different athletic teams illustrate the problem of selective deposit.

5. The owners and management control who plays on their teams. The management of some teams may select more aggressive players to play on their teams and they may also choose to have their team wear black uniforms to fit their image of having a more aggressive team. Put simply, this alternative states that more aggressive teams wear black and not that teams wearing black are more aggressive. One finding in the summary can be used to challenge this new alternative. When players on a team already formed changed to black uniforms, their play was more aggressive. Since the team was already formed the selection of the players by the management cannot have been what made the team play more aggressively when they changed to black uniforms.

B. The Kremer, Barry, and McNally (1986) misdirected-letter study:

1. The independent variables in the first experiment (misdirected letters) were the two areas of West Belfast (Catholic and Protestant) and the names to which the misdirected letters were addressed (Patrick Connolly and William Scott). The independent variables in the second experiment (quasi-questionnaires)

were the two different households that received the quasi-questionnaire (Protestant and Catholic); the two different towns, one of which had a history of sectarian conflict and one of which had been relatively free of conflict; and the names on the cover letter and return envelope (Patrick Connolly and William Scott).

2. The dependent variable of whether or not a letter was returned represents a nominal scale of measurement. Nominal scales are those that classify responses into exclusive categories such as returned or not returned.

3. Once respondents at the intended households decide to return the misdirected letters to the return address the misdirected letters must again be processed through the mail system. Mishandling by the postal workers could result in the misdirected letters not being delivered to the return address. This potential problem could be especially troublesome if the failures to deliver the letters to the return address were to vary with the area of West Belfast (Catholic or Protestant) or with the name of the addressee (Patrick Connolly and William Scott). The investigators would not be able to determine what percentage of non-returned letters represented mishandling by postal workers since the letters would not reach the return address. Thus, the influence of this potential problem would be hard to assess, and so a technique such as the quasi-questionnaire that avoids this problem would be a preferred alternative.

4. Examples of the use of institutional sponsorship as an independent variable in the quasi-questionnaire technique would be to identify the questionnaire as having come from two different political parties or from two different government agencies or from two different civic groups. Examples of other factors that might be meaningfully manipulated as independent variables with the quasi-questionnaire technique would be the gender or the ethnic background of the person distributing the questionnaire.

IV. PROBLEMS AND EXERCISES

A. Problem 1

1. The concept of a romantic personal ad needs to be given a clear operational definition prior to collecting data.

2. Selective deposit could be a problem if the cost of placing a personal ad (or the space available for ads) changes over time making it more difficult for students to place ads in the newspapers. A problem of selective survival seems less likely, but it could be a problem if editorial policies changed over the years such that more censoring of personal ads took place recently.

3. The frequency of personal ads may have varied over time due to the variable of cost of placing the ad. Another important factor that is not controlled in the study is the change over time in alternative ways to communicate romantic messages besides personal ads in the newspaper. Also, we do not know whether enrollments have been decreasing at the colleges in question. There may be fewer students more recently to place the ads.

B. Problem 2

1. The student's operational definition of anxiety is biting or chewing on a pencil during the test.

2. If you assume that using a pencil is a natural part of taking standardized tests and that leaving marks on the pencil from chewing is an accretion of something on the pencil, then the student's measure is a natural accretion measure. Different assumptions about how natural using pencils for tests is and about the effects of chewing (erosion?) on pencils could reasonably lead to different classifications of the pencil-chewing measure.

3. Selective deposit could pose a problem if natural science and social science students were differentially likely to forget to drop off their pencil after the test. This would be especially troublesome if the differential likelihood of dropping off the pencil were systematically related to the anxiety level of the students. Are more anxious students, for instance, more likely to forget to return their pencils?

V. DATA ANALYSIS

1. The statistical description of a z score is the difference between the score (X) and the mean (M) divided by the standard deviation (s). In symbols the equation is $z = (X - M)/s$. The z score expresses the distance of each score from the mean in standard deviation units. You can use z scores to determine your percentile rank in a distribution (you need special tables to do this). For example, a z score of 1.0 corresponds to a percentile rank of 84. That is, 84 percent of the scores are below a z score of 1.0. Positive z scores indicate values above the mean, and negative z scores indicate values below the mean; it is essential, therefore, to pay attention to the sign and the numeric value of a z score.

2. A z score measure controls for changes in the mean and standard deviations across several distributions of scores being compared like the case in this study where comparisons are being made across 17 years. The same number of yards penalized could be a below-average number in one year and an above-average number in another year. Similarly, a given number above the mean in a

distribution of scores could be relatively a lot or a little above the mean depending upon the size of the standard deviation. The z score controls for differences in the means and standard deviations across sets of scores.

3. The average (mean) z scores for the black and nonblack teams were .94 and -.20, respectively.

VI. REVIEW TESTS

A. Completion

1. past behavior
2. planned
3. accretion measure
4. selective deposit
5. coding
6. accidentally related
7. multimethod

B. Multiple Choice

Numbers in parentheses following each answer refer to pages in the fourth edition of Research Methods in Psychology (1997), by Shaughnessy and Zechmeister, which contains discussion of these concepts.

1. a (167)
2. a (167)
3. b (168)
4. b (179)
5. d (179)

Unit 6 INDEPENDENT GROUPS DESIGNS

III. QUESTIONS ABOUT EXPERIMENTAL STUDIES (INDEPENDENT GROUPS)

A. The Langer and Piper (1987) mindfulness study:

1. (a) The independent variable was the three different ways in which the unfamiliar object was described. The three levels of this variable were: unconditionally, conditionally, and conditionally unknown. (b) The independent variable was a manipulated independent variable because the experimenter determined (controlled) the "value" of each level of the independent variable. (c) The dependent variable was whether or not the participant came up with a creative solution to the problem by suggesting that the unfamiliar object could be used as an eraser. (d) The dependent variable was measured on a nominal scale including two categories, coming up with a creative solution or not coming up with a solution.

2. The control method of balancing was used when the undergraduates were randomly assigned to the three experimental conditions. One condition that is specifically described in the summary as having been controlled by being held constant is that all the participants were tested in the same room. It is likely that other factors such as the pictures and objects shown in the room, the descriptions of these pictures and objects, the questions asked about the pictures and objects, and the instructions given to the participants during the experiment were held constant across the three experimental conditions. In general, any factor that can be held constant across experimental conditions should be held constant.

3. (a) One possible source of experimenter effects could be that the experimenters would give subtle verbal and nonverbal cues to participants in the two conditional conditions to encourage them to come up with creative solutions. These cues would not be given to participants in the unconditional condition. The experimenters might even give these cues unknowingly because of their expectation that the participants in the conditional groups were supposed to come up with more creative solutions. (b) There are two procedures that can be used to try to control for experimenter effects. The first is to keep the experimenters "blind" such that they do not know the hypothesis being tested in the experiment. A more common procedure is to alert experimenters to the possibility of experimenter effects and to train them to follow the experimental procedures very closely so as to minimize experimenter effects.

4. The three different psychology classes represent intact groups--groups that had previously been formed on some systematic basis. It is very unlikely that

such intact groups will be comparable even if the groups are randomly assigned to the conditions of the experiment. The solution to the problem of intact groups is a simple one. Don't use them!

5. (a) The primary goal of block randomization is to form comparable groups in the experiment by using randomization to balance individual differences across conditions. A secondary benefit of block randomization is that the same number of subjects is assigned to each group--a relatively unlikely outcome if each subject is simply randomly assigned to one of the groups. (b) Because there are three groups (one for each level of the independent variable) in the Langer and Piper study, the block size would be three; since there are 20 participants in each group, there would be 20 blocks in this study. To create the first block, you prepare a random order of the three conditions; each condition must appear in each block once and only once. The random order can be made by putting three pieces of paper (one with each condition's name on it) in a hat and drawing the papers out one at a time. More commonly, each condition is assigned a number, e.g., Unconditional=1; Conditional=2; and Conditional Unknown=3. A random number table is then used to make a random order of these three numbers. The condition corresponding to each number is then entered in the randomized sequence for the first block. In this case, nineteen additional random sequences would be made to construct the complete block randomized schedule for the experiment. (c) The use of two different experimenters would represent an extraneous variable. In general, the presence of extraneous variables decreases the sensitivity of the experiment and increases the generality (external validity) of the experiment. (d) To balance the extraneous variable of the two experimenters, each experimenter could test ten blocks of the block randomized schedule described in part b. Since each block includes each condition once, by having each experimenter test ten blocks we ensure that each experimenter tests the same number of participants (10) in each group.

B.   The Clinton and McKinlay (1986) anorexia nervosa study:

1. The independent variable in this study was the four groups of females representing the four levels of: acutely ill anorexics, recovered anorexics, psychiatric controls, and normals.

2. (a) The dependent variable was scored on a 6-point scale to 40 statements on the Eating Attitudes Test (EAT). (b) We can assume that the dependent variable was measured on an interval scale.

3. Causal inferences based on the natural groups design are difficult because individual differences (subject) variables are naturally confounded. For example, in the present study the group of acutely ill anorexics likely differ in

several ways from the group of normals besides their being anorexic. These other differences, just like any confounding variable, could be responsible for the obtained differences on the EAT. The differences among these four groups of females in their eating attitudes provide useful correlational information. Once again, however, we must be careful not to draw causal inferences solely on the basis of demonstrated correlations.

4. There are reasons to be concerned about the external validity of the results of the Clinton and McKinlay study. Three of the samples are relatively small (15 or fewer), and smaller sample sizes make it harder to generalize. It would likely not be easy to increase the sample sizes for the three groups that have or have had emotional problems, but the small sample size still does limit the external validity of the findings. The group of normals has the largest sample size, but this group is made up of all nursing students and only a brief questionnaire was used to determine that none of these students had an eating disorder. Nursing students may well not be representative of "normal" females; again, this characteristic of the study would limit its external validity. Perhaps the most serious threat to the external validity of the study arises in the recovered group. Here, only 14 of the 26 women initially identified for the study completed the EAT. These women are likely different from those recovered anorexics who did not participate in ways other than their participation in the study. This is a particularly troublesome problem because a key finding in the study involves the comparison of the recovered group with the acutely ill anorexic group and with the normals. Finally, external validity is influenced by the robustness of the results, that is, how strong the effects in the study are. The small sample sizes again indicate that the comparisons were not especially sensitive tests of differences. This would be particularly a problem for conclusions that groups did not differ (e.g., the currently ill group did not differ from the recovered group). This potentially important finding has limited external validity because of the relatively weak statistical test the small sample sizes necessitated. This study illustrates well that establishing external validity for findings in important research areas is a challenging endeavor.

IV. PROBLEMS AND EXERCISES

A. Problem 1

1. The independent variable was the nature of the physical fitness programs. The levels were Plan N with diet/nutritional requirements for all participants and Plan E emphasizing a regular exercise program without a diet modification.

2. The dependent variables were amount of absenteeism monitored during the 6-month program and attitudes toward the company and toward the fitness program that were assessed using a questionnaire.

3. One potentially serious threat to the internal validity of this experiment is selective subject loss. Not all participants completed the program in either group, but there was greater loss in Program N than in Program E. This differential loss across groups is one indication of selective subject loss. Although there were several possible reasons for the loss, it is reasonable to expect that some of the loss occurred because of characteristics of the participants related to the experiment. For example, participants in Group N who were unwilling or unable to comply with the recommended dietary changes would not have been likely to complete the program. These participants' attitudes toward fitness and even toward the company may have been systematically different from those who completed the program. Stated another way, those who completed the program in Group N may have been the ones who most benefited from the program. Their attitudes toward the program, therefore, would likely have been more positive. The psychologist was correct in judging that the final sample sizes were large enough to obtain reliable findings. The problem of selective subject loss, however, makes it unlikely that these reliable findings will be interpretable. The comparability of groups necessary in the random groups design has likely been lost because of the selective subject loss.

B.   Problem 2

1. The independent variable was the way in which the confederate-observer was introduced to the participant with the three ways intended to indicate increasing status. The levels of the independent variable were: an undergraduate working for the psychology department, an undergraduate honors student working for the faculty member, and a graduate student working for the faculty member.

2. The dependent variable was the number of participants who moved their chair (even slightly) while the confederate-observer sat 6 inches from the participant for 5 minutes.

3. Only one confederate-observer was randomly assigned to each level of the independent variable. Thus, the differences among the characteristics of the three confederate-observers were confounded with the intended differences in status across the levels of the independent variable.

4. The experimenter should have controlled the confounding variable by balancing the three confederate-observers across the three levels of the independent variable. That is, a third of the participants in each condition should have been tested with one of the three confederate-observers. This breaks the confounding of differences in the characteristics of the confederate-observers and the intended independent variable. If all three confederate-

observers appear equally often in each status condition, then any differences in chair movement have to be due to the intended independent variable.

V. DATA ANALYSIS

A. Descriptive Statistics

1. The mean EAT scores with standard deviations (based on $\underline{n}$ and on $\underline{n}$-1) in parentheses for the four groups are: Acutely Ill--Mean=49.0(8.5/9.0); Recovered Anorexic--Mean=45.1(7.5/7.9); Psychiatric Control--Mean=11.4(5.4/5.7); Normal Control--Mean=11.1(5.4/5.8). NOTE: We have reported two values for the standard deviations; the smaller value is the sample standard deviation and the larger value is the estimate of the population standard deviation. See Problem A.2 in the Data Analysis section of Unit 3 in this Appendix for an explanation of these two different values for the standard deviation.

2.

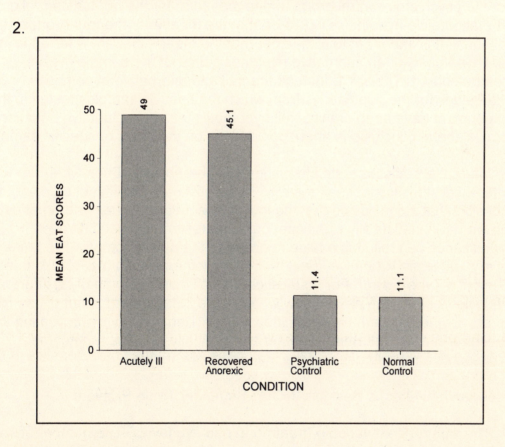

Fig. 6-1 Mean EAT (Eating Attitude Test) scores as a function of condition.

B.   Inferential Statistics

1. Differences among means such as those calculated from Table 6.1 indicate that the independent variable may have had an effect. The mean differences alone cannot be used to confirm the effect of the independent variable because the differences could occur even if the independent variable had had no effect. That is, the differences among the means could be the result of error variation (chance) alone. To confirm that the mean differences are due to the effect of the independent variable it is necessary to perform an inferential statistics test (analysis of variance) to show that the mean differences are larger than would be expected if they were due only to error variation.

2. The null hypothesis would be that the means for the four groups of females would be equal. Or it could be stated that the mean for the acutely ill group would be equal to the mean for the recovered anorexic group and to the mean for the psychiatric control group and to the mean for the normal control group. The alternative hypothesis would be that the means for the four groups are not all equal. It is important to remember that the means that are referred to in a null hypothesis or an alternative hypothesis are not the sample means computed from Table 6.1. Instead the null and alternative hypotheses refer to the means for the populations from which the specific samples tested in the experiment have been drawn. Null hypothesis testing is inductive because we draw general conclusions about populations on the basis of specific samples.

3. Inferential statistics tests always involve probabilities. Even when an inferential statistics test has resulted in a statistically significant outcome, it is possible that a conclusion that the independent variable has had an effect could be wrong. A statistically significant outcome tested at the .05 level of significance can result in a false rejection of the null hypothesis five times out of every 100 tests. When we reject the null hypothesis even though it is true, we commit a Type 1 error. For a statistically significant outcome of an inferential statistics test we can never know whether the independent variable has had an effect or whether we have committed a Type 1 error. Only by replicating the outcome can we determine whether a statistically significant outcome represents a reliable effect of the independent variable.

3.   Independent Groups Design: ANOVA Summary Table Problem

1. The independent variable (treatment) had five levels. The number of levels of an independent variable can be determined in an ANOVA summary table by adding 1 to the df for that variable; in this case, Treatment has 4 df and so there are five levels of this independent variable.

2. Because this is a random groups design we know that each level of the independent variable is represented by a separate group. There are five levels of the treatment variable (see question 1 of this problem) and so there are five groups in the experiment. The number of subjects in each group can be determined from an ANOVA summary table using the df for the within groups source of variation. The df for within subjects is determined by multiplying the number of groups by the df within each group. Knowing that the df for within-groups in this experiment is 45 and that there are five groups the df within each group must be 9 (45/5 = 9). The df within each group is equal to the number of subjects minus 1. So, if the df within each group in this experiment is 9, the number of subjects in each group is 10.

3. The estimate that reflects only error variation in a random groups design is the mean square within groups. In this experiment the value representing error variation is 15.01, the mean square within groups.

4. The effect of the independent variable was not statistically significant. The F ratio testing the effect of the independent variable was 2.04 with a probability of .10. Because the probability of the obtained F ratio is greater than the .05 level of significance, the effect of the independent variable is not statistically significant.

5. When an omnibus F-test is not statistically significant, we conclude that there is no overall effect of the treatment variable. This does not prove that the null hypothesis is correct, however. For example, it is possible that the experiment was not sensitive enough to detect an effect of the treatment variable.

4. Independent Groups Design: Calculation Problem

a. Appropriate statistical software was used to carry out the computations for an omnibus F-test based on the data from the EAT measure presented in Table 6.1. An $F(3,32) = 73.7$ was obtained; the Mean Square Within Groups (error variation) for this analysis was 52.4. The probability of this F ratio if the null hypothesis were true is .0001. This probability is less than the .05 level of significance and so we would conclude that there are differences among the means for the four conditions (Acutely Ill = 49.0; Recovered Anorexic = 45.1; Psychiatric Control = 11.4; Normal Control = 11.1). In other words, the independent variable of condition had an effect. Analytical comparisons like those described in the next two questions would be required to determine the source of this statistically significant omnibus F-ratio.

b. The null hypothesis for the analytical comparison of the Recovered Anorexic group with the Acutely Ill group is H_o: $\mu_{RA} = \mu_{AI}$. The alternative hypothesis is that the two means are not equal. The computation of this comparison yielded a

Sum of Squares for the comparison of 68.45. Because analytical comparisons always involve only 1 $\underline{df}$, the Mean Square for the comparison is also 68.45. The Mean Square Error for the $\underline{F}$-ratio for this comparison is the Mean Square Within Groups (52.4) from the omnibus $\underline{F}$-test computed in the previous problem (4.a.). The $\underline{F}(1,32) = 1.31$ for this comparison with a $\underline{p}$ value of .26. This outcome indicates that we should fail to reject the null hypothesis and conclude that the mean EAT score for the Recovered Anorexic group was not reliably different from the mean for the Acutely Ill group.

c. The null hypothesis for the analytical comparison of the two anorexic groups with the two control groups is H_0: $(\mu_{AI} + \mu_{RA})/2 = (\mu_{PC} + \mu_{NC})/2$. The alternative hypothesis is that the two combined means are not equal. The computation of this comparison yielded a Sum of Squares of 11,534.8, and, again, the Mean Square for this comparison remains the same, 11,534.8. The Mean Square Error for the $\underline{F}$-ratio for this comparison is again the Mean Square Within Groups (52.4) from the omnibus $\underline{F}$-test computed in problem 4.a. The $\underline{F}(1,32) = 220.1$ for this comparison with a $\underline{p}$ value of .0001. This outcome indicates that we should reject the null hypothesis and conclude that the mean EAT score for the combined anorexic groups (47.0) was statistically significantly higher than the mean for the combined control groups (11.2).

VI. REVIEW TESTS

A. Matching

1. R (random groups)
2. N (natural groups)
3. R (random groups)
4. M (matched groups)
5. M (matched groups but with a natural groups independent variable)

NOTE: In the matched groups design random assignment is typically used to balance individual differences other than the variable on which the groups have been matched (see Number 4 in this section). In number 5, however, an individual differences variable is used to form the groups after the matching has been done. The two groups can be considered comparable only on their standardized test scores. It will be difficult, therefore, to conclude that any differences in spelling performance between the children from the city and suburban schools is due to the school variable alone.

B. Identification of Confoundings

The confounding results in this study because the investigator used intact groups in forming the conditions of the experiment. Children at School A used the new method and Children at School B used the traditional method. The obtained difference in favor of the new method could have arisen because the children in School A were better at cognitive operations regardless of the method used to present the problems. To break the confounding the investigator would need to use a random groups design in which children from the two schools who had not participated in the first study were randomly assigned to the two methods.

C. Multiple Choice

Numbers in parentheses following each answer refer to pages in the fourth edition of <u>Research Methods in Psychology</u> (1997), by Shaughnessy and Zechmeister, which contains discussion of these concepts.

1. b (196)	6. b (212)	11. c (225)
2. d (192)	7. a (213)	12. c (225)
3. b (208)	8. c (209-210)	13. a (229)
4. c (207)	9. a (222)	14. d (229)
5. c (211)	10. a (224)	15. d (231)

Unit 7 REPEATED MEASURES DESIGNS

III. QUESTIONS ABOUT EXPERIMENTAL STUDIES (REPEATED MEASURES)

A. The Stroop (1935) attention study:

1. (a) The independent variable was the two types of stimuli, color squares and color words. (b) The dependent variable was the time taken to read each 10 X 10 array.

2. (a) Each participant was given the color squares and the color words twice, so this experiment is classified as a complete repeated measures design. (b) The counterbalancing technique used to present the four arrays was ABBA counterbalancing. (c) There would be two stages of practice in this experiment. The first stage would include the first presentation of the two conditions (CS-CW or CW-CS). The second stage would include the second presentation of the two conditions (CW-CS or CS-CW). To describe the practice effects you would determine a score for each participant for each of the two stages by adding the times for the first two trials and the times for the second two trials. Then the mean time across the participants would be calculated for each stage. The difference between these two means would reflect the practice effect, if any, in this experiment.

3. (a) The two counterbalancing techniques that could be used with 16 participants to control for practice effects are the two types of selected orders in the incomplete repeated measures design (specifically, a Latin Square or random starting order with rotation). It would take 24 participants to use all possible orders which is the third option for controlling practice effects in the incomplete repeated measures design. (b) In the incomplete repeated measures design each ordinal position (i.e., the first, second, third, and fourth positions in which the four conditions were presented) represents a stage of practice. To compute the practice effects, therefore, you simply compute the mean for the first position across all participants and then do the same for the other three positions. Differences, if any, among these four means represent practice effects that are interpretable because each condition appears in each position equally often, in this experiment four times. (c) The best design for investigating differential transfer effects is a large incomplete repeated measures design with complete counterbalancing. This allows for a test of differential transfer in each condition of the experiment because the complete counterbalancing ensures that every condition precedes and follows every other condition equally often at every ordinal position. Although complete counterbalancing could not be used in this situation, there is an analysis that can be done. This analysis examines the pattern of results to test for differential transfer rather than testing for differential transfer in each condition. There can

be no differential transfer in the first stage of practice since no conditions have preceded the condition tested first. A comparison of the performance across the four conditions at the first stage indicates what performance is like in the control and experimental conditions without differential transfer. This pattern of results can then be compared with the results including all four stages of practice which does have the potential for differential transfer. If differential transfer has occurred then the pattern of performance will be different in the analysis using all stages from that in the analysis of only the first stage.

B.   The Landauer and Bjork (1978) memory study:

1. One way to break the confounding between the six item types and the specific names to be recalled is to rotate the names across the six item types. The first step would be to assign the 12 names to six sets of two (i.e., one set for each of the six item types). The next step would be to rotate each of the sets of two names such that each set of names appeared with each item type once. This would result in six versions of the study list, and then participants could be assigned to the versions such that the same number of participants was tested with each version. The logic of this rotation procedure is similar to that of the counterbalancing techniques (specifically, the random starting orders with rotation) used to control practice effects in the incomplete repeated measures design. This problem illustrates that a relatively small number of balancing techniques can be used to solve control problems in repeated measures experiments.

2. Each participant was tested on two instances of each of the six item types. Because the participants were tested on each condition more than once the study list is more like a complete repeated measures design. To balance practice effects across the study list the most reasonable balancing technique is block randomization. The study list could be divided in half and one instance of each of the six item types could be assigned to each half. The six versions of the list described in Part 1 of this problem would then be used to fill in the block randomized list skeleton. With this procedure the specific names would be well distributed across both item types and positions in the study list.

IV. PROBLEMS AND EXERCISES

A.   Problem 1

1. (a) The independent variable in this experiment is the participants' preferred or nonpreferred mode of learning. (b) The dependent variable in this experiment is the number of words recalled of a possible 20 on each list.

2. Each participant is tested on his or her preferred and nonpreferred mode only once, so this experiment is classified as an incomplete repeated measures design.

3. (a) The first confounding resulted because the participants are always tested first on their preferred mode and second on their nonpreferred mode. Any difference in performance as a function of the mode could have been due to practice, causing performance on the first task to be better than that on the second task. The second confounding resulted because the same 20 words were always used for the preferred task and a different 20 words were always used for the nonpreferred task. Again, any differences between the two modes could have been due to the differences in difficulty of these two sets of words. (b) The mode variable should have been manipulated using the incomplete repeated measures design with half of the participants tested in the order Preferred Mode-Nonpreferred Mode and half in the order Nonpreferred Mode-Preferred Mode. The two sets of 20 words should be balanced across the two modes such that half of the participants tested in each mode order should have the first set of 20 words with the Preferred Mode and the second set with the Nonpreferred mode. The other half of the participants tested in the other mode order would similarly have the two word sets balanced across the two modes. With this design interpretable findings could be obtained for the effects of mode, practice effects, and word sets.

B. Problem 2

1. Violence is operationally defined in this study on the basis of a formula using the number of "hits" and "kills" depicted in cartoon episodes.

2. For both the violence classification and the "comfort" index reliability could be established by having several observers rate stimuli for these dimensions. These observers would need to be trained and given operational definitions of terms such as "hits," "kills," and "comfort." Inter-rater reliability (see Unit 3) could then be computed to determine whether the concepts of violence and "comfort" could be measured reliably.

3. (a) Experimenter bias could play a role in this experiment because the investigator is responsible for rating the violence of the cartoon episodes and for computing the children's "comfort" index. (b) Experimenter bias can be controlled if independent raters who are unfamiliar with the hypothesis being tested rate the violence of the cartoon episodes and the "comfort" index from the children's responses.

4. The investigator has chosen to test only the six most violent episodes from the original set of 24. These six most violent episodes may not be

representative of the violence in cartoons that children typically watch on television.

5. The most serious problem with this study is that the investigator has not included any comparison against which to evaluate the effects of the violent cartoon episodes. Perhaps children's "comfort" index would have increased if they had viewed pleasant or even neutral episodes. In addition, the six episodes that were presented may have differed in the "comfort" index they would have evoked in children regardless of how many prior episodes the children had seen. If the ones with the higher "comfort" index happened to fall at the end of the sequence, then it would appear that viewing several episodes had led to an increase when this was not the case. The solution to this problem is to balance the six episodes across the six positions using procedures for the incomplete repeated measures design.

V. DATA ANALYSIS

A. Descriptive Statistics

1. (a) The overall means for the conditions are: S = 7.44; W = 5.44; and C = 3.75. The means for each participant in each condition are shown below.

	Cond S	Cond W	Cond C
participant #1	7.75	6.00	3.75
participant #2	7.50	5.50	3.50
participant #3	7.75	5.50	4.00
participant #4	6.75	4.75	3.75

(b) The means appear to decrease from the highest in Condition S to an intermediate value in Condition W to the lowest value in Condition C. Inferential tests would need to be done, however, to determine if these apparent differences are statistically significant.

(c) There are four stages of practice in this complete repeated measures design with each stage defined as the presentation of the three conditions once. The mean for Stage 1 (Trials 1-3) is 4.00; the mean for Stage 2 (Trials 4-6) is 5.42; the mean for Stage 3 (Trials 7-9) is 5.83; and the mean for Stage 4 (Trials 10-12) is 6.92. Practice effects do appear to be present with the increasing means from Stage I to Stage 4. These practice effects have been balanced through the use of ABBA counterbalancing and so the practice effects do not affect the interpretability of the experiment.

2. (a) The means for the four levels of the independent variable are: (1) = 25.12; (2) = 33.88; (3) = 27.62; (4) = 34.75.

2. (b) The administration of each condition constitutes a stage of practice in the incomplete repeated measures design. Each ordinal position, therefore, also defines a stage of practice. The means for the four stages of practice are: Stage 1 = 31.00; Stage 2 = 30.00; Stage 3 = 30.00; Stage 4 = 30.40. Even though the means differ slightly, there do not appear to be practice effects in this experiment.

B. Inferential Statistics

2. Repeated Measures Design: ANOVA Summary Table Problem

a. Overall differences among subjects are one of the sources of variation in a repeated measures design (the first one listed in the ANOVA summary table). In this summary table there are 14 df for subjects so there are 15 subjects in the experiment (df = n - 1).

b. The independent variable, treatment, is shown in the summary table to have 2 df. the number of df is one fewer than the number of levels of the independent variable so the number of levels of the treatment variable is 3.

c. The numerator of the F-ratio for this analysis is the estimate that includes variation due to the independent variable (treatment). The Mean Square for treatment provides this estimate and has the value of 13.22 in this analysis.

d. The null hypothesis should be rejected based on this analysis. The obtained F-ratio of 10.75 is statistically significant because its probability of .001 is less than the .05 level of significance. This indicates that the outcome of this experiment is unlikely if the null hypothesis were true; thus, the null hypothesis should be rejected.

e. Because the omnibus F-test in this summary table is statistically significant, we can conclude that there was an overall effect of the independent variable of treatment. Analytical comparisons would need to be done, however, to specify the source of the omnibus effect.

3. Repeated Measures Design: Calculation Problem

a. The means for this analysis are Level 1 = 25.12; Level 2 = 33.88; Level 3 = 27.62; and Level 4 = 34.75 (see section A.2.a.). Statistical software appropriate for a repeated measures analysis of variance was used to compute an omnibus F-test for these means. The resulting summary table is presented below.

Source	df	SS	MS	F	p
Independent Variable (A)	3	532.1	177.4	46.8	.0001
Subjects (S)	7	107.5	15.4		
Residual (Error Term)	21	79.7	3.8		
Total	31	719.2			

The obtained probability (.0001) is less than the significance level of .05, so the effect of the independent variable is statistically significant.

b. The null hypothesis for an analytical comparison of the mean for the combined first two levels (29.5) with the mean for the combined third and fourth levels (31.2) is: H_0: $(\mu_1 + \mu_2)/2 = (\mu_3 + \mu_4)/2$. The alternative hypothesis is that these two combined means are not equal. The Sum of Squares (SS) for this comparison is 22.71 and since the comparison (like all analytical comparisons) has one df, the mean square (MS) for the comparison is also 22.71. The error term (3.8) from the summary table in Part 1 was used to compute the F-ratio for this comparison. The resulting $F(1, 21) = 5.98$ is associated with a p value of .02 which is less than the level of significance of .05 and so the comparison is statistically significant. Notice that the absolute size of the difference is quite small but it is still a statistically significant difference. The repeated measures design is typically more sensitive because the variation due to subjects is eliminated from the analysis rather than being part of the error variation as is the case in the between-subjects (independent groups) designs. This increased sensitivity allows small differences between means to be detected in repeated measures designs.

VI. REVIEW TESTS

A. Identifying Designs and Counterbalancing Techniques

1. (a) Because each participant rates each inkblot once the study is a repeated measures design. (b) Because each participant rates each inkblot only once the study is an incomplete repeated measures design. (c) There are only 20 participants to be tested, so some form of selected orders counterbalancing would have to be used. Random starting orders with rotation would probably be the easiest to use. The first participant would be tested with a random order of the 20 inkblots. Nineteen additional orders would be constructed using rotation and each of the other 19 participants would be tested with one of these orders.

2. (a) Because each participant is tested on each of the six intervals the study is a repeated measures design. (b) Because each participant is tested more than once (four times) on each interval the study is a complete repeated measures design. (c) ABBA counterbalancing would not be advisable in this experiment

because participants could come to anticipate which interval would be presented next. Block randomization would be the preferred balancing technique. There would be four blocks in which the six intervals would be randomly ordered. A separate block randomized schedule could be made up for each of the 12 participants, but it would also be acceptable to use the same block randomized sequence for all the participants.

3. (a) The independent variable is the form of the questionnaire with two levels, and each participant is randomly assigned to only one form, so this study uses a random groups design. (b) Types of repeated measures designs do not apply to this problem. (c) Types of counterbalancing do not apply to this problem.

4. (a) Because each child is tested on all four cereal creatures the study is a repeated measures design. (b) Because each child is tested on each cereal creature only once the study is an incomplete repeated measures design. (c) The use of all possible orders is preferred for this study because there are only four levels of the independent variable and there are 24 children available to be tested. After preparing the 24 possible orders these orders should be randomized and then each of the 24 participants should be tested using one of the orders. Randomizing the orders is the equivalent of randomly assigning the children to the orders.

5. (a) Because each participant is tested under both methods the study is a repeated measures design. (b) Because each participant is tested more than once (twice) under each method the study is a complete repeated measures design. (c) ABBA counterbalancing is the preferred choice for this experiment because two times with each method would not be sufficient for block randomization to be effective. There seems to be little reason to expect nonlinear practice effects or anticipation effects so ABBA counterbalancing should be effective. Two different ABBA sequences should be used, one beginning with each of the two methods. Four of the participants should be randomly assigned to each of the two sequences.

B. Multiple Choice

Numbers in parentheses following each answer refer to pages in the fourth edition of Research Methods in Psychology (1997), by Shaughnessy and Zechmeister, which contains discussion of these concepts.

1. a (241)   6. d (255-256)
2. a (245)   7. d (257-258)
3. c (252)   8. a (258-259)
4. c (249-250)   9. a (259-260)
5. a (250)   10. b (263)

UNIT 8 COMPLEX DESIGNS

III. QUESTIONS ABOUT COMPLEX DESIGN STUDIES

A. The Arkes et al. (1987) decision making study:

1. (a) The first of the two major independent variables in this study was the nature of the first five questions, and this variable had two levels: questions that looked easy but were difficult and questions that looked difficult and were difficult. The second independent variable was the presence or absence of feedback. Half of the participants given each of the types of questions were given feedback and half were not. Thus, these two independent variables were combined factorially. (b) The first dependent variable was the number correct, and this dependent variable was used for two different analyses--one analysis was on the number correct for the first five questions and one analysis was on the number correct on the final 30 questions. The second dependent variable was the average confidence for each participant for the first five questions. The third dependent variable computed for each participant was the participant's average confidence for the final 30 items minus the participant's proportion correct on these items. This last dependent variable allowed an estimate of the overconfidence (a positive score) or underconfidence (a negative score) for each participant.

2. Manipulation was used to control the two independent variables. For the first five questions, half of the participants were given easy-looking questions and half were given difficult-looking question. In each of these two question conditions, half of the participants were given feedback and half were not given feedback. Booklets with the questions were likely used to hold constant the order and the format of the presentation of the questions. The researchers controlled the difficulty of the final test by using the same 30 questions across groups. Balancing was used as a control technique when participants were randomly assigned to the four groups.

3. The researchers intended that the easy-looking items would look easy (and thus increase participants' confidence that they knew the answers to these items) but that the easy-looking items would actually be as difficult as the difficult-looking items. (a) The analysis of the number correct showed that the easy-looking items were answered no better than the difficult-looking items and so the two types of items were of comparable difficulty. (b) The analysis of the confidence scores showed, however, that the average confidence was higher in the groups given easy-looking items than in the groups given difficult-looking items. These analyses confirm that the researchers' manipulation had the intended effect: In the easy-looking condition participants thought they knew the answers but they did not.

4. (a)

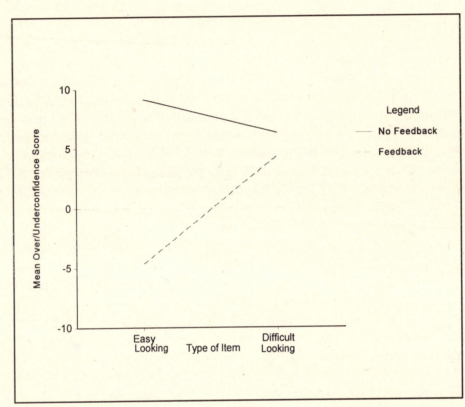

(b) The difference between the feedback and no feedback groups was greater for the easy-looking items than for the difficult-looking items. As predicted by the researchers, the feedback had its greatest effect in lowering the confidence of participants for the easy-looking items. The interaction can also be described in terms of the differences due to the type of item at each level of feedback. That is, there was little difference in the mean over/underconfidence scores for the easy-looking and difficult-looking items when there was no feedback, but there was a much lower score for the easy-looking items than for the difficult-looking items when feedback was given. Interactions are not usually described both ways (except when trying to teach students that there are two ways to describe an interaction). The choice of which way to describe the interaction is typically determined by the theoretical basis of the experiment.

5. The main effect of the feedback variable is represented by the difference between the mean for the feedback groups (-.16) and for the no feedback groups (7.71). Overall, the no feedback groups were more overconfident than were the feedback groups. An inferential test showed that this difference was statistically significant.

B. The Rodman and Burger (1985) depression study:

1. Because the 16 participants who were classified as depressed scored above the criterion for depression on the BDI there is good reason to believe that their results would generalize to other depressed students. However, we cannot assume that the results would generalize to college students who are depressed to the extent that they are not able to function enough to participate in an experiment. Also, we cannot be sure that the results would generalize to individuals who are diagnosed as depressed on the basis of a clinical interview instead of the BDI. The external validity of the results for the other two groups is more questionable. The participants having the 20 lowest scores on the BDI represent a select sample and they may not represent adequately all those who might be classified as nondepressed. Classifying the slightly depressed group as intermediate between the depressed and nondepressed groups may also pose a problem. If, for example, the scores for the nondepressed group are very low, then selecting students between the depressed and the nondepressed group may still include many students with relatively low scores. This could result in the slightly depressed group's being more similar to the nondepressed group than to the depressed group. If, on the other hand, those between the depressed and nondepressed groups had mostly higher scores, then the slightly depressed group would be more similar to the depressed group than to the nondepressed group. Without a more specific operational definition of the slightly depressed group it is difficult to know how well the results for this group would generalize to other studies involving slightly depressed students.

2. Several characteristics of the accident description were held constant across conditions. First, the accident was always a three-car accident. Second, the description was written to give all three drivers a role in the accident. Third, the description was written to allow for the role of uncontrollable factors. All participants also were told to read the description as if they were members of a jury.

3. The severity of the accident was a manipulated independent variable because half of the participants in each depression group were assigned to the mild accident condition and half to the severe accident condition. The depression variable represents a nonmanipulated individual differences (subject) variable because participants were selected for the three levels (depressed, slightly depressed, and nondepressed) of this independent variable based on their score on the Beck Depression Inventory.

4.

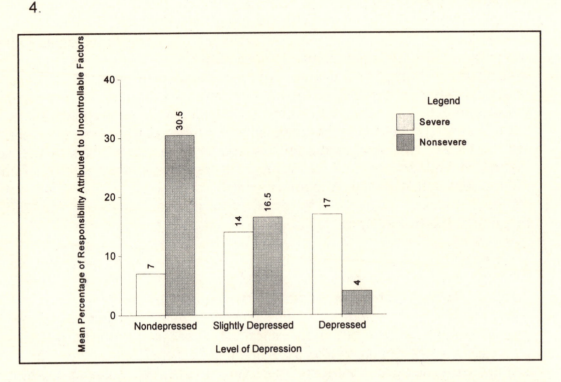

5. (a) Rodman and Burger identified that the thinking of nondepressed and depressed individuals are distinguished in the way they make causal attributions, specifically, the extent to which they exhibit a defensive attribution bias. The researchers manipulated the severity of the accident in order to influence the likelihood that the defensive attribution bias would come into play. In the nonsevere accident neither nondepressed nor depressed participants were expected to show a defensive attribution bias. In the severe accident condition, however, the nondepressed participants were expected to show a defensive attribution bias while the depressed participants were expected to show less of a defensive attribution bias. In this way the researchers planned to produce an interaction of the accident severity and depression variables.

(b) For purposes of this problem we will consider only two levels of the depression variable, depressed and nondepressed. As shown in Table 8-1 (p. 153), the depressed participants assigned more responsibility to uncontrollable factors than did nondepressed participants in the severe accident condition. If the severe accident condition had been the only condition in the experiment it would not be possible to conclude that depressed participants are less likely to show the defensive attribution bias because it may be that depressed participants are just generally more likely to attribute responsibility to uncontrollable factors. The findings in the nonsevere accident condition in Table 8-1, however, indicate that depressed participants assigned less responsibility to uncontrollable factors than did nondepressed participants. If there had been no interaction, the depressed participants would have assigned more responsibility to uncontrollable factors in both the severe and the nonsevere conditions. If there had been no interaction, therefore, it would have been impossible to refute the alternative hypothesis that depressed participants generally attribute more responsibility to uncontrollable factors than do nondepressed participants. The interaction shown in Table 8-1 indicates that this alternative hypothesis can be refuted because the depressed participants attribute more responsibility to uncontrollable factors than do nondepressed participants only in the severe accident condition. The interaction supports the researchers' hypothesis that depressed individuals would be less likely to exhibit a defensive attribution bias than would nondepressed individuals. Interactions play a powerful role in experiments like this one in which individual differences variables are involved.

IV. PROBLEMS AND EXERCISES

A.   Problem 1

1. (a)   TRUE--There are two independent variables (grade and type of story) in this experiment and each independent variable has two levels.
(b) TRUE--The grade independent variable involves selected levels that represent characteristics of the participants.
(c) FALSE--The second independent variable (type of story variable) was manipulated between subjects (random groups design).
(d) TRUE--The 2nd graders are expected to remember less than the 6th graders (main effect of grade) and the logically ordered story is expected to be recalled better than the disrupted story (main effect of type of story).

2. The following table (design matrix) shows two main effects and an interaction involving the two independent variables of type of story and grade. The absolute values in the table are not critical since these are hypothetical data. What is critical is that: (1) the overall mean for the logically ordered story is larger than the overall mean for the disrupted story; (2) the overall mean for the 6th graders is larger than the overall mean for the 2nd graders; and (3) the difference between the means for the logically ordered and disrupted stories is larger for the 2nd graders than for the 6th graders.

	Type of Story	
Grade	Logically Ordered	Disrupted
2nd	55	25
6th	75	60

3. The following table (design matrix) shows the same pattern of results as in question 2, but this time the level of recall for the 6th graders indicates that a ceiling effect may be present. The maximum score possible is 100. The real difference between the means for the logically ordered and disrupted stories for the 6th graders may be larger than 5, but this real difference cannot be measured because of the potential ceiling effect. The apparent interaction may have been "forced" by the presence of the ceiling effect.

	Type of Story	
Grade	Logically Ordered	Disrupted
2nd	55	25
6th	100	95

B. Problem 2

1. The three independent variables are grade (2nd and 6th), type of story (nondisrupted and disrupted), and length of story (original length and one-third longer).

2. Yes, this replication does represent a mixed design. A different design is used for each independent variable: natural groups for the grade variable; repeated measures for the type of story variable; and independent groups for the length of story variable.

3. The type of story variable is manipulated using a repeated measures design (most likely incomplete repeated measures although this is not specified in the summary). Practice effects must still be balanced when a repeated measures design appears within a mixed design experiment. Thus, all possible orders could be used for the type of story variable. That is, one half of the participants would have the order nondisrupted then disrupted, and one half would have the order disrupted then nondisrupted.

4. Because the length of story variable is manipulated using an independent groups design half of the children will be tested with each story length. Thus 40 children will be tested with each story length.

5. Because the type of story variable is manipulated using a repeated measures design, each participant will be tested on both the disrupted and the nondisrupted stories. Therefore, 80 children will be tested at each level of the story-type variable.

V. DATA ANALYSIS

A. Descriptive Statistics

1. The means for the six cells in this experiment are: A1-Communication A = 32.9; A1-Communication B = 15.8; A1-Communication C = 12.4; A2-Communication A = 13.6; A2-Communication B = 14.4; A2-Communication C = 3.0.

2. The following is a table of the results of this experiment presented in APA format.

Table 8-2

Mean Anxiety Scores as a Function of Type of Communication and Diagnostic

 Category

Diagnostic Category	Type of Communication		
	A	B	C
A1	32.9	15.8	12.4
A2	13.6	14.4	3.0

3. The mean anxiety scores for diagnostic category A1 are consistently higher than those for category A2. The overall mean anxiety score is highest for Communication A, intermediate for Communication B, and lowest for Communication C. These overall effects, however, must be viewed in light of the apparent interaction of diagnostic category and type of communication. The difference between the mean anxiety scores between the two diagnostic categories is different for the three types of communications. Most noteworthy is that the mean difference between the categories is much larger for Communication A than for either Communication B or Communication C.

B. Inferential Statistics

1. The major consideration in deciding whether to carry out simple main effects or analytical comparisons is whether a statistically significant interaction effect has occurred in a complex design. If there is an interaction, then the source of the interaction is sought using simple main effects. If there is no interaction, then analytical comparisons are used to locate more precisely the source of statistically significant main effects.

2. Simple comparisons are analyses that are used in conjunction with simple main effects to identify the source of a statistically significant interaction. Simple main effects can be used when an interaction includes an independent variable with only two levels. If the simple main effect of the independent variable is statistically significant, however, there is no reason to break the simple main effect down further since there is only one difference present. Simple comparisons are intended to break down simple main effects further and so they are used only when the independent variable entering into the interaction has three or more levels. Similarly, analytical comparisons are used to break down statistically significant main effects. If a main effect results from an independent variable with only two levels, there is no reason to analyze the main effect further. Analytical comparisons are used, therefore, to analyze the main effects of independent variables with three or more levels.

2. Complex Design: ANOVA Summary Table

1. There were two independent variables in this experiment: Type of Problem and Presentation Rate. These are indicated in the first two rows of the summary table with the F-ratio for each independent variable reflecting the main effect of that independent variable.

2. The Type of Problem independent variable had three levels and the Presentation Rate independent variable had two levels. The number of levels for each independent variable can be determined from the summary table by adding 1 to the number of df for each independent variable. This can be done because the number of df for an independent variable is equal to the number of levels minus 1.

3. The most direct way to determine from a summary table how many individuals participated in a complex design experiment when both independent variables represent the independent groups design is to add 1 to the df for the total source of variation. So, with a df of 47 for the total source of variation in this experiment, the number of participants in the experiment would be 48.

4. The first step in determining how many individuals participated in each condition of the experiment is to determine the number of conditions in the

experiment. In question 2 we determined the number of levels of each of the two independent variables. There were three levels of the Type of Problem variable and two levels of the Presentation Rate variable. The overall design of this complex design experiment can be described as a 3 X 2. In a 3 X 2 design there are six conditions; this is obtained by multiplying the number of levels of the two independent variables. In question 3 we determined that there were 48 participants in the experiment. If we assume equal number of participants in each condition (i.e., equal cell sizes), then we can divide the number of conditions into the total number of participants to determine the number of participants in each condition. In this case, with 6 conditions and 48 total participants there would be 8 participants in each condition. One way to check that there are 8 participants in each group is to use this value to compute the df for the within-groups error in the summary table. If there are 8 participants in each condition, then there would be 7 df in each condition. With 6 conditions there would then be 42 df within groups. The value listed for the df for the within-groups error is 42 and so our check has confirmed that there were 8 participants in each condition.

5. The F-ratio and corresponding probability (p) for the main effect of Type of Problem are listed in the first row of the summary table. Because the probability of the F-ratio for this main effect is .03 which is less than the .05 level of significance, the main effect of Type of Problem was statistically significant. Analytical comparisons developed on the basis of the research questions being investigated in this experiment would likely be used to locate the source of the main effect of the Type of Problem variable. The F-ratio and corresponding probability for the main effect of Presentation Rate are listed in the second row of the summary table. The F-ratio of 1.27 is associated with a p value of .26 which is greater than an alpha of .05. Therefore, the main effect of Presentation Rate was not statistically significant.

6. The F-ratio and corresponding probability for the test of the Type of Problem X Presentation Rate interaction are listed in the third row of the summary table. The probability of .41 associated with the F-ratio for the interaction is greater than the .05 level of significance and so the interaction was not statistically significant.

3. Complex Design: Calculation Problem

    a. Appropriate statistical software was used to carry out the computations for the omnibus analysis of variance. This complex design involved two variables, each represent an independent groups design. The results of these computations are presented in the following ANOVA summary table.

Source	df	SS	MS	F	p
Category (A)	1	1200.0	1200.0	44.7	.0001
Communication (B)	2	1939.3	969.6	36.1	.0001
A X B	2	641.4	320.7	11.9	.0002
Ss/AB (Error)	42	1128.0	26.9		
Total	47	4908.7			

2. The interaction is the first source of variation that should be examined in a summary table for a complex design. The obtained probability for the F-test of the interaction of the category variable and the communication variable in this analysis was .0002. Because this probability is less than the .05 level of significance, the interaction was statistically significant. Similarly, the obtained probabilities for the main effects of the category and communication variables are both less than the .05 level of significance. Thus, both main effects were statistically significant.

3. When the results of an omnibus F-test for an interaction are statistically significant, simple main effects (and, if necessary, simple comparisons) are used to locate the source of the interaction. In the omnibus analysis of this experiment the interaction of communication and category was statistically significant. Therefore, it would be necessary to test the simple main effects. One set of simple main effects would be the effects of the category variable at each level of the communication variable. These analyses would indicate whether the difference between the two categories was statistically significant or not for each type of communication. Alternatively, the simple main effects of the communication variable at each level of the category variable could be examined. Because there are three levels of the communication variable simple comparisons could be used to analyze the simple main effects in greater depth. For example, a simple comparison of Communication A with the average of Communications B and C could be done for the simple main effect of communication at category A1. Simple comparisons like this one provide much more specific information about the sources of variation in an experiment than can be obtained from an omnibus test of an interaction. Simple main effects and simple comparisons can be best used, however, when an analysis plan for the experiment is developed based on specific research questions that are being examined in the experiment.

VI. REVIEW TESTS

A. Main Effects and Interactions

1. Computations using the means in the table show overall means of 15, 20, and 25 for the three levels of Factor A and so a main effect of Factor A is indicated. The means for Factor B are 21.7 and 25 and so there may be a small main effect of Factor B. An interaction is indicated because the effect of Factor B at level A3 of Factor A is opposite those for Factor B at levels A1 and A2.

2. In order to complete the matrix such that there is a main effect of Factor A, no main effect of Factor B, and an interaction of Factors A and B, the missing cell must have a value of 10.

3. In order to complete the matrix such that there are two main effects and no interaction, the missing cell must have a value of 50.

4. (a) The pattern depicted in this graph shows no main effect of Factor A (flat lines), a main effect of Factor B (space between the lines), and no interaction of Factors A and B (parallel lines). (b) The pattern depicted in this graph shows a crossing interaction of Factors A and B, but no main effects of either Factor A or Factor B.

B. Multiple Choice

Numbers in parentheses following each answer refer to pages in the fourth edition of Research Methods in Psychology (1997), by Shaughnessy and Zechmeister, which contains discussion of these concepts.

1. b (269)	6. c (278)
2. b (270)	7. c (292-293)
3. b (274)	8. d (290-294)
4. a (270)	9. a (295)
5. d (277)	10. c (287)

UNIT 9   SINGLE-CASE RESEARCH DESIGNS

III. QUESTIONS ABOUT SINGLE-CASE RESEARCH

A.   The Glover (1985) kleptomania study:

1. Two components of the treatment in addition to the covert sensitization procedure per se are the use of hypnosis in the last two sessions and the fact that the woman left at home the particular bag she had used when shoplifting.

2. One factor that may have contributed to the shoplifting and that may have changed during the time of treatment is the condition for which the woman had taken antidepressant medication. Another potential factor that may have led to the shoplifting was the deterioration of the woman's relationships with her husband and her friends. If these relationships improved the shoplifting may have lessened even in the absence of the treatment with covert sensitization.

3. (a) The therapist might have overestimated or underestimated the improvement made by the woman based on the therapist's subjective impressions of how she looked and what she said. This case study may have been free of such bias because the treatment was designed to modify a relatively objective aspect of the woman's behavior--her shoplifting. (b) Unless the shoplifting behavior of the woman was monitored by an independent observer, it would have been possible for the woman to bias the results by underreporting how often she shoplifted. In general, self-reports are subject to problems of bias.

4. (a) Because this case study involved the treatment of a relatively specific problem with a relatively specific technique the study is not likely to be an important source of hypotheses about behavior. (b) It is not clear from the summary how well established the covert sensitization technique is so it is reasonable to argue that this case study does provide an opportunity for clinical innovation. (c) The relatively short length of the treatment makes it unlikely that this case study will permit the intensive study of a rare phenomenon (even considering, for the moment, that shoplifting is a rare phenomenon). (d) This case study could be seen as a challenge to theoretical assumptions about the psychological bases of the problem of shoplifting. Covert sensitization focuses on changing the shoplifting behavior, and its success in changing this specific behavior, as well as improving the client's overall well-being, could be taken as evidence against theoretical approaches that propose that the shoplifting is only a symptom of underlying psychological conflict. (e) In the same sense that this case study could be taken as evidence against theoretical approaches it can also be taken as tentative support for a psychological theory proposing that covert conditioning can modify shoplifting behavior.

B.   The Matson et al. (1990) infantile autism study:

1. The percentage of trials on which the child said "please" (the target behavior) during the baseline period should have been near zero and should not have shown improvement across baseline sessions. The percentage of trials on which the child gave the target response during treatment sessions should have risen rapidly at the onset of the treatment sessions and stayed relatively high throughout the treatment sessions. The percentage of trials on which the child said the target response during the baseline periods for the target behaviors of "thank you" and "you're welcome" should have been near zero with no improvement across sessions. However, the percentage of trials on which the child said the target response (e.g., "thank you") should have risen rapidly at the onset of the next treatment session and stayed relatively high throughout the treatment sessions. It is important to remember that application of the treatment is "staggered," first showing an "effect" for one behavior, then the next, and finally for the third behavior. Multiple-baseline designs demonstrate the effectiveness of a treatment best when the change in performance from baseline to treatment is abrupt and large.

2. Several sources of evidence serve to increase the external validity of the results of this study. First, it can be noted that the treatment was successful for three different children and the effects were obtained with three different target behaviors. Another source of evidence is that the children responded appropriately to novel objects presented at the follow-up sessions one and six months later. Additional evidence enhancing the external validity of the results was the informal data from parents and teachers indicating that spontaneous use of the target behaviors occurred in the home and in other situations.

3. To verify that the change in the children's use of the target behaviors was the result of the specific treatment, it is important that behaviors should change only when the treatment is given for a particular target behavior. If the target behavior "thank you" changed before the treatment had been given for that specific response, it is possible that there was generalization from the treatment for the "please" response. If the children began to use the "thank you" response "prematurely," this would be a problem for drawing causal inferences in the multiple-baseline design. It would not be clear what "produced" the change in behavior. This would not be a problem in terms of the clinical significance of the change because the children's verbal responsiveness would be increasing.

4. (a) Subjective evaluation is a measure of the clinical significance of a treatment in which the judgments of people who have contact with the child are used to assess whether the behavior of the child is perceptibly different after treatment than it was before treatment. This basis of clinical significance trusts

the judgments of "expert" observers to assess the change from before to after the treatment. Social comparison, on the other hand, is a measure of clinical significance in which the researcher compares the behavior of the child after the treatment with the behavior of a "normal" or "comparison" group of children. With social comparison the standard for clinical significance is whether the improvement in the child's behavior has moved the child closer to the behavior typical of other children. (b) In the Matson et al. study it is unlikely that the use of social comparison would involve a comparison with "normal" children given the very low verbal responsiveness of the autistic children. Social comparison could still be used, however, by selecting a group of children whose verbal responsiveness is higher than that of the autistic children. As you can see, social comparison as a measure of clinical significance is somewhat of a "sliding scale." The choice of the comparison group will influence how difficult it will be to demonstrate a clinically significant finding.

C. The Horton (1987) facial screening study:

1.

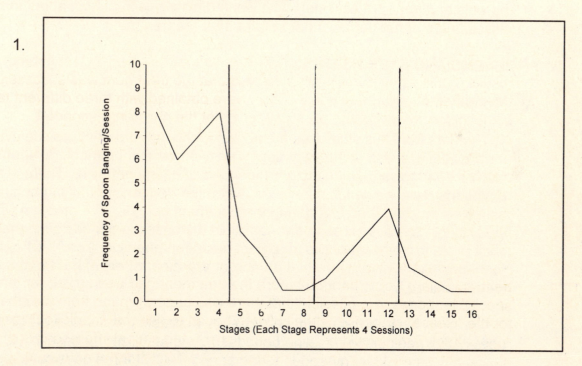

2. If the facial screening was effective in reducing spoon banging in a multiple-baseline design across situations, then at breakfast, lunch, and dinner the pattern of results would have been the same. Frequency of spoon banging would have been high during the baseline period and the frequency would have dropped during the treatment period. The pattern should look much like the pattern in the first two panels of the graph shown in the answer to question 1, but, of course, with the effect of the treatment appearing at different times.

3. It is difficult to say how well the results of the Horton (1987) study would generalize to other situations, responses, and populations. In general, the ABAB design with only one child makes it difficult to assess the external validity of the study. There are reasons to think, however, that the results would generalize to other situations, responses, and populations. The effects of the facial screening were large and the spoon banging behavior was not observed even after six months, indicating that the effects of the treatment persisted. The best test of the external validity of these results is to apply the facial screening technique to other situations, responses, and populations for which it appears to be applicable.

4. The social comparison measures of clinical significance likely included comparisons with the disruptive behavior of other severely retarded children and with the behavior of children who were developmentally more advanced than the severely retarded child to see if her behavior had improved. The subjective evaluation measures of clinical significance likely involved asking the parents and para-professionals who worked closely with the girl about their assessment of her behavior before and after the treatment.

IV. PROBLEMS AND EXERCISES

A. Problem 1

1. The data from this study that are shown in the graph do not provide evidence for the effectiveness of the treatment. The two treatment periods do seem to show a trend toward decreasing frequencies of hitting behavior. There are times during the baseline periods, however, when the frequency of hitting behavior is as low as or lower than that during the treatment periods. The problem with this study is that there is excessive variability in the baseline periods such that it is impossible to tell whether the treatment has been effective. The $\underline{N}$ = 1 designs require a stable baseline so that an abrupt and clear effect of the treatment can be determined by visual inspection.

2. One possible solution using the presently available data is to average across days of the week in the baseline periods to try to stabilize the baseline (e.g., the first two days could be averaged together and the last three days could be averaged together). This is not a preferred solution in this situation because you end up with only two data points in each baseline period and you are averaging over only two or three days. A better solution for "stabilizing" a baseline via averaging would be to extend the baseline over longer periods of time or to take measurements more often during the baseline period (e.g., determining the frequency of the target response every 15 minutes instead of only every hour). Another approach to this problem of excessive variability is to seek out those factors that are likely contributors to the variability and attempt to remove them.

B. Problem 2

1. The data from this study do not provide evidence for the effectiveness of the treatment even though the baselines are relatively stable for all three players. The problem in this case is that the target behavior changes for Carol and Arlene <u>before</u> the treatment is administered to them. If the treatment is the cause of their changed behavior then the change must occur after the treatment is administered and not before.

2. It is likely that Carol and Arlene have seen the feedback given to Beth (the record of her shooting posted on her locker), and may also have heard the coach affirming Beth when she takes more "good shots." Carol's and Arlene's data suggest that they may have decided to modify their shot selection prior to being given the treatment. One potential solution to the contamination of the treatment across players in this study would be to give the feedback to the players privately.

3. (a) Observer reliability could be increased by having a good operational definition of a high percentage shot. Reliability would also be increased by training the observers in the use of the operational definition prior to beginning the study itself. (b) Information about observer reliability could be obtained by having two independent observers categorize every shot during a practice scrimmage as a high or a low percentage shot. The responses for these two observers would then be tallied according to the number of times their classifications of shots agreed. The number of agreements would then be divided by the total number of opportunities to agree (i.e., the total number of shots). This value when multiplied by 100 would yield a percent agreement measure of interobserver reliability.

VI. REVIEW TESTS

Numbers in parentheses following each answer for the True-False and Multiple-Choice questions refer to pages in the fourth edition of <u>Research Methods in Psychology</u> (1997), by Shaughnessy and Zechmeister, which contains discussion of these concepts.

A. True-False

1. F (314-315)   6. F (325)
2. T (315)   7. T (323)
3. F (321)   8. F (330)
4. F (323)   9. T (329)
5. T (325)   10. T (331)

B. Multiple Choice

   1. d (311)   6. d (325-326)
   2. c (315-317) 7. b (329-330)
   3. b (322)   8. b (329-330)
   4. c (325)   9. a (322)
   5. c (328)   10. c (331)

UNIT 10 QUASI-EXPERIMENTAL DESIGNS AND PROGRAM EVALUATION

III. QUESTIONS ABOUT QUASI-EXPERIMENTAL STUDIES

A. The Levitt and Leventhal (1986) environmental study:

1. (a) The specific quasi-experimental design used in this study was a time-series with nonequivalent control group design. (b) The time-series aspect of the design is indicated by the repeated measurements at 2-week intervals both 14 weeks prior to and after the implementation of the bottle bill. If it had been a simple time-series design, then data would have been collected only in New York where the "treatment" had been administered. This study included a nonequivalent control group by gathering data in the nearby state of New Jersey, and so it was a time-series with a nonequivalent control group design.

2. The operational definition of "litter" in this study was: "all bottles and cans, returnable and nonreturnable, of which at least one-half of the container was visibly present or intact."

3. In general the most likely threats to the internal validity of a time-series design with a nonequivalent control group involve interactions with selection (e.g., the interaction of selection and history or the interaction of selection with maturation). There are at least two such possible interactions with selection in this study, both of which involve interactions of selection with history. It is likely that there was publicity surrounding the environmental issues related to the bottle bill during the time that the bill was being proposed. It is also likely that this publicity would increase to a peak around the time of the passage of the bottle bill. Finally, it is likely that this publicity would be more extensive in New York than in New Jersey. The information contained in the publicity materials in favor of the bottle bill may have caused the change in people's littering that was found in this study. Just as those in New York were subject to the bottle bill and those in New Jersey were not, those in New York could have been subject to publicity that changed their views about littering while those in New Jersey were not subjected to this publicity. A second possible interaction of selection and history builds on the finding that a significant change in littering occurred in New York at highway sites but not at railway sites. If the bottle bill had been the cause of the decreased littering, then it seems reasonable that it would have affected littering at both sites in New York and at neither site in New Jersey. Perhaps part of a campaign to educate the public about littering was begun in conjunction with the passage of the bottle bill. Suppose further that this campaign was focused on billboards along highways. This possibility may seem far-fetched, but it is consistent with the pattern of results reported in the summary. The key to developing alternative plausible hypotheses in quasi-

experimental designs is to develop testable "leads" (like those used by detectives). If these leads don't "pan out," then the evidence in favor of the effect of the treatment (in this case, the bottle bill) is stronger. For example, if there was no billboard campaign related to littering at the time of the bottle bill, then that potential threat to the internal validity of the study would be refuted. Finally, it is also useful to note how the time-series design with a nonequivalent control group does control for several threats to internal validity. If only a simple time-series design had been used in this study testing only New York, for example, it would be very possible that people's increasing awareness and concern over environmental issues led to decreased littering with little or no effect of the bottle bill. The addition of the New Jersey test makes it much less likely that the decreased littering in New York is the result of people's increasing awareness and concern over environmental issues. Quasi-experiments need to be subjected to vigorous challenges with regard to potential threats to their internal validity, but we must not lose sight of the fact that well-done quasi-experiments provide invaluable information in applied research settings.

4. One potential threat to the external validity of this study is whether the people of New York are representative of the people of states in other regions of the country, especially with regard to their attitudes about environmental issues and government regulations. A second potential threat to the external validity of this study has to do with the procedures followed in New York in the drafting and enforcement of the bottle bill. It is possible that certain critical details of the bill and its enforcement would not be applicable in other states. It is difficult to replicate the procedures of a laboratory-based experiment; it is much more difficult to replicate a legislative bill. Unless those critical details are replicated, however, the generality of the effects of the original bill is likely to be limited.

B.   The Taylor (1988) vocational study:

1. (a) The specific quasi-experimental design used in this study was the nonequivalent control group design. (b) The nonequivalent groups were the interns (the treatment group) and the noninterns (the nonequivalent control group). The nonequivalent control group design does include a pretest and posttest before and after the treatment, but it is distinguishable from the time-series design with a nonequivalent control group because the time-series design involves multiple measurements before and after the treatment as was the case in the first study in this unit.

2. (a) In general the potential threats to the internal validity of a nonequivalent control group design involve interactions with selection (e.g., selection and history or selection and maturation). (b) A selection and history interaction that may have affected the internal validity of this study involves the fact that the interns volunteered for the internship experience and the noninterns did not. It

is likely that this willingness to seek out opportunities may affect other aspects of the interns' academic and work experiences during the time of the internship. These differences between the two groups in these other experiences may have been responsible for the effects that are being attributed to the internship itself. It is important to recognize that this alternative explanation is plausible (and testable) only if there are specific events or experiences that can be identified that are different for the interns and the noninterns. In general, plausible alternative hypotheses like the hypotheses being directly investigated in a study are useful only insofar as they are testable. A second potential threat to this study's internal validity involves an interaction of selection and maturation. It again centers around the fact that the interns volunteered and the noninterns did not. Perhaps those who volunteer develop in a different way and at a different rate from those who don't volunteer. The interns may have developed greater potential for successful job placement than the noninterns even if they hadn't had the specific experience of an internship. Because of their willingness to volunteer (and thus taking the risk of challenging themselves) the intern group may have had more experiences or benefited more from their experiences than did the nonintern group.

3. Those in the intern group had the chance to demonstrate their abilities "on the job." If the intern performs well, it is possible that the employer will offer the intern a permanent position doing the same or similar work. The internship serves in this case as a potential contact for a job. In the original article, the author mentions that interns also may acquire technical skills that are valuable to employers. She states further that employers may assume interns are more qualified in general and this, too, may give them an edge in a competitive job market.

4. The instrument used to measure "reality shock" may not have been sufficiently sensitive to pick up differences that may have existed between the interns and the noninterns. At the extremes the instrument may have resulted in a basement or ceiling effect that would not show differences between the groups. The instrument may also have been affected by social desirability factors; even if the participants had been "shocked" when starting a new job, they may not have judged it appropriate to say that they had been shocked. The nature of the participants tested may also have contributed to the finding of no difference in "reality shock." The interns needed to meet certain criteria to be eligible for an internship and the noninterns had been selected to be similar to the interns on these criteria in order to form an appropriate nonequivalent group for comparison with the interns. These selection criteria may have resulted in participants in the two groups who were very similar in their potential for experiencing "reality shock." It is also quite possible that the noninterns would have had experiences such as part-time employment that would have served to prepare them for "reality shock" in a way comparable to the effect of the

internship experience on the interns. You may remember that the groups did <u>not</u> differ in terms of prior part-time work experience.

5. One question that an investigator might address regarding the external validity of this study is whether an internship experience would be beneficial for students who met the criteria but who had not volunteered for the internship program. For example, psychology departments might judge that an internship should be a requirement for all psychology majors. The success in this study of the internship experience may have been dependent upon students' willingness to volunteer for the experience. Before instituting a requirement for all majors it would be advisable to extend the test of the beneficial effects of internships to nonvolunteers. A second question related to the external validity of this study would be to test whether other work-related experiences (e.g., part-time work) would have beneficial effects like those shown for the internships.

IV. PROBLEMS AND EXERCISES

A. Problem 1

1. One possible threat to the internal validity of this study is maturation. Because the study includes no comparison group there is no way to refute the possibility that these students might have improved as part of their own development as college students (independent of the special program). A second possible threat to internal validity in this study is regression. This threat may be particularly likely given that students were selected for their poor performance. If the instrument used to identify these students as having reading comprehension deficiencies was not perfectly reliable, then the students' apparent improvement may have reflected their regression toward the mean. Finally, history could have posed a threat to the internal validity of this study. Perhaps the professors or teaching assistants in the courses in which these students were enrolled gave them additional tutoring or instruction in study skills. This could easily have gone on while the students were enrolled in the special program. The absence of a comparison group again makes it impossible to tell whether the program or their experiences in their courses was responsible for their improvement.

2. In the previous answer reference was made to the absence of a comparison group in the present study and how this contributed to an inability to refute alternative plausible hypotheses for the effects of the special program. A nonequivalent control group design would add this comparison group and would provide both pretest and posttest measures for both the treatment and the control groups. It is unlikely that a comparable control group could be formed using a true experiment because students would have to accept being randomly assigned to the treatment and control groups. Thus, the nonequivalent control

group design would be the most practical way to obtain a comparison group. The nonequivalent control group should be made up of students as similar as possible to those identified as needing the special program. For example, students who have been identified by their teachers as performing poorly in these areas might constitute a comparison group. They would differ from the treatment group because they would not receive the treatment. They would represent a nonequivalent control group because the treatment and control groups would not have been formed through random assignment.

3. If the population of students at her school was substantially different, the administrator would be concerned with generalizing the results of the present study to those likely to be obtained at her institution. She might also be concerned about the external validity of the findings of the present study if her institution did not have the resources to implement the special program in the same way it was done in the present study.

B. Problem 2

1. The social scientist has been asked to conduct an outcome evaluation because the local police department asked for <u>an evaluation of the effectiveness</u> of a program aimed at reducing juvenile delinquency (and the program obviously had been planned and implemented prior to the psychologist's arriving on the scene).

2. A time-series design would involve examining the police department records for the incidence of juvenile delinquency and any other measures that would be pertinent to the potential effectiveness of the program. The investigator then would examine records prior to the beginning of the program. The investigator would continue to monitor these measures during the program and after the program had been completed. The time-series design would demonstrate that the program had been effective if there was an abrupt change in the critical measures coincident with the implementation of the program.

3. The major threats to the internal validity of a time-series design are history and instrumentation. In this situation history seems to be the more plausible threat because archival records are being used to measure the dependent variables. If the police department is sufficiently concerned about juvenile delinquency in the community to have begun such an extensive program, it is likely that others in the community are also concerned and may have introduced other programs. This general level of concern and possible concurrent programs addressing problems of juvenile delinquency would provide potential history threats to the internal validity of the police department's study. A potential instrumentation threat exists if there is a change in the ways delinquent activities are recorded during the period of observation.

4. (a) The social scientist might consider a similar neighboring community to serve as a nonequivalent control group in this study. The sample drawn from the neighboring community should be as similar as possible to the sample undergoing the program. (b) The treatment group and the nonequivalent control group should be assessed on the same dependent variables both before and after the program was implemented.

VI. REVIEW TESTS

A. Matching

1.	g	6.	c
2.	b	7.	i
3.	f	8.	h
4.	d	9.	a
5.	e	10.	j

B. Multiple Choice

Numbers in parentheses following each answer refer to pages in the fourth edition of <u>Research Methods in Psychology</u> (1997), by Shaughnessy and Zechmeister, which contains discussion of these concepts.

1.	c (341)	6.	d (350)
2.	a (342)	7.	b (354)
3.	b (346)	8.	a (372)
4.	d (347)	9.	b (372)
5.	c (346)	10.	d (373-374)

DATE DUE

AP 5 '03			
NOV 2 3 2003			
ILL			
2574793			
2/27/04			
DE 18 '04			
FE 2 4 '05			
MY 24 '05			
GAYLORD			PRINTED IN U.S.A.